Kathy Ivens
Brian Proffit

OS/2 Inside & Out

Osborne **McGraw-Hill**

Berkeley New York St. Louis San Francisco
Auckland Bogotà Hamburg London Madrid
Mexico City Milan Montreal New Delhi Panama City
Paris São Paulo Singapore Sydney
Tokyo Toronto

Osborne **McGraw-Hill**
2600 Tenth Street
Berkeley, California 94710 U.S.A.

For information on translations and book distributors outside of the U.S.A., please write to Osborne **McGraw-Hill** at the above address.

OS/2 Inside & Out

1234567890 DOC 99876543

ISBN 0-07-881871-0

Publisher	**Technical Editor**
Kenna S. Wood	John Mueller
Acquisitions Editor	**Proofreader**
Frances Stack	Pat Mannion
Associate Editor	**Indexer**
Jill Pisoni	Richard Shrout
Project Editor	**Computer Designer**
Kelly Barr	Barry Bergin
Copy Editors	**Illustrator**
Vivian Jaquette	Susie C. Kim
Ann Krueger Spivack	**Cover Designer**
Editorial Assistant	Mason Fong
Judith Kleppe	

To Catherine Pearlman, who provided a needed retreat for shedding writer's block when deadlines and other crises overwhelmed.
—Kathy Ivens

To Tiffani and Eric — I now return control of my evenings to you.
—Brian Proffit

Contents at a Glance

Contents

Acknowledgments

When we started writing *OS/2 Inside & Out*, one of our pivotal aims was to pass along our enthusiasm for this wonderfully productive operating system. A programmer and a consultant bring different views to computing and we wanted our diverse backgrounds to produce a volume that gives information and explanations in ways that are understood by all users, while providing technical insights unavailable in normal documentation. In addition, we wanted to make sure that everyone who read the book understood that OS/2 is more fun than the other operating systems.

With the help of the talented people at Osborne, we met our goals and enjoyed the process. Special thanks to Jill Pisoni, Kelly Barr, John Mueller, and especially Frances Stack for their commitment to quality, their humanism, their patience, and, especially needed, their humor.

Introduction

This book is written specifically for OS/2 version 2.0, the 32-bit version of IBM's multitasking operating system. Whether you've already installed OS/2 2.0 or are planning to, this book is written to help you use this new, powerful operating system as productively and easily as possible.

Some of you may already be using earlier versions of OS/2 and are aware that version 2.0 is substantially different. Upgrading is not difficult and this book should help make it fairly painless and rapid.

For those making their first foray into this new technology, this book will help you understand what to do, how to do it and when to do it as you move into the enhanced productivity available in a multitasking operating system.

While the authors assume that a user contemplating OS/2 already has at least an elementary knowledge of DOS and the primary DOS commands, we do not presume that you have advanced technical knowledge about the hardware or electronics of a computer, nor any prior knowledge of OS/2.

Our intent is to provide information that is consequential enough to give you some insight into the tangible and potential power inherent in the state-of-the-art technology represented by OS/2.

Throughout the book, references to OS/2 should be interpreted as meaning version 2.0 unless specifically indicated otherwise, and references to the 80386/80486 processors include all versions of the chips (SX, SL, SLC, DX).

As you experiment with the power of OS/2, this book will help you configure your hardware, software, peripherals, and files. You will learn how to create protocols and design conventions that fit your own needs and make your computer a productive tool. Above all, you will have fun. OS/2 is a joy to use!

How This Book Is Organized

This is not a manual or a listing of commands. This is a reference source and the authors approached its development with the goal of helping you understand the thinking that went into the development of OS/2 and the theories upon which it operates. There will be, of course, explanations and examples of the commands, the files, and the tools available.

If you have not yet installed OS/2, you may want to read each chapter, in order, as a guide to installation, use, and enhanced productivity. If you are already using OS/2, it might be advantageous to head right for those chapters that suit your needs or answer some of the questions you may have.

It is probably a good idea, in either case, to gain some understanding of the relationship between your computer and an operating system like OS/2, which takes advantage of the protected mode of your computer's processor. Chapter 1 will give you an easy-to-understand overview of what it takes to run a true multitasking operating system.

The next group of chapters provide the basic information you need to install and use the operating system. Chapters 2 and 3 will help you install OS/2 and access the robust Help facility built into the operating system. Chapters 4 and 5 will give you an understanding of the power of the Workplace Shell, the graphical environment in which you will spend most of your time.

In Chapter 6, those users comfortable with DOS and its command structure will learn how and when to use OS/2 via text-based instructions. To write, edit, or view text files (your own or those belonging to applications), you'll use the OS/2 System Editors, described in Chapter

7. And, if you are accustomed to writing batch files, you'll find the power of OS/2 command files described in Chapter 8.

Chapters 9 and 10 cover the ins and outs of printing and fonts—important subjects because OS/2 gives you a lot of room to be creative when using its built-in screen and printer fonts.

To help you get the most out of your DOS and Windows applications, Chapters 11 and 12 provide important and essential information, as well as some tips for enhanced performance. There is also plenty of information on known compatibility problems.

To further enhance performance, Chapter 13 discusses the various options available within OS/2 that can make things even faster and more productive.

Chapter 14 is an overview of the productivity applications that are built into OS/2, while Chapter 15 discusses the games available at the click of a mouse button.

With a new operating system that takes advantage of the power of your hardware, you will find yourself being more selective as you decide your future software purchases. Chapter 16 will help you set your new standards.

Chapter 17 is filled with tips, tricks, and shortcuts culled from some of the folks at IBM who helped develop and test OS/2. In addition, we picked the brains of some of the OS/2 beta testers, as well as some of the long-time users of earlier versions of OS/2 who are recognized experts in this operating system.

If you want to build powerful batch files and other easy-to-write programs to help your day-to-day computing, Chapter 18 is a guide to REXX, the powerful programming facility built into OS/2. You don't have to be an experienced programmer to use REXX.

Chapter 19 provides a reference of some of the error messages you may encounter while using OS/2, along with explanations regarding the probable cause of each error and suggested solutions.

When you need a quick reference, there are appendices. Appendix A offers a guide to most of the commands you're likely to use when you work at the command line. Appendix B contains an overview of the configuration possibilities available for your system, including explanations of the choices. Appendix C is a map for locating the OS/2 operating system files. Appendix D provides information you will need if you change or add hardware and peripherals.

OS/2 Inside & Out is written under the assumption that you will develop your expertise in this operating system at your own pace, turning to the topics you need to cover when the need arises. The chapters, therefore, are not dependent upon any special order of reading. Head for the things that interest you most. And don't forget that there is plenty of online help available once you've installed OS/2.

Conventions Used in this Book

The conventions used in this book are similar to those used in other books and manuals:

☐ User input that you are to type from the keyboard is indicated by **boldface** text, as in "type **HELP**", "type **N**", and "enter the command **PRINT /C**".

☐ Computer keyboard keys that you are asked to press are represented by SMALL CAPS, as in "press ENTER" and "press ALT". Keystroke combinations are indicated by a connecting plus sign (+): "press CTRL+ALT".

☐ Items you are asked to choose, select, or click on—such as menu selections, dialog box options and buttons, and dialog box fields— are shown in a **special font**: "choose **Save** from the File menu", "click on the **OK** button", "select the **Import text file** option", "enter the word in the **Search** field".

CHAPTER

Your Computer and OS/2

With a new operating system as powerful as OS/2 version 2.0, you can make the time you spend working on your computer more productive and more fun. The more you know about OS/2, the more you will get out of it. The relationship between a computer's hardware and its operating system is important, and this is especially true for OS/2. The multitasking capabilities of OS/2 are directly related to the connection it has with the parts of the computer. Understanding how computers and operating systems interact helps you take advantage of the differences between earlier PC environments and the enormous power of this new one.

History of the Computer

The development of the personal computer is one of the shortest yet most eventful scientific sagas in history. Not so long ago, probably within your own lifetime, a computer was a gargantuan assemblage of tubes, pipes, tapes, and metal. A large room had to be constructed to hold the computer, and controlling the environment of that room was terribly important. In some cases, people even donned special "clean" suits when entering the computer room.

Programmers who worked on these behemoths (many of whom are still actively working with computers, since this was not so long ago) tell stories of formulating code to force the computer to multiply a 3-digit number by a 4-digit number. When the computer spit out the correct answer, the programmers were elated; they knew the answer was correct because they'd had plenty of time to calculate the total themselves, using pencil and paper, before the computer was ready to return its answer. Today's computers fit neatly on desktops (with plenty of room left for telephones, memo pads, file folders, and pictures of the children), and do far more complicated calculations in far less time.

It's equally surprising to note that DOS, the operating system that until now ran almost every PC, made its first appearance less than a dozen years ago.

While this rapid evolutionary process has produced some changes in the internal elements of the personal computer, the basic operation of the computer hasn't really changed very much.

The Hardware

The standard personal computer does three things: accepts input, processes information, and produces output. Therefore, all computers have at least a keyboard, a system unit, and a monitor, as shown in Figure 1-1.

Input and Output Devices

Some peripherals, shown in Figure 1-1, are clearly for input, others for output. Some can be used for both.

Modem

A *modem* is an example of an input/output device. Using telephone lines, data can be transferred in either direction between your computer and another computer. The faster the modem, the better, of course, but

Basic hardware components and some peripherals

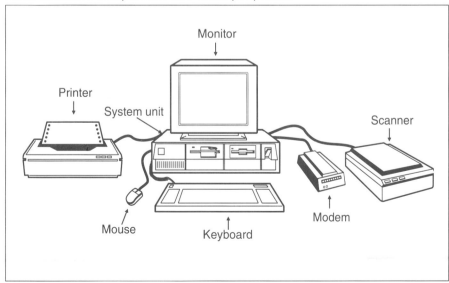

it should be noted that there are not yet any universally recognized standard protocols for modems operating at 9600 baud or above, and you may not be able to connect with other modems at that speed. Your modem either connects to one of your serial ports or acts as an internal device with its own controller/port attached.

 Tip   If you use a modem, you'll have better performance in the multi-tasking environment if you install communications software that is designed to run under OS/2.

Mouse

A *mouse* is another powerful input device, in addition to the keyboard. With the popularity and proliferation of graphical user interfaces, the mouse has become an important factor in maintaining an appropriate level of productivity. Since OS/2 2.0 uses a graphical interface, a mouse is almost a necessity. It is possible to use OS/2 with only a keyboard, but the technique is awkward and cumbersome and will tend to slow you down.

The mouse attaches to your system through a port. You can use either a port specifically designed for the mouse (a controller card purchased with a bus mouse or a designated mouse port on the computer) or one of the serial ports. OS/2 will want information about your mouse during installation.

Scanner

Another useful input device is a *scanner*, which gives you the ability to bring printed images into your data files.

In order to use a scanner effectively, you also need software to "clean up" or edit the images you capture. Most scanners come with this software, which lets you save the scanned images in a variety of file types so that you can use them with your favorite software.

These images will be received as graphics unless you also have optical character recognition software, which will permit you to edit any text in the images.

Monitor

Monitor technology has advanced so far that today there are enough variations in size, resolution, color palette, and scanning speed to suit every taste and pocketbook. To get the most out of OS/2's graphical capabilities, you should have a VGA color monitor capable of good, clear resolution.

Printers

Printers are available in a number of different models and configurations, from draft-quality dot-matrix printers to laser printers capable of near typeset-quality output. Your choice of printers will depend upon your output needs. For most business database and accounting programs, a fast dot-matrix printer is the printer of choice. For letters and other external correspondence, a dot-matrix printer with near letter-quality output capabilities serves many businesses well. A laser printer produces more attractive output and, combined with a powerful word processor, supports graphics, special effects, and some desktop-publishing features. If you will be doing full desktop publishing or other graphical production, consider a high-end laser printer capable of at least 400 dots-per-inch resolution. Regardless of the printer type attached to your system, if it has any capability at all to produce graphics, you can print multiple fonts thanks to the built-in capabilities of OS/2.

Other Input/Output Devices

There are a variety of other peripherals that may be useful for your software applications or your own work style. They include trackballs, tablets, play boards, and CD ROM and video/audio capture devices. Your own needs determine whether you require these additional peripherals.

The System Unit

The system unit contains the most complex structure, housing the motherboard, the power supply, video controllers, disk drive controllers, and any additional controllers added by the user. While different manufacturers arrange components in various ways, there is a measure of similarity among all system units, as shown in Figure 1-2.

Controllers

Controllers are circuit boards that act as interfaces between pieces of equipment attached to the computer and the motherboard that is the basis of the system unit. There is generally some type of cable connecting

FIGURE 1-2   The system unit

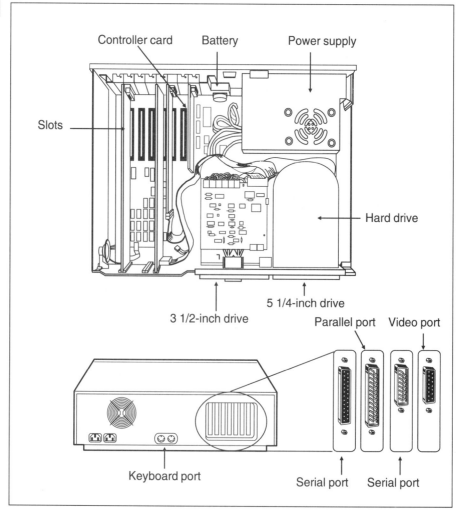

the controller to the device. It is the controller that determines the nature and characterization of the attached part. For instance, it is the video controller to which you attach your monitor that determines whether you have EGA or VGA display output.

The disk drive controllers rule the type and operation of the floppy and hard drives. Sometimes a single controller card supports the floppy drive (or drives) and hard drive (or drives) on your system. Other configurations may entail one controller card for your floppy drives and another for the hard disk. Some disk types may not be attached to a controller card in the system unit; instead, a cable connection is made directly to a controller imbedded in the motherboard.

If you add other devices to your system—for example, a tape backup unit—you will probably also have to add a controller card. Some tape backup units permit you to attach the unit to the floppy drive controller. Usually these backup units are less expensive, but they yield a much slower performance; which is best for you depends on your own priorities. Tape backup units come with the software to run them, and OS/2 versions of that software are available from some manufacturers.

Floppy Drives

To run OS/2, your computer must have at least one high-density floppy drive, either a 1.4MB 3 1/2-inch drive or a 1.2MB 5 1/4-inch drive. Many computers have both. Some people like to set up software so that data is written to a floppy disk instead of to the hard disk, feeling that this system increases the security or portability of the data. Be aware that there is a sizable tradeoff in performance with this protocol, since accessing a floppy drive is a much slower process than working with the hard disk.

Ports

Most 80386 and higher machines contain 2 RS-232 serial ports (usually one with a 9-pin connection and another with a 25-pin connection) and 1 parallel port. You may also have a game port, extra parallel ports, or any other piece of equipment you added.

Some personal computers come with a dedicated mouse port, frequently located near the port to which the keyboard attaches.

The Motherboard

The *motherboard* is a printed circuit board that holds chips (the manufacturer's BIOS, memory, numeric coprocessors, and so forth), wires, and other components, including the controllers. The most important chip is the *CPU* or central processing unit, usually referred to as the processor.

The Processor

The maturation of the PC processor is the most important factor in the progression of the power of personal computers. The original 8086/8088 processors found in early personal computers produced the first version of DOS and enjoyed such a large degree of public acceptance that software companies couldn't seem to form fast enough to keep up with the applications PC users wanted to buy. Complicated databases, accounting programs, powerful word processors, and spreadsheet applications were developed, and users rarely complained about the fact that waiting for the screen to change to the next screen page took multiple seconds. Waiting was part of the process, but it was worth it, because the process provided relief from the tedium of working with typewriters and pencils.

The development of the 80286 chip marked a major turning point in PC capabilities. The architecture of this chip included extended abilities to address memory and also the capability to run the computer in protected mode, a capacity that until then was found only in mainframes. *Protected mode* means that the computer's components, such as memory and ports, can be protected by the operating system. Software and users have no direct access to them; they are "out of bounds." Only the operating system can interact directly with them. Software has to ask permission from the operating system to use these parts. DOS, however, is unable to perform these functions, and software running under DOS has the ability to grab what it wants without regard to the needs of other tasks.

An important consideration built into the design of this chip was an emulation mode for the original 8086 architecture so that there was downward compatibility for software applications that had been previously purchased. Since DOS is not able to use the extended capabilities of this chip, these machines were merely perceived as fast personal computers by the users who purchased them.

The increase in speed of 80286 machines was due to the faster megahertz rates at which they operated and their 16-bit data path. The 8086/8088 processors were 8-bit processors, meaning they used an 8-bit data path. To picture the difference, imagine a highway 8 lanes wide with several dozen cars zooming along. If the highway suddenly widened to 16 lanes, every car would get to its destination faster.

Operating system advances have been precipitated by these changes in processor capabilities. An *operating system* is software that works directly with the hardware; it is a liaison between the computer and the software you install. The software you use has to obey the rules established by the operating system just as you do. In DOS, for example, there is a rule about naming files—you cannot have more than 8 letters in a filename nor more than 3 letters in an extension. The filename cannot contain any spaces and there are other forbidden characters. Your software, as it names its program files and permits you to name your own data files, has to obey the same rules.

Serious computer users (the people called "techies") as well as hardware and software developers understood that the power of the 80286 would never be utilized until an operating system was designed to take advantage of the extended architecture. This was the genesis of OS/2, an operating system that exploits all of the possibilities inherent in the hardware it controls.

The 80386 and 80486 chips, which followed the 80286, were designed with multitasking in mind. They take advantage of protected mode capabilities, address large amounts of memory, and provide a 32-bit environment. OS/2 version 2.0 is designed for the 80386 and higher processors.

When you moved up to a 32-bit computer, probably the first thing you noticed about it was its speed. Your search through a large database took a fraction of the time it used to, and file retrieval and saving may have seemed instantaneous. But these 32-bit machines offer a great deal more than speed. They are, in fact, dual-personality computers capable of operating in real mode (8086/8088) or protected mode. Downward compatibility is built into the chip.

The Operating System

Loading DOS as your operating system means you are using the real-mode character of your dual-personality machine.

With DOS, the computer's processor directly interacts with the hardware—video, ports, memory, and so on. Every program you run also interacts with the components in your computer. If your word processor is ready to print, it asks DOS for direct access to your printer port and DOS complies (or, depending on how rude the programmer was, the word processor may just take what it needs without asking—behavior that doesn't really follow the rules but is frequently tolerated by DOS). When your database is searching for information in order to fill in a screen, the screen belongs to the database and waits (along with you) for the information to arrive.

Using OS/2 means that the programs you run are prohibited from accessing the components of your computer directly. This feature is important because it allows you to do more than one thing at a time. If you are running two or more programs at once, they are both going to want access to the memory, video, keyboard, and so on. In order to make multitasking possible, there has to be a cooperative, amicable environment.

Multitasking

If two or more applications are running at the same time, only one can update the screen. If you are entering information at the keyboard while you have several programs running, the data must be sent to the right program. When your software is ready to print a report for you, the data has to be spooled in a way that ensures that data from other concurrently running programs isn't mixed in.

Virtual Devices

OS/2 presents the devices contained in your computer to you and to the programs you install in a new way. They are virtual devices, not real devices. *Virtual* means they appear the same as real devices, and neither you nor your software programs can tell the difference in your day-to-day work. The program thinks it is putting information on the screen, but it is really using a virtual screen, created and held in the computer's memory, presented to it by the operating system. OS/2 takes the information that is presented to these virtual devices and passes it to the actual devices. OS/2 creates as many of these virtual devices as it needs, and it is never confused about which data is connected to which program.

You might also be interested to know that OS/2 "marries" your virtual input devices (keyboard, mouse) with a virtual screen and keeps them together in an entity called a *screen group*. The output of each program that is running is written to its own unique screen group, and the keyboard or mouse input for each program is sent to its own screen group. In this way data that is entered is always processed through the right program and passed to the right screen group.

When you switch between applications in your multitasking environment, the application you are working on directly is the *foreground* application. The other applications that you are running concurrently are, at that moment, in the *background*. With true multitasking, work continues in the background, tasks are completed, and updates take place. However, the definition of "background" shouldn't be taken literally. If you are working full-screen, the continuing actions of other applications will indeed be in the background, hidden behind the window you've opened for your work. However, if you are opening multiple windows on your screen, you will be able to see the work continuing in the "background" within the windows of the screen groups. The screen you are working on, the application you switched to, is just the screen group that is in the foreground.

Memory

Like virtual devices, virtual memory is created as needed and data is passed along to real, physical memory when the program needs it. Physical memory, of course, is measured by the number of memory chips in the computer. The ability to create virtual memory makes a few megabytes of physical RAM go a very long way. When a program requests more memory than is physically available, the operating system allocates virtual memory on the fixed disk. That means the amount of memory available to software applications is limited only by the amount of space available on the fixed disk.

One implementation of this movement of memory is called *swapping*, as the operating system swaps pieces of programs back and forth between the fixed disk and RAM. Windows and earlier versions of OS/2 used swapping, but since the pieces weren't all the same size, there were some gaps created in memory and on the hard disk. Attempts to solve this problem created other results that affected the performance of the system.

OS/2 version 2.0 is designed to take advantage of a special feature of the 80386 processor called *paged* memory mode, which is designed to move memory in pages of 4K. Having a specific size for a memory page means that memory is always allocated in blocks of the same size, eliminating the need for extra processes to be running in the background in order to keep memory and the swap file organized properly. This speeds these memory functions.

Under OS/2 your software cannot access memory directly, since memory is protected as are other parts of the computer. Software must request memory from the operating system. Not only does OS/2 create virtual memory in order to provide enough memory for each program to run, it also manages the memory so that programs and the data attached to them don't bump into each other.

Still, even under OS/2 a program must reside in the computer's real memory in order to complete tasks. It must have its own address in that memory, and the operating system has to track that location. OS/2 creates a map of each section of memory and permits software to allocate whatever memory size it will require. The ability for software to use as much memory as it wants is another enormous, wonderful difference between DOS, with its absolute 640K limit for software, and OS/2. The breaking of the 640K barrier has unleashed all the imagination and creativity of programmers who have been limited by DOS; as a result, applications written to take advantage of OS/2 are powerful and productive.

Using its map, OS/2 can move the program code and its associated data between virtual and physical memory as the need arises. With the ability to create enormous amounts of virtual memory, OS/2 has plenty of room to maneuver. By being able to control this virtual-to-physical memory mapping, OS/2 can map diverse programs to the same memory location, meaning that parts of the physical memory can be shared by separate processes.

Time Slices

Inherent in OS/2's multitasking character is its ability to act as a director of operations and a referee. Remember, even though you are multitasking, your computer has only one CPU, which can only perform one function at a time. OS/2 is permitting the execution of one task for a specific time period and then allowing another task to perform. That specific time period is called a *time slice*. OS/2 gives the CPU to each function that needs it, using a variety of criteria to allocate the size of the time slice and the frequency with which it is granted. This scheduling is done in a round-robin fashion much of the time, but any program that needs the computer to complete a task will be given priority. Using a method bordering on artificial intelligence to determine when a task needs CPU time, OS/2 boosts the priority of tasks to ensure that every application gets what it needs and the user remains productive. OS/2 has several classes of priorities and will regularly check on the progress of the tasks being performed to see if one of them needs to be given a resource in order to execute its next step. If there are a lot of time-critical tasks being performed, OS/2 will make sure that less critical tasks get a turn by using *preemptive scheduling*, a process that involves temporarily raising the priority levels so that every thread of every program running on your computer gets the resources it needs.

This ability to do preemptive scheduling gives OS/2 the power of a parallel multitasking system, like a mainframe. That means that for all intents and purposes, and in appearances, it really is doing more than one thing at a time, which is *parallel multitasking*. Another example of parallel multitasking is the ability of a person to walk down the street and chew gum or to drive a car and talk.

Because of the limitation of working with one CPU, technically OS/2 is serially multitasking, but the ability to be flexible and accommodating gives it the power (and appearance) of parallel multitasking.

Serial multitasking is like reading a book and talking to your spouse at the same time. These may appear to be simultaneous actions, but in reality you are reading, and then talking, and then reading, and so on. If you tried to combine these tasks, either you would be unable to absorb the book's contents or you would be chattering unintelligibly.

Every time OS/2 switches from one task to another, it remembers the state of each task, just as when you finish a sentence and go back to reading your book, you remember where you were and what happened in the plot development. When any task gets its turn at the CPU, OS/2 presents the computer's resources to that task so that it seems as if there had been no interruption. This amazing ability is called *context switching.*

Device Drivers

Since the video, parallel, and serial ports of your computer are also part of the protected mode operation of OS/2, they work a little differently than they do under DOS (although you won't notice, since your day-to-day work in any software will proceed as it always did). In fact, any peripheral attached to the computer and controlled by a device on the motherboard has to cooperate with the protected-mode personality of your computer. None of them can be addressed directly by you or the software you use. OS/2 uses special software called *device drivers* to translate general requests from a program into specific instructions tailored for the specific device. For instance, if your software program needs to read data from the diskette in drive A, the OS/2 device driver generates the appropriate functions, moving the heads on the floppy drive, reading the data, and so on. The functions would be different if the instructions were to read from keyboard input. There are hundreds of device drivers, many of them for specific brands of printers, included in OS/2.

The 32-Bit Environment

OS/2 version 2.0 is written expressly for a 32-bit computer. Unlike previous versions, it cannot be run on a computer with an 80286 processor. It does, however, maintain compatibility with 16-bit applications and resources.

Operating with a 32-bit data path provides a meaningful difference in speed and productivity. Not only is your software, along with its data, operating in a 32-bit path, but so are the operating system instructions and other operating system chores. In addition, it is the 32-bit 80386 processor that provides the memory technique called *paging*, discussed earlier.

Using DOS and Windows

The fact that you've moved to OS/2 doesn't mean you have to abandon DOS or Windows and the software applications attached to those systems. The ability to run both of those environments is built into OS/2. Most of your software will operate quite happily in the OS/2 DOS/Windows climates, blissfully unaware that you have not invoked the "real" operating systems. If necessary, you can continue to use native DOS or Windows. In fact, you can have several different DOS programs operating at the same time, and they can be running in different versions of DOS.

There are several ways to implement this under OS/2. They are explained in the following chapters, and instructions are given on setting up your computer to execute your choices.

CHAPTER

Installing OS/2

*I*n this chapter, you learn how to install OS/2 from a diskette. It is also possible to install OS/2 from a CD or to download OS/2 from a network.

Installation Decisions

As you install OS/2, there are a number of choices to consider. Some of the decisions should be made before you begin the installation process. Others can be made as you go through the operation and can be altered afterward if you change your mind. Some of the decisions you make involve tradeoffs. For instance, you may opt for power and flexibility, but in doing so you create a more complicated environment in which to work. Your own priorities and work needs determine your personal choices.

How Many Operating Systems Do You Need?

An OS/2 computer can support multiple operating systems if you choose to add them. You have the option of installing (or keeping) DOS on your computer in addition to OS/2. However, you probably don't need to do this since most DOS software runs perfectly well under OS/2.

The same is true of Windows—you can use the Windows component of OS/2 or install a copy of Windows. (Remember that Windows is not really an operating system and needs to be installed on top of DOS.) You can also install UNIX, XENIX, or AIX in addition to OS/2.

If you have been using DOS 5.0 and have any software that requires the use of the SETVER function, you can modify the OS/2 DOS settings so that it does the equivalent of a SETVER for an application automatically. DOS in OS/2 is based on DOS 5.0.

Keeping a Copy of DOS

If DOS is already installed on your computer, you can install OS/2 in addition to DOS. If you use DR DOS, you will be happy to hear that you do not have to give up your operating system either, since OS/2 is perfectly happy with DR DOS; people who are using OS/2 with DR DOS report that they work beautifully together. (Any generic mention of "DOS" in this book should be interpreted as including DR DOS.)

There are some software programs that don't work well (or at all) under OS/2. If you wish to use one of these programs, you have no choice but to have an installed copy of DOS. You might, however, want to look for an OS/2 program that performs the same functions.

In addition, any software that demands direct access to hardware is prevented from doing so under OS/2. If you do any programming, you should be aware that many DOS 386 debuggers typically go directly to the 386 control registers, a process that requires DOS and isn't allowed under OS/2. There are also some known problems with certain internal fax boards. A guide to OS/2 compatibility is provided in the README file.

Keeping a Copy of Windows

As with DOS software, there are some Windows applications that do not work well under OS/2 Windows, and you should install (or keep) native Windows. Any Windows program that must run in Windows enhanced mode will not run under OS/2. Actually, to be technically correct, Windows enhanced-mode applications that require WINMEM32.DLL don't run under OS/2, but enhanced-mode applications written for DPMI do. The software packages give the information you need regarding software requirements. While these Windows applications are in the minority, their number is growing; if you think you may need such software, you are better off installing native Windows.

 Note   If you purchased the DOS or Windows Upgrade version of OS/2, you must have DOS on your disk because the installation program will look for a DOS partition.

Dual Boot with DOS

If you are going to run DOS, the easiest way is with the dual boot option. *Dual booting* means your computer boots into whatever operating system was active the last time you turned it off. It allows you to shift between running under DOS or OS/2 with a simple command.

Once dual boot is installed, switch between the two operating systems with the BOOT command. When running OS/2, type

BOOT /DOS

at a command line to switch to DOS. After executing a normal OS/2 shutdown, rebooting brings up the DOS operating system. When running DOS, type

BOOT /OS2

to set up OS/2 to be started at the next boot.

The BOOT command moves the correct COMMAND.COM, CONFIG.SYS, and AUTOEXEC.BAT files to the root of the C drive and rewrites the boot sector to start the correct operating system. It does not execute the boot automatically; you must reboot the computer yourself.

To establish this dual boot configuration, you can simply install OS/2 on top of your existing DOS or, if this is a new machine, install your favorite version of DOS prior to beginning OS/2 installation. The installation program detects DOS and installs dual boot automatically.

Most people who opt for this configuration end up spending most of their time using OS/2; it is possible to eliminate a lot of DOS files and save disk space, since many of these functions are available in OS/2.

To install dual boot, you must be running DOS 3.3 or higher. If you are installing OS/2 version 2.0 onto a computer that contains earlier versions of OS/2, be aware that version 2.0 is larger than the earlier versions. Even if you have an existing dual boot configuration, make sure your partition is large enough to hold OS/2 2.0.

Tradeoffs to Consider

In general, dual boot is simpler, but it has the potential for trouble. Users who have accidentally edited or deleted one or more of the important boot files (AUTOEXEC.BAT or CONFIG.SYS, for example) have created unusable systems for themselves. If, for example, your CONFIG.SYS is inadvertently altered, you may have problems booting OS/2.

While the potential for trouble may complicate things, dual boot does simplify the OS/2 installation because it does not require you to repartition your hard disk.

Multiple Operating Systems

You can install OS/2 so that your computer contains multiple operating systems. In order to do this, however, plan on repartitioning all or part of your hard disk.

 Caution If you partition, you should make a backup of any files currently on your hard disk because the partitioning process deletes all data from the hard disk.

Partitioning

The most straightforward way to configure your system is to put each operating system in its own partition on your hard disk. As in DOS, you can separate your disk into primary partitions and use the areas outside them for extended partitions that contain logical drives.

OS/2 permits up to four partitions on your hard disk, and you can configure them in the way that is most efficient for you. You may choose to have four primary partitions, or three primary and one extended, and so on. The extended partition can have multiple logical drives within it. One example of a partition plan is shown in Figure 2-1.

When you use primary partitions to install multiple operating systems, you must dedicate one of them to hold the OS/2 programs that manage the multiple operating system configuration. This partition is referred to as the Boot Manager partition. You must have at least one primary partition in addition to the Boot Manager partition.

One difference between logical drives and primary partitions is that each logical drive is identified by a unique drive letter while all the primary partitions share the same drive letter. On the first disk in your computer, that drive letter is "C." While you are operating your computer, there is actually only one drive C, since only one primary partition can be active

FIGURE
2-1

Sample partition scheme for DOS 5.0

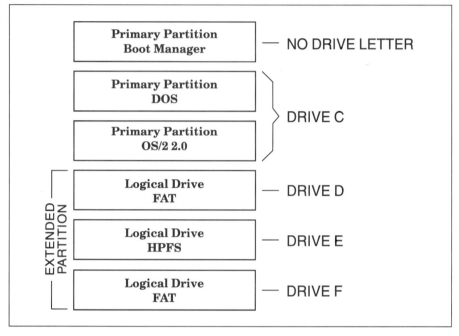

at a time; any other primary partitions that share that designation are not active and therefore are not *mapped*, not given a drive letter. This means that any data in a primary partition cannot be accessed by an operating system in another primary partition.

The next available drive letter, "D," is assigned to the first logical drive in the first extended partition. If you have more than one logical drive in that extended partition, they would become drive E, drive F, and so on. If you have two hard disks in your system, the primary partitions on the second hard disk become drive D, and then the logical drives are mapped, beginning with drive E. The Boot Manager partition is not assigned a drive letter.

Mappings

Mapping is performed automatically by the operating system that is active when you start your system. An operating system only maps those drives with a file system format that it supports. A *file system* is the component of the operating system that provides access to files and programs on a disk. The file system used under DOS is the File Allocation Table (FAT). With OS/2 you have an installable file system—the High Performance File System (HPFS)—available if you choose to use it, in addition to FAT, which is discussed later in this chapter. As you set up your partitions, you are asked to choose the file system assigned to any logical drives you create.

If DOS is the active operating system when you start, and you have chosen the HPFS file system for one of the partitions, it is possible that there will be logical drives that DOS cannot recognize, and therefore they will not be mapped. To make things a little more complicated, versions of DOS earlier than 5.0 will stop the mapping process as soon as they see a file system they don't recognize.

Using DOS 5.0, a computer configured as shown in Figure 2-1 would change the drive mappings illustrated. Logical drive D would remain the same, logical drive E would not be recognized, and logical drive F would be mapped to drive E. Earlier versions of DOS would stop mapping at drive D and go no further. Any software and data contained in drive F, as shown in Figure 2-1, would be inaccessible even though the file system is compatible. Therefore, as you design your installation of OS/2, you should plan to put logical drives that use the HPFS at the end of the hard disk.

Incidentally, it is possible to install OS/2 version 2.0 onto a logical drive instead of in a primary partition. (Earlier versions of OS/2 could only be placed in primary partitions.) However, this is a much more complicated way to operate and can cause a lot of confusion for those inexperienced with computing or with OS/2. For that reason it is an avenue not generally recommended, and you should plan to put any and all operating systems you wish to install into primary partitions.

Partition Size

As you plan your installation you should consider partition sizes, since the capacity of your hard disk is finite. First of all, if your hard disk is not larger than 60MB, there is no real performance advantage in using the High Performance File System. The Boot Manager partition requires 1 megabyte of disk space. Assigning 3 megabytes of disk space to DOS partitions should be sufficient. You can, of course, make a DOS partition larger and use the remaining space for software and data. If you do that, you need to remember that some versions of DOS (such as DOS 3.3) must be installed in a primary partition that is within the first 32MB of the hard disk.

The OS/2 partition needs to have disk space allocated in a large enough supply to handle the components you want to install. Plan on a minimum of 15MB and if you are contemplating the use of every feature available in OS/2, you need about 30MB.

Remember that the decisions you make during installation regarding the features you want to install are not etched in stone. OS/2 has a built-in Selective Install option that allows you to add all of these features in the future. You do, however, need enough room in the OS/2 partition to add them.

If sufficient hard disk space is available, you should probably assign at least 25 to 30 megabytes of it to the OS/2 partition.

You can use the multiple operating systems installation option and still have a dual boot system. To do so, install both DOS and OS/2 in the same primary partition.

Tradeoffs to Consider

Multiple booting is more complex and it takes longer to set up because of the necessity of partitioning your hard disk. Once installed, the system takes a little longer to boot because every time you boot it displays the selection screen asking which operating system you want. On the other hand, the DOS and OS/2 files are protected from each other.

If you need to partition or repartition your hard disk anyway in order to install OS/2, you should probably use the multiple boot system.

OS/2 File Systems

With OS/2 you have a choice of *file systems*, the way the operating system keeps track of your files. As information is stored, retrieved, and stored again on hard disk, the operating system must keep track of where each file or portion of a file is located. OS/2 is capable of handling this chore in two ways: using FAT (File Allocation Table), or HPFS (High Performance File System). DOS supports only the FAT file system. OS/2 also supports the FAT file system but has enhanced it so that it adds extended attributes to your files. Operating as a 32-bit application, this version of FAT runs much faster than FAT under prior versions of OS/2 or DOS. The somewhat oversimplified explanations and distinctions that follow may help you decide which system to use.

FAT

A portion of your disk, located at the beginning sector of the partition, is reserved by the operating system for storage of the FAT system. The FAT system not only keeps track of where the files are, but, if they have been split up, it remembers the order in which the separate pieces of the file should be retrieved.

The FAT system places files, or portions of files, by finding disk space large enough to hold them. When you first begin using a new hard disk and install software files, and then begin to use that software to create data files, the operating system can generally find portions of the disk large enough to put an entire file in one contiguous spot. As you begin to fill up your hard disk, however, finding one spot large enough to hold a file becomes more difficult. As you retrieve data files, add information to them, and then save the new, larger files, the operating system has to start splitting those files up, placing them all over the disk. The "address book" the operating system uses to keep track of scattered files is FAT—the File Allocation Table.

Eventually the disk and the files it holds can become quite fragmented, with many files scattered, in small pieces, all over the hard disk. Retrieving and saving files takes longer. You can sometimes hear the hard disk churning away as it puts together files for you. There are some utility programs on the market that, if used with proper caution and under the right circumstances, can be used to *defrag* the hard disk, moving files around so that pieces of the same file occupy contiguous space on the hard disk.

The FAT system follows the conventional 8.3 file-naming system, where filenames cannot exceed 8 characters and extensions cannot exceed 3 characters. Certain keyboard characters cannot be used in filenames, and spaces are not allowed.

HPFS

The *High Performance File System* available in OS/2 operates differently and more efficiently than the FAT system. It keeps its directory of files in the center of the partition, which increases its speed in finding files. HPFS is designed to allocate contiguous space for files, preventing the kind of disk fragmentation that can happen with FAT. HPFS also deals with write errors by reserving alternate space on the partition to write to. The filenames under HPFS are not limited to the 8.3 standard (although like FAT, there are some forbidden characters). HPFS permits you to use 254 characters, allowing for descriptive filenames.

Tradeoffs to Consider

If you have DOS programs that must run by booting native DOS, you have to make sure these programs and their data are in a FAT partition. DOS software cannot get to anything in an HPFS partition. As robust and advanced as HPFS is, there is not the high level of compatibility that you have if you use FAT.

Installing OS/2

At this point you should have enough information to make a decision about whether you need to have copies of native DOS or Windows on your system. Your conclusion regarding the installation choices—whether you want to operate solely under OS/2, under a dual boot system, or in a multiple operating system environment—should be easy to make once you think about the types of applications you expect to run, as well as the size and condition (new or already full of software and data) of your hard disk. The decision on the file system or systems you want to use must also be made at this point.

 Caution   If you are going to repartition your hard disk, at least back up all of your data files (your software files can be reinstalled from their original diskettes). For safety, you might want to format a fresh set of diskettes for this backup and discard any diskettes that report any bad sectors.

During the installation process, you will be presented with a large set of choices for customizing your OS/2 installation (see Figure 2-2). Each option has the amount of disk space it requires listed alongside it. In addition, a separate window at the bottom of the screen keeps a running tally of the amount of disk space required for the set of functions you have selected. This allows you to determine intelligently which features fit on your disk.

The OS/2 disk labeled Disk 1 is not the first disk you will use. You begin your installation with the Installation Disk.

Basic Installation

If you are installing OS/2 on a computer that does not contain any operating system and you do not believe you will have any need for a separate installation of native DOS, the easiest procedure is basic installation of OS/2. Begin by inserting the OS/2 Installation Disk and following the instructions on the screen.

FIGURE 2-2

OS/2 installation options *

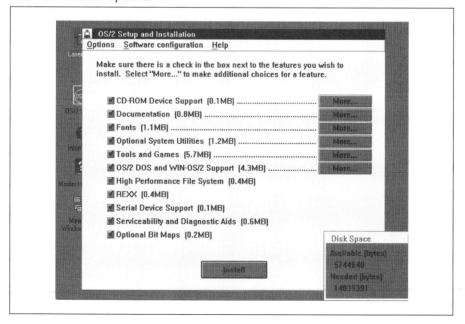

During the installation process, you are asked to make choices about the system setup. Each time there is a choice, a default choice is provided. There is more information about these choices in the following sections of this chapter.

Installing with Dual Boot

All of the DOS commands and utilities, including COMMAND.COM, must be in a subdirectory. Most people name the subdirectory DOS. You have to check the contents of CONFIG.SYS and AUTOEXEC.BAT as well as DOSSHELL.BAT if you are using the DOS shell. Make sure the SHELL, COMSPEC, PATH, and APPEND statements point to the DOS directory, not to the root. If you don't have an AUTOEXEC.BAT, you need to create one with at least:

```
SET COMSPEC=C:\DOS\COMMAND.COM
PATH C:\DOS
COPY C:\DOS\COMMAND.COM C:\ >NUL
```

The CONFIG.SYS file must have at least:

```
SHELL=C:\DOS\COMMAND.COM /P
```

If you are using the DOS shell, edit DOSSHELL.BAT to change

```
@CD C:\
```

to

```
@CD C:\DOS
```

Once the changes are made, reboot your computer to have them take effect. If you have any DOS or Windows programs you want to install, do so before installing OS/2.

Begin the Installation

Insert the Installation Disk into drive A and reboot your computer. The first installation screen appears, illustrated in Figure 2-3.

Initial installation screen ✿

```
        IBM Operating System/2 Installation
                  Version 2.00

(C) Copyright IBM Corp. 1981, 1991, 1992. All rights reserved.

Remove the diskette from drive A

Insert the Operating System/2 Diskette 1 into drive A
Then, press Enter.
```

Following the instructions on the screen, insert Disk 1. After reading Disk 1 for awhile, OS/2 displays a prompt asking you to press ENTER to continue or ESC to cancel. Press ENTER. You receive several screens of information on how to make selections during the installation process, after which you are prompted to insert Disk 2. After processing Disk 2 for a few seconds, OS/2 tells you where it intends to install itself, as shown in Figure 2-4.

When you are asked to select an installation drive, make sure you choose drive C. Do not choose to format your hard disk during the installation process.

You will continue to be prompted by the installation program to answer questions and make choices. A more complete description of these choices is provided in the section of this chapter on installing multiple operating systems. If you are not sure about any of the choices, press F1 for help. The system will prompt you to place diskettes into drive A several times before the program completes the process of copying information from the diskettes to your hard disk.

FIGURE
2-4

Choosing an installation drive ✿

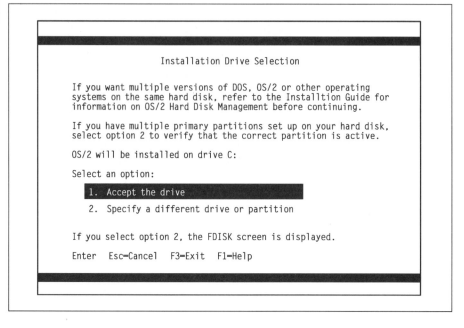

```
                    Installation Drive Selection

  If you want multiple versions of DOS, OS/2 or other operating
  systems on the same hard disk, refer to the Installtion Guide for
  information on OS/2 Hard Disk Management before continuing.

  If you have multiple primary partitions set up on your hard disk,
  select option 2 to verify that the correct partition is active.

  OS/2 will be installed on drive C:

  Select an option:
     1.  Accept the drive
     2.  Specify a different drive or partition

  If you select option 2, the FDISK screen is displayed.

  Enter   Esc=Cancel   F3=Exit   F1=Help
```

Modifying Bootup Files

Once OS/2 is installed, if you are in OS/2 and want to modify the DOS CONFIG.SYS or AUTOEXEC.BAT file, look in the \OS2\SYSTEM sub-directory for the files CONFIG.DOS and AUTOEXEC.DOS. Likewise, when you are running DOS and want to modify the OS/2 files, look in the SYSTEM subdirectory for CONFIG.OS2 and AUTOEXEC.OS2.

Installing with Multiple Operating Systems

Insert the OS/2 Installation Disk into drive A and boot (or reboot) the computer. The opening screen portrayed in Figure 2-3 will appear. You will then see the screens of information on how to make selections during the installation process. You will be prompted to insert Disk 2.

After reading Disk 2 for a few seconds, OS/2 asks you to specify a drive (see Figure 2-4). Select option 2, which brings up the FDISK screen after warning you that changing partitions will cause you to lose your data.

Remove Existing Partitions

To put the Boot Manager at the beginning of your disk, you need to remove all partitions that currently exist. Move the highlight to the last partition on the disk by selecting it with the left mouse button. Then open the Options menu by clicking on **Options** on the menu bar (see Figure 2-5), and select **Delete partition**.

Note It is possible to put the Boot Manager partition somewhere other than in the first partition, perhaps to leave an existing DOS partition intact. However, the possible complications make this a less desirable choice.

FIGURE 2-5

Selecting **Delete partition** from the Options menu ✿

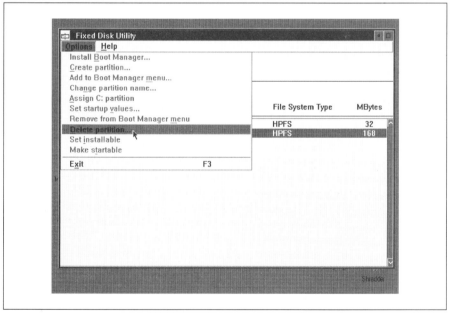

You get one last warning message, shown in the following illustration, so you can change your mind (or check the quality of your backup if you think you should) before proceeding. ✿

Follow these same steps to delete all existing partitions on your disk.

Install Boot Manager

Now when you select **Options**, the **Install Boot Manager** option is highlighted. Select that option, and a 1MB partition will be created at the beginning of your fixed disk to contain the Boot Manager. You now need to create a partition to contain your first operating system. Move the highlight to the undefined partition below the Boot Manager and again click on **Options**. You need to select **Create partition** to make a place for the first operating system. You will be asked if you are creating a Primary Partition or an Extended Logical Partition. Choose **Primary**, since this is an operating system partition.

Create Primary Partitions

The next prompt asks for the size of the partition to create. It is recommended that the first operating system be the one for DOS. (This recommendation is based on the assumption that only DOS users would be using multiple boot. It is indeed possible that you might want to install UNIX/AIX in this partition rather than DOS, but that is the exception rather than the rule.) For most versions of DOS, a 3MB partition should suffice.

At the next prompt, tell OS/2 that you want to create this partition at the next available space; you will be asked to name the partition. Select a name that reflects the contents of the partition, such as "DR DOS 6" or "DOS 3.3." You also have to set this partition as Startable so that you can install the operating system into the partition. After installation of the operating system, the status of the partition changes to Bootable. Finally, select **Options** and **Add to Boot Manager menu** so that this operating system can be selected for startup.

Now you need to create a partition for the next operating system. Most likely, that will be OS/2 2.0. This should also be set as a primary partition. The size required is going to vary a good bit based on the options you wish to install. Name this partition in the same way you did the first, with a name like "OS/2 2.0," and add it to the Boot Manager menu. Finally, select **Options** one more time, and make sure that partition is set to Installable so that OS/2 can be loaded there.

Create Logical Partitions

Now establish one or more program/data partitions. These should be extended logical partitions, so they can be accessed by either of the operating systems installed. Remember that later you have to format these partitions and you also have to choose a file system, either FAT or HPFS.

Exit the Fixed Disk Utility by pressing F3 and saving your changes. You will be asked to insert the Installation Disk and reboot so OS/2 can recognize the new partitions.

Choosing What to Install

When the computer has booted, accept the default installation drive. Now you are ready to tell the OS/2 installation program which features of OS/2 you want to install onto your hard disk. Following are some guidelines to help you decide.

Documentation

The installation program presents the following dialog box to find out which parts of the online documentation you wish to install: ✿

If you are new to OS/2, you should install the tutorial; it is an excellent introduction to OS/2. After reviewing the tutorial, you can delete it to reclaim the disk space. Everyone should install the OS/2 command reference. It is an invaluable resource for looking up OS/2 commands and the meanings of their parameters. Even users who are familiar with OS/2 will find times when they can't recall specific parameters for a command. Version 2.0 does not provide this information in the printed documentation that comes with the system, but even if it were supplied it is always easier to look it up online.

The online REXX information is especially important for those who will be writing programs in REXX (see Chapter 18 for more information on using REXX). If you use REXX only to create command files, however, this information is probably not that important and you may want to save the disk space it would occupy (about .2MB).

Fonts

The next installation category is Fonts. Clicking on **More** brings up a confusing list of available font choices. As you can see in Figure 2-6, some fonts are listed more than once.

The difference is that some are system fonts and some are Adobe Type Manager (outline) fonts. It is probably a good idea to install all three outline fonts. These can be used by a wide variety of applications and can be resized to almost any dimension imaginable. This flexibility does have a price, however. In order to be *scalable* (sized to order by the user) these fonts are stored differently than standard fonts. With system fonts, an actual picture of each character is stored and can be instantly called to the screen. With outline fonts, a description of how to draw each character is stored. That way, the font can be made any size, simply by

FIGURE
2-6

Installing fonts ✿

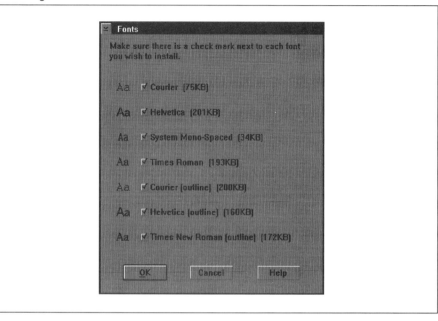

following the instructions but making each segment of the character a different size. Thus, it takes a little longer to display each character because its appearance has to be calculated based on the current point size.

In practice, this delay isn't a problem for most applications. For word processing applications that display an entire page of text, the delay can be quite noticeable. Using draft mode during the initial entry stage of a document and turning to the WYSIWYG view of the document later in the process circumvents this problem. If you have lots of free disk space, install all of the fonts. If you don't, eschewing the non-outline versions of Times Roman, Courier, and Helvetica can save nearly half a megabyte of disk space. The System Mono-Spaced font should definitely be installed.

System Utilities

Your next choices concern the system utilities, shown in Figure 2-7.

FIGURE 2-7

System utilities choices ☼

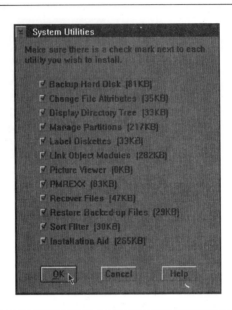

Unless you have an OS/2 application that you prefer to use for file backup, you should check the **Backup Hard Disk** and **Restore Backed-up Files** system utilities.

Caution If you are using the High Performance File System, your DOS backup program will not work properly. There are backup systems available for OS/2 HPFS.

Change File Attributes The ability to change file attributes and display a directory tree is now included in the Workplace Shell, so command-line versions may safely be deselected. If you happen to have one of the few applications that calls one of these commands directly, it is easy to put these command lines back later.

Manage Partitions Probably the only time you would change the partitions on your fixed disk would be to install a new operating system, so the Manage Partitions program is one that can usually be left out.

Again, it is easy to install it later if you find you need it; in the meantime, save the disk space.

Label Diskettes This utility is superfluous for many people. The typical time to label a diskette is when it is formatted, and the FORMAT utility can give a label to a diskette without the LABEL utility.

Link Object Modules The ability to link object modules is only important to those who are developing programs for OS/2. You don't need this utility to write REXX programs, so virtually all end users can save the .3MB of disk space that this program uses.

Picture Viewer This is an interesting utility for viewing PM bitmaps. Probably any program you use to create such a bitmap would have a view ability built into it, so you may choose not to install this feature as well.

PMREXX This is a shell for REXX programs that allows them to run in a PM window rather than a command window. It also adds the ability to scroll back through the program's output. This is a convenient utility that doesn't take much disk space. On the other hand, if all you're going to be doing is running commercial applications, you probably won't use PMREXX very much.

Recover Files Here is a potential way to recover data from a disk that develops defective sectors. While it is certainly not guaranteed to recover data from a bad disk, if you ever encounter this situation, you will probably want every tool at your disposal.

Sort Filter This filter provides you with a way to rearrange data in files via a command you can use at the command line or in a REXX program. In today's world of high-powered applications and databases, it is rare for an end user to go through this step manually. It does, however, provide a "quick and dirty" way for a user to rearrange data files created with one of the OS/2 editors. This should not be used with files created by applications, however, since they are usually stored in a binary form and you won't know the exact locations of the information in each record. All in all, unless you are planning to do some REXX programming, you will probably never use this program.

Installation Aid This is a program some companies have used to create an installation program for their applications. IBM did not publish the interface to this program widely, however, and for the most part it is only IBM programs that use it. If you are going to use IBM applications such as OS/2 Extended Services, install this aid. Otherwise, this is a quarter of a megabyte of disk space that can be put to better use. As always, should you get a program which requires this, it is easy to add later.

Choosing Optional Programs

There are a number of mini-applications, programs, and functions available that are not absolutely necessary if you plan to spend all your time working in application software under OS/2. If disk space is available, however, many of these programs will add to your productivity and fun.

Tools and Games

To decide which of the tools and games shown in Figure 2-8 you want to install, you might want to read Chapter 7, which describes the Enhanced Editor; Chapter 14, covering the productivity applications; and Chapter 15, which goes over the games. This will give you an idea of the value of these programs.

DOS, Windows, and Memory Management

If you are only going to be running OS/2 programs, deselect the **OS/2 DOS + WIN-OS/2 Environment** option and save yourself a whopping 4MB of disk space.

To decide upon memory management extensions for DOS, shown in Figure 2-9, take a look at the DOS applications you plan to run. Determine which, if any, of the techniques your applications use. You can mix and match DPMI, EMS, and XMS as needed. Note that if you're going to run Windows applications, you should install DPMI support since many Windows applications will require it. If you are going to be

Tools and games available with OS/2 *

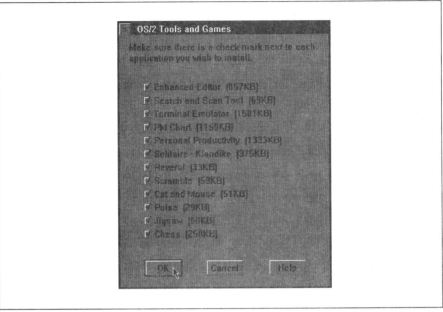

Memory management options *

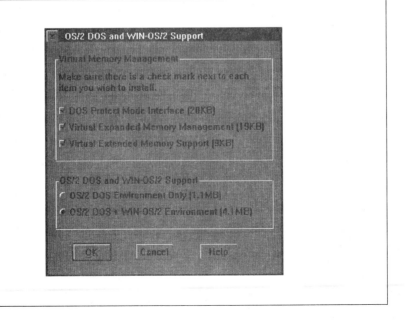

running DOS programs but not Windows programs, select the **OS/2 DOS Environment Only** option and save 3MB of disk space.

HPFS and REXX

The High Performance File System was discussed earlier in this chapter. You can decide whether to install it based upon your needs. The same is true of REXX. Note that many applications are starting to use REXX as their macro or extension language, so it may be of value even if you don't intend to write programs of your own.

Serial Device Support

If you are planning to use a modem or any other serial devices, you should install serial device support, even if you plan to use Extended Services.

Serviceability and Diagnostic Aids

These can be useful to trained service personnel in tracking down a problem you might have with your system. The situations in which you would use them, however, are probably rare. Unless you are using Extended Services, which requires these tools, you can delay installing these until a service representative asks you for the information they provide.

Bitmaps

The optional bitmaps are simply pictures that can be used as the background for the desktop, or can be brought to the screen when the system goes into a security lockup. The actual images vary based on the resolution of the display adapter and monitor you have. If you think you may be using them, go ahead and install them. If disk space becomes a problem, it is easy enough to delete them later.

Installing Printer Drivers

Once you've completed the above selections, the OS/2 installation continues through the rest of the diskettes. You are then prompted to insert the first printer driver disk. In past versions of OS/2, a lack of printer support was often cited as a major handicap to its acceptance. With version 2.0, however, there are well over 100 printers supported on the diskettes shipped with the product. There are many more printer drivers available on bulletin boards and IBM's IBMOS2 forum on CompuServe. Select your printer from the list and follow the instructions to insert the appropriate printer driver disk as instructed.

Installing Devices

Finally, you will be shown a dialog box that first asks if you have a device support diskette to install. IBM has published an interface that hardware developers can use to provide easy installation of device drivers for their products. If you have received such a disk with a device, select this option.

Migrating Applications

Next, you're asked if you want to migrate applications. If you installed for dual boot without repartitioning or reformatting your hard disk, you probably still have applications on your disk. The migrate option instructs OS/2 to look through your disk and try to identify those applications. Those that it recognizes it will add to an applications folder on your desktop automatically. Note that this recognition is based on a database of major programs. It is likely that there are some programs that are not listed in the database and thus not automatically added to a folder. Chapter 4 discusses how you can add these yourself.

Configure Windows Desktop

The third option on this dialog box allows you to configure your WIN-OS/2 desktop. If you are not going to run Windows applications, ignore this option entirely. If you are running Windows applications now and didn't format your disk, OS/2 will detect the desktop configuration from your existing Windows implementation and use it for the WIN-OS2 desktop.

Completing Installation

After your final entries, there is a pause while OS/2 finishes configuring your disk. You are then prompted to remove the last diskette and restart the system. The first time you boot OS/2, there is a somewhat lengthy delay as it initializes the Workplace Shell parameters. It boots much more quickly thereafter.

The First Bootup

Once OS/2 installation is complete, reboot your computer. Select OS/2 as the operating system, open an OS/2 command line, and run FDISKPM. This is the same Fixed Disk Utility you saw when first setting up for the Boot Manager. This time, highlight the DOS partition, click on **Options,** and select **Make Bootable** so that at the next boot that partition will be active. Exit the Fixed Disk Utility by pressing F3, save the changes, and shutdown OS/2 (click the right mouse button with the pointer anywhere on the desktop, and select **Shutdown**).

 Caution   You should not run DOS or Windows programs the first time you boot OS/2. There is a minor bug with version 2.0 that can cause problems only on this first boot. Once you have shutdown and restarted, the problem goes away.

Install DOS

Now that the OS/2 installation is complete, it is time to install the DOS partition. Put your DOS or DR DOS Installation Disk into drive A, and press CTRL+ALT+DEL to reboot and begin DOS installation. Follow the manufacturer's instructions for installing DOS into its partition. After DOS installation, run the FDISK program included in the version of DOS you just installed. Set the 1MB Boot Manager partition as the starting partition.

That's all there is to it. From now on, when you start your system, you'll get the Boot Manager menu shown in Figure 2-10, which allows you to select the operating system you want to start.

One of the options of the Fixed Disk Utility allowed you to select an operating system as the default. In other words, if you don't select a specific operating system within a specified period of time, the default operating system starts automatically. Therefore, if you are one of those users who turns on a computer and goes to the coffee machine, when you return your default operating system will be mounted. You can then begin to work just the way you did before you installed OS/2.

FIGURE 2-10　　The Boot Manager Menu ✿

```
                           Boot Manager
                              Menu




         DOS
         OS/2 1.3
         OS/2 2.0




         No selection within 30 seconds, boots OS/2 2.0.
         Press Esc to disable timer.
         Use ↑ or ↓ to select.  Press Enter to Boot.
```

CHAPTER

Getting Help

*T*he container that held your copy of OS/2 was smaller than most software boxes, especially when you consider the large number of diskettes enclosed. This is because there is not a lot of written documentation included with your OS/2 software. When you need help in the day-to-day use of OS/2, you can get it directly from your computer. There are several online mechanisms that provide whatever information or assistance you need.

Menu Bar Help

OS/2 applications typically have a menu bar that contains an entry marked **Help**. (If you want to follow along with the text and illustrations, use the Daily Planner. From the desktop select OS/2 System, open the Productivity folder, and select the Daily Planner.) Clicking on **Help** pulls down a general help menu, shown here, that is much the same for all OS/2 applications.*

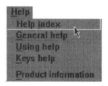

Index

The first item in the menu is the one you probably will use most often: **Help index**. Click on **Help index** to bring up the help window shown in Figure 3-1. There are many topics available and the list is presented in alphabetical order. Use the scroll bar to move up and down through the list. Because the window you are viewing may be smaller than the widest line of text within the window, some of the lines may not be entirely visible. To resize the window, move your cursor to the right edge, where your pointer becomes a double arrow, and drag the right edge over until you see all of the text. Alternatively, you can click on the upper right corner of the window to maximize the window size.

The Help Index ✲

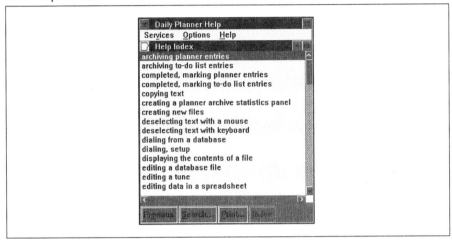

Table of Contents

In addition to the index of help topics, there is also a table of contents. Click on **Options** on the menu bar and then click on **Contents** to bring up a table of contents like the one shown in Figure 3-2.

Table of Contents ✲

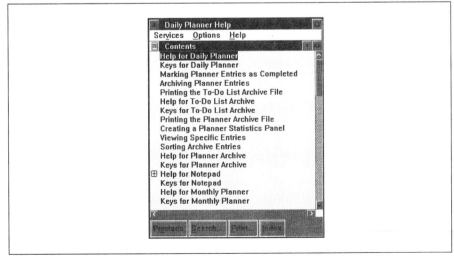

Step-by-step instructions in Help ✿

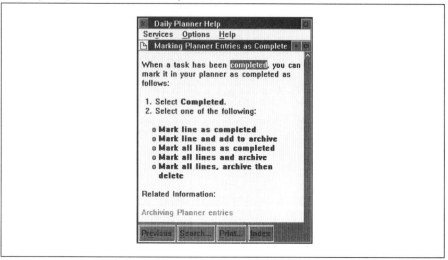

Viewing the Entries

From either the index or the table of contents, double-click on the item of interest to bring up the help text on that topic. For example, open the help text information on **Marking Planner Entries as Completed** as shown in Figure 3-3. The window contains step-by-step instructions for the topic selected. Since the help text is in a separate window, you can move it off to the side of the Daily Planner window and follow the instructions as you do your work. If you also want to print the instructions for later reference, simply click on the **Print** button at the bottom of the window.

Viewing Linked Entries

Notice in Figure 3-3 that the word "completed" is highlighted in gray. This indicates that there is a further definition of this word available. Double-clicking on the word causes a search of the glossary for that entry, as shown in the following: ✿

This is an example of a *hyperlink*, a section of text that is linked to another section of text because there is some relationship between them.

Scroll down to the bottom of the help text to see another type of hyperlink. The entry **Archiving Planner Entries** is in a different color. Double-clicking on that phrase transfers you immediately to a window with text on that topic. To return to the original text, simply click on the **Previous** button at the bottom of the window. To return to the index, just click on the **Index** button.

Using Search

There will be times when you want help on a certain topic but can't find an exact match in the index. For example, suppose you want help with setting alarms in order to have your computer alert you when it is time for a meeting or time to perform a task. There is no index entry for "alarm." Click on the **Search** button to bring up the dialog box shown here: ✿

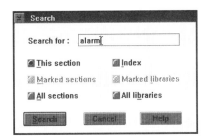

Type the word you want to search for (in this case, "alarm") and a window with a list of all the help topics that contain the word "alarm" will be presented, as shown in Figure 3-4.

Notice that the list of topics given in response to your query contains only one entry with the word "alarm" in it. When you ask OS/2 to search for a word, it searches the text of the topics in the help files, not just the titles. Even though the word you searched for is not part of each listing presented to you, double-clicking on any entry will bring up text that contains the search word (which is shown in a different color).

Results of searching in Help ✿

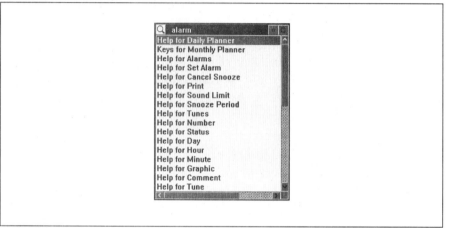

Note   The Search dialog box allows you to set the range of the search you want to perform. Limiting the search to **This section** means that only information in the current area of inquiry will be scrutinized. If you click on **All sections,** the OS/2 help feature will search all the help files in the system.

The F1 Key

Another way to get help from within an application is with the F1 key. Use of F1 as the help key is defined in IBM's Common User Access (CUA) specifications.

Note   Programs that conform to CUA all share a number of attributes such as menu bar appearance, control keys, and so on. The advantage of a common form of software presentation is that even when approaching an unfamiliar application, you can use the help function. You can perform many tasks using keystrokes familiar to you from software you've already learned.

In a CUA application, the help text that appears when you press F1 is determined by where you are in the application at the time. For example, from the Daily Planner, click on **View** in the menu bar to get to the pull-down menu. As illustrated here, **View complete entry** is highlighted:✿

Pressing F1 at this point brings up help information specific to the **View complete entry** selection, as shown in Figure 3-5.

Start Here

Help is also available for OS/2 itself. After installing OS/2, you probably noticed the Start Here icon. Double-clicking on this icon brings up a list of OS/2 topics for you to peruse when you need specific advice. As seen in Figure 3-6, the list covers all the tasks you are likely to perform.

FIGURE 3-5

Specific help on a menu bar item ✿

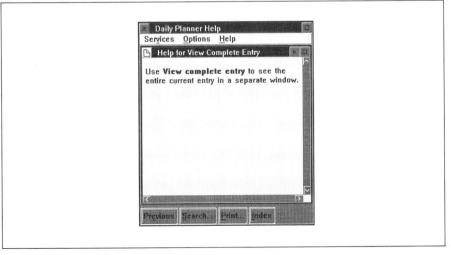

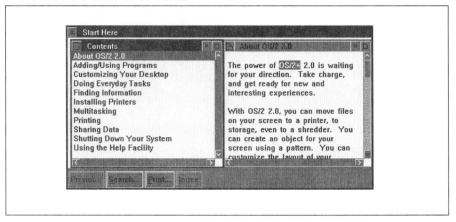

FIGURE 3-6   The Start Here table of contents ☼

Selecting a Topic

Choosing a topic brings up a list of individual menu items related to your selection. For example, selecting **Doing Everyday Tasks** from the list brings up a comprehensive table of contents covering the functions you use on a daily basis. Select one of the functions to get an explanation, step-by-step instructions on using the function, and some suggestions about where else to look for help with that function.

The Information Folder

Several other types of online help are available in the Information folder. To access the Information folder, select the Information icon, which presents the window shown in Figure 3-7.

The README File

The first item in the folder is a file named README. Selecting this file causes the OS/2 System Editor to load and display the README file, as shown in Figure 3-8. This file contains valuable information that IBM

FIGURE 3-7

The Information folder *

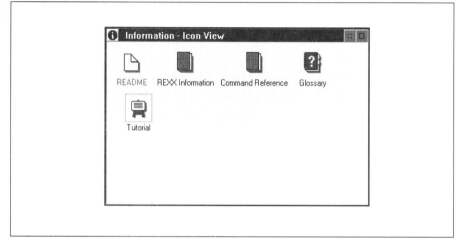

collected during the late testing phases of the product and didn't have time to include in the documentation. Everyone should review this file, particularly those who will be running DOS or Windows applications. Most of the information in the first version of this file is included in this book.

FIGURE 3-8

The OS/2 README file *

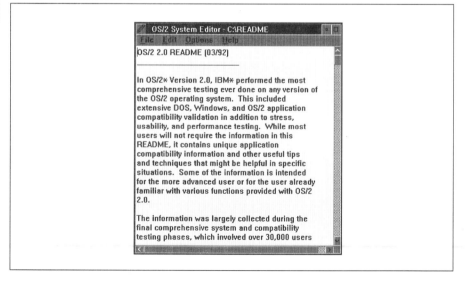

REXX Information

The second item in the Information folder is REXX Information. Whether you use REXX to create simple command files or more advanced programming functions, the information available on REXX, shown in Figure 3-9, is extremely helpful. The breadth of functions available with REXX is discussed in Chapter 18.

Command Reference

The third item is the Command Reference, an online "book" containing detailed information on all the OS/2 commands. When you first open it, you are looking only at the list of available topics. Clicking on the plus sign beside a topic reveals a more detailed table of contents. Figure 3-10 shows the topics under **OS/2 Commands by Name** that are shown after you click on the plus sign.

Choose a command about which you would like more information. For example, selecting the command FIND produces the details about that command, as shown in Figure 3-11. This syntax diagram shows the format and potential parameters of the command. The items beneath the

| FIGURE 3-9 | Table of contents for help on REXX ✿ |

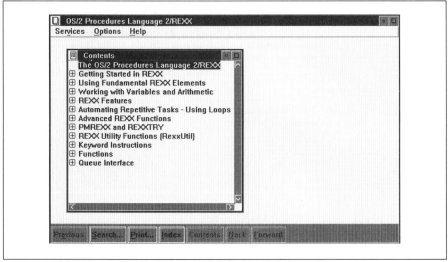

FIGURE
3-10

Table of contents for the Online Command Reference ☼

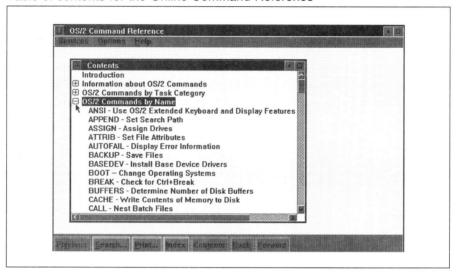

FIGURE
3-11

Syntax diagram of a command ☼

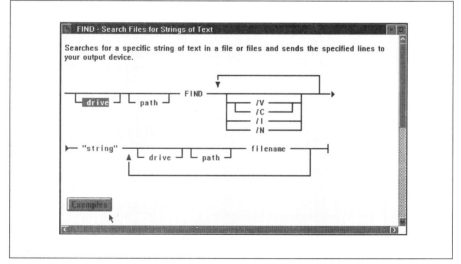

main line, such as "drive" and "path," indicate optional items in the command. Items on the main line, such as "FIND" and "string," are required entries. The arrow looping back over the line indicates that more than one of the single-character parameters can be strung together.

The color highlighting for the parameters indicates that more information is available. To learn what the /C parameter means, just select it to bring up more information, as shown in Figure 3-12.

Many people prefer to learn by example. The Command Reference provides examples of each command, describing what will happen with each combination of parameters. Just click on the **Examples** button (seen in Figure 3-12) to get the information you see in Figure 3-13.

FIGURE 3-12 Help for command parameters ✿

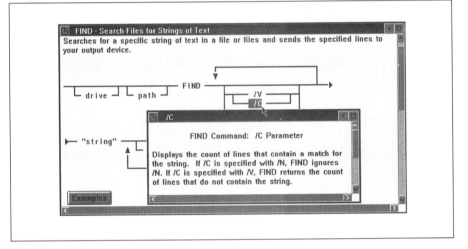

FIGURE 3-13 Command-line help examples ✿

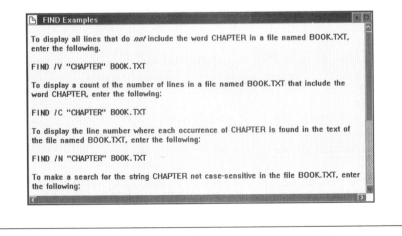

The Glossary

The last item in the Information folder, the **Glossary**, is a dictionary of key terms related to the use of OS/2. The implementation of the Glossary is done via the Workplace Shell notebook control, as seen in Figure 3-14. The Workplace Shell notebook control is a graphical interface in which the information, arranged alphabetically, is presented like a notebook with tabs for each letter of the alphabet.

To get to the page you need, open the notebook at the appropriate section. Since the screen presents only a limited number of sections (letters of the alphabet), use the arrows on the lower right side of the window to move to other sections. You can also click on **Search**, enter the topic or phrase you need information about, and move rapidly to the correct section of the Glossary. Once there, an easily understood definition is presented.

Master Help Index

The Master Help Index notebook is installed on the desktop for easy access. As with all notebooks, the Master Help Index has tabs to allow you to move quickly to the section you're interested in (see Figure 3-15). This index is extremely thorough and provides more information together

FIGURE 3-14   The Glossary ✿

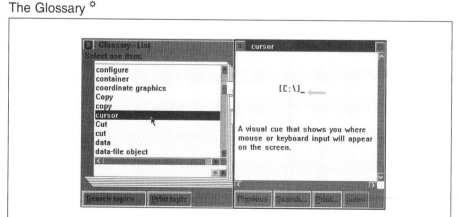

in one place than does most printed documentation. Selecting a topic brings directions on implementing that function as well as pointers for getting more help once you have begun to use it.

Command-Line Help

When you are at a system prompt, just type **HELP XXX** (where *XXX* is the OS/2 command for which you need help). The Command Reference window, illustrated in Figure 3-11, will open for the appropriate command.

OS/2 provides exhaustive documentation without forcing you to find, and then thumb through, several different books to unearth the required information. OS/2 also makes it easy for developers to use the same standardized format for documentation in the applications you purchase.

**FIGURE
3-15**

Master Help Index ✿

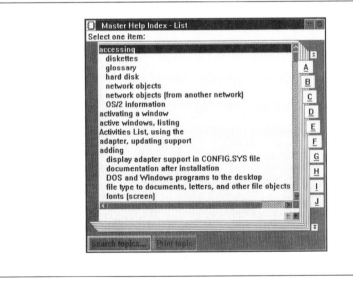

Summary

Since there are so many places to find help as you work in OS/2, it might be beneficial to summarize this chapter.

To Get Help with Applications

☐ Menu bar **Help** entry produces a pop-up menu.

☐ F1 key produces contextual help.

To Get Help with OS/2

☐ The Start Here icon produces a list of topics about OS/2.

☐ The Information folder contains a README file, a folder on REXX, a Command Reference folder, a Glossary notebook, and an icon to launch the tutorial.

☐ Master Help Index produces a notebook with alphabetical tabs.

☐ Command Line help offers information about a specific command while you are working in a command session.

CHAPTER

The Workplace Shell

Your main interface to OS/2 is the Workplace Shell. This may present a somewhat different interface than most computer users are accustomed to. A look at some of the basics, then, is appropriate for the computer newcomer as well as the seasoned computer user.

The computer screen is an electronic representation of a desktop. Many of the items found on your real desktop are there, as are other things that are in your office but not necessarily on your desk. For instance, like your desk, your computer desktop can have an appointment book, a letter you need to read, or even a printer. Like the file cabinets in your office, the computer screen offers ways to combine and arrange files that belong together.

The Startup Desktop

The first thing you see is the OS/2 startup desktop, shown in Figure 4-1. It contains a number of icons, which are pictorial representations of objects.

FIGURE 4-1   The startup desktop ✿

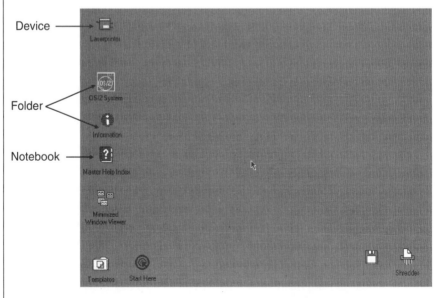

Objects

With OS/2 version 2.0, the model for thinking about computer tasks has moved to object orientation. An *object* is anything you use as you work at your computer, including files, devices, and utilities. Previously, whether you used a DOS menu system, the DOS command line, or Windows, you thought in terms of applications. You chose and launched specific software applications whether you did so with a mouse or a keyboard entry. Once in the application, you chose the files you needed to work on.

Now that you are using the Workplace Shell, everything is an object— even the desktop itself. You can work with objects pretty much the way you work with physical objects on your desk or in your file cabinets. You can select them, work on them, move them, copy them, or get rid of them.

Data File   *Data file* objects are related to information. Text files, word processing documents, and spreadsheets are all data file objects.

Program   A *program* object represents an executable program. The text editors that produce text files, database programs, word processing software, and any program files that actually execute software all are program objects.

Device   *Device* objects are physical devices such as printers, modems, or any other physical peripheral attached to a computer.

Folders   *Folders* are objects that contain other objects. You can use folders to organize objects so that the objects you use frequently are together. In fact, the objects they contain can be other folders.

The OS/2 System Object

One of the icons on the startup desktop is the OS/2 System icon. This folder, filled with other folders, is where you can find OS/2 system utilities. This is a good place to begin, to practice using the mouse, and to learn to get around the graphical interface.

Using a Mouse

As you move the mouse around, you see a pointer on the screen move in a corresponding fashion. Most of the time the pointer looks like an arrow, but its shape changes under certain circumstances. For instance, when you are entering text, the pointer will look like a tall, thin capital letter "I".

Customizing the Mouse

If you are left-handed or have gotten so used to environments other than OS/2 where some of the mouse button functions are different than the OS/2 defaults, you may want to customize the way the mouse works. You can configure the mouse button by going into the System Setup folder in the OS/2 System folder.

Mouse Speed

Double-click with the left button on the mouse object and then click on **Timing** to bring up the Mouse Settings screen illustrated in Figure 4-2.

Mouse timing settings screen ✿

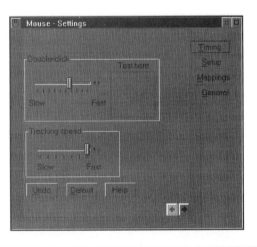

This dialog box allows you to set the speed at which the mouse operates to match your double-clicking coordination and the speed with which the cursor follows your mouse movements.

Mouse Settings

Click on **Setup** to choose between right-handed and left-handed configuration. As shown in Figure 4-3, it is easy to go back to the default OS/2 setup if you are not comfortable with the changes you've made.

Mouse Mappings

Click on **Mappings** to access the screen depicted in Figure 4-4. You can make very specific changes to the way the buttons work and, if you find later that you are not comfortable (or you don't remember the changes you made and therefore aren't moving as quickly as you'd like), you can always reset the mouse to the default settings.

Default Mouse Functions

If you do not make changes to the mouse button mappings, the left button is button #1 and the right button is #2. If you do make changes,

Mouse setup screen ✿

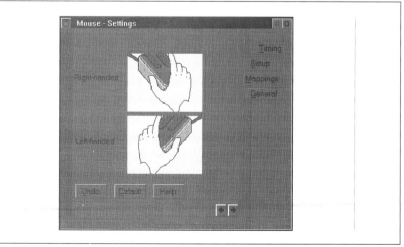

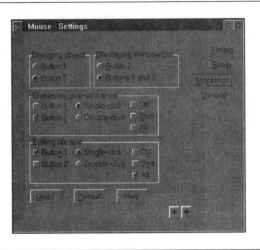

FIGURE

4-4

Mouse mappings screen ☼

substitute the appropriate buttons for the references used throughout the rest of this book.

Clicking button #1 when the pointer is positioned on an item selects that item.

Clicking button #2 when the pointer is on an item brings up the attributes of that item so that you can view or change them. *Attributes* are the set of characteristics that determine the behavior of an object.

Double-clicking (clicking the button twice, quickly) mouse button #1 opens an item so that you can use it.

Dragging an item from one place to another on the screen is accomplished by positioning the pointer over the item and holding down button #2 instead of simply clicking and releasing it. Drag the object along until it is where you want it to be, and then release the button.

Opening a Window

Open the OS/2 System folder by double-clicking on the System folder icon. When the folder opens, you are looking at a window. A *window* on the computer screen gives you a view of the programs, data, and utilities inside your computer much as the windows in your house give you a view of the outside world.

Since most people have several work projects going on simultaneously, they usually have papers of many different types on their desk at any point in time. The computer screen is similar to your desk in that respect. Just as on your desk, these papers can overlap each other so that you see parts of some items sticking out underneath the items on top. Your computer windows can be moved around on the screen the same way you shuffle papers on your desktop.

The Elements of a Window

Figure 4-5 shows the window that is displayed when you select the Daily Planner (to follow along, double-click on the Productivity folder and then double-click on the Daily Planner). There are a number of elements illustrated that you will be using regularly.

FIGURE
4-5

Parts of an OS/2 window ✿

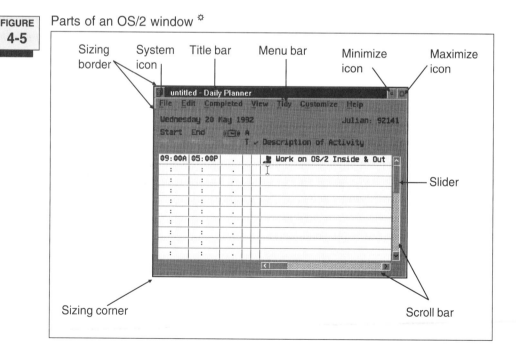

Title Bar

The title bar is an information bar on the top of the window that tells you the name of the object you are using.

Minimizing Icon

Just as you occasionally need to clean off your desk—or at least pile some of the items neatly into a corner—you can move objects totally out of sight on your desktop workspace. You don't even have to worry about where you put them, whether there is space in your filing cabinet if you need to file them, or what name you filed them under when it is time to retrieve them.

The process of reducing a file's size is called *minimizing* a window. If you look in the upper right corner of Figure 4-5, you see two icons side by side at the right edge of the title bar. The one on the left is the minimize icon. Clicking on that icon will cause the window to disappear from the screen. Actually, it has not really vanished, it has merely been changed to a minimal size and tucked out of sight. This is a very fast way to get one program off the screen so you can view the information in another.

When you want the hidden information back, just open the Minimized Window Viewer on the Startup Desktop by clicking on its icon. All the windows you've minimized will be shown in a folder. Double-clicking on the icon of the program you want to restore will cause that program's window to be reopened exactly as you left it.

Maximizing Icon

The maximize icon, to the right of the minimize icon, enlarges a window so that it fills the screen. Any other open windows will be hidden behind the maximized window, as will any icons that were visible anywhere on the screen when the window was smaller.

Scroll Bar

The presence of a scroll bar indicates that the information visible in the window is only a part of the total amount of information available.

You can access the information not visible on the screen in several different ways. Click on the arrows on either end of the scroll bar to move the entire view one "unit" up or down. The definition of a unit varies depending on the type of window being accessed. If you are looking at a text window, that unit would probably be one line vertically, or five or so columns horizontally. If you are looking at a folder, the view would move one row or one column of icons.

Slider

The slider provides a shortcut for moving through a window in larger increments than a few lines or a page at a time. (The definition of a page will vary based on the type of information being displayed, but in general it represents one window full of information.) Moving the slider in either direction will move the contents of the window proportionally in the same direction. The slider is moved by pointing to it and then dragging it.

The size of the slider indicates the percentage of the window that is visible. If the slider is nearly as big as the scroll bar, you know that there is very little information not shown. If it is quite small, you know that there are several pages not shown in the window. This terrific visual cue is a graphical function unique to OS/2. Clicking on the scroll bar at a point between the slider and the arrow will move the window one page.

Menu Bar

The *menu bar* presents a menu of available functions, which vary depending on the application you are using.

Manipulating Windows

No matter how many windows you have open at any time, it is quite easy to change them, move between them, exchange one for the other, or maneuver them around your screen.

Moving Windows

To relocate a window, move the arrow pointer to the title bar of the window and press and hold down mouse button #2. The border of the window becomes highlighted. Now, move the mouse around the screen, still holding down button #2. The highlighted border outline moves along with it. When you get the border to the place you'd like the window, just release the mouse button. The window moves to the position occupied by the highlighted border.

Sizing Windows

Applications may have a default window size with which they open, or they may depend on OS/2's default window size. Either way, it is not unusual for users to find some other size more suited to their tastes. The Workplace Shell is designed to allow you to set up your desktop to suit your particular preferences, including the ability to change the size of windows.

The size of a window can be altered in a couple of different ways. If you move the pointer to the border on any side of the window, the pointer changes its shape to indicate that it is in position to size the window. If your pointer is on either side of the window, the shape of the pointer changes to a left-right arrow: ✷

At the top and bottom borders of the window, the pointer changes to an up-down arrow. You can drag whichever border you are accessing and the window will grow, or shrink, in that direction.

Frequently, however, you will want to change the window both vertically and horizontally in order to maintain the original ratio regardless of size. You can do both at the same time by moving the pointer to a corner of any window until your pointer changes to a two-way arrow on an angle as shown in the following illustration: ✷

You can then drag that corner, and both sides of the window that meet at that corner will grow.

If you want the window to grow to full size, just use the maximize button.

Switching Among Windows

Aside from minimizing a window to access the window beneath it, there is another way to move from one window to another. If you click on any part of a window that is sticking out from underneath the top window, it will immediately be moved to the top of the screen and be totally uncovered. The original top window remains the same size, but it is now underneath the new top window. You can move the new top window so that you see parts of the windows placed underneath (making it easy to bring one of them to the top at the click of a mouse button). Shifting between windows rapidly in this fashion is a productive way to move between tasks because you can always see the "paper work" waiting for you in the other windows. Try to do that with payroll ledgers on your desk when they're covered by accounts payable.

Suppose there are no parts of any other windows visible that you can click on to bring them to the foreground. Click on the system icon in the upper left corner of the window. This pops up the system menu. This menu differs depending on whether the window in question is a folder or an application. For instance, if you are in the OS/2 System folder, you see the detailed menu in Figure 4-6. Clicking on the **Window** option brings up the secondary menu with **Restore**, **Close**, and other options listed. (This secondary menu is the only one you will see when you click on the System icon from an application window.) The last item on this screen is **Window list**. Selecting this option brings up the *Task Manager* window. The Task Manager is a list of every window you have opened. You can double-click on any item in this list in order to bring an item to the foreground immediately.

System menu ✿

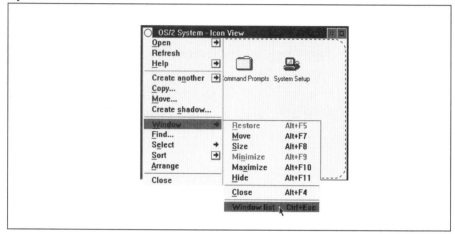

 Tip   The Task Manager can also be accessed by pressing both mouse buttons simultaneously or by pressing CTRL+ESC.

Changing the current window's size is another way to get to other windows. Minimizing a window reveals the window beneath it, and restoring a minimized window switches back to that window.

Closing Windows

If you want to remove a window from the desktop completely, you can close it via the system menu. Notice that there is a **Close** option in the menu shown in Figure 4-6.

 Tip   There's an even easier way to close a window. Simply double-click on the system icon in the upper left corner of the window to send a close message to the window.

Remember that closing a window is not the same as minimizing it. Closing shuts down the application completely, the same way pressing the sequence of keys to exit an application does.

Accelerator Keys

If you look at Figure 4-6, you see that beside the **Close** option on the menu is the key combination ALT+F4. This is an example of an accelerator key. These are listed frequently beside menu options. If your fingers are comfortably on the keyboard and you'd rather not move to the mouse, you can close a window just as easily with the ALT+F4 key sequence.

There is a second type of accelerator key. If you look at a menu bar such as the one shown in Figure 4-5, you can see that each of the entries has one letter underlined. These highlighted letters are a type of accelerator key too. When a window is active, pressing ALT highlights its menu bar. You can then select any of the items on the menu bar simply by pressing the letter that is underlined. If the menu selection causes the appearance of another menu, you will usually find underlined letters in the items in that menu as well, which means that you simply have to press the appropriate letter to select the next action.

Folders

The idea behind a folder is simply to help you organize information within your system. For example, you might want to have a Text Processing folder, including a word processor, a grammar checker, a thesaurus, and a spell checker. Similarly, you can group any number of things in whatever manner best suits your particular needs. The idea is to be able to customize the desktop to match the way you think and the way you work.

Creating Folders

If you look in the lower left corner of the desktop (see Figure 4-1), you will see a folder labeled Templates. Open that folder by double-clicking on the icon. The window that opens contains templates for the creation of all sorts of Workplace Shell objects, shown in Figure 4-7. To create any of these objects, simply move the pointer to the desired template, then

**FIGURE
4-7**   Templates *

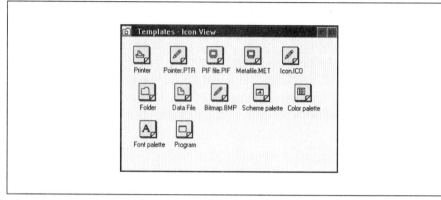

drag that template to the desired position and release the mouse button to drop it.

Suppose you want to create a folder containing your calendar management functions. Drag the Folder template to an empty spot on the desktop and drop it. You have just created a new folder with the generic name Folder. Since this isn't very descriptive of the folder's contents, you should change the name.

If you click on mouse button #2 while your pointer is on the new folder, you get a menu of things you can do with this folder, illustrated here: *

The arrow that appears to the right of **Open** indicates that there is a secondary menu for this option. Clicking on that arrow produces a number of aspects of this folder that you can open.

   Note   The system menu is different for applications than it is for other types of folders. Clicking with button #2 on a program icon rather than a folder icon would present much the same first set of selections, but the secondary menu under the **Open** selection would include only those options appropriate for that particular program: the settings notebook and the program itself.

For your folder, click on **Settings** to open the Settings notebook (see Figure 4-8). The notebook is a new type of object for the Workplace Shell, introduced with version 2.0 of OS/2. As you can see, it looks much like a physical notebook. It has tabs on the side to allow you to move quickly to the section of the notebook in which you're interested. The arrows at the bottom right of the page allow you to move through the pages of the notebook one at a time. All objects have a Settings notebook associated with them, but the pages of each notebook vary greatly to reflect the items of significance for that particular object.

It is somewhat unusual for the casual user to change the settings of any of the sections of the Settings notebook except the last one, and details regarding using the tabs are discussed in Chapter 3. For now, click on the **General** tab to move immediately to the last section. Your screen looks like Figure 4-9.

Changing a Folder Name

To change the text that appears underneath the new folder, move the pointer into the **Title** field and click. The text cursor begins flashing there,

Settings notebook ✧

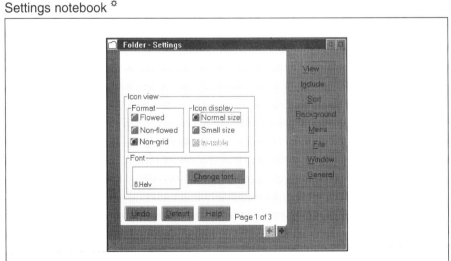

FIGURE
4-9

Changing general settings *

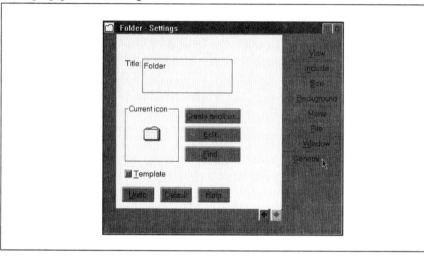

indicating that you can begin typing text. Modify the title to whatever is appropriate; for the purpose of this exercise, enter **Calendar** as the title.

Note OS/2 offers insert mode for typing by default. Whatever you type will be inserted and any characters to the right of your typing will remain in the field, unless you press DEL.

Since you are replacing the word "folder", it is easier to mark that word by moving the cursor to the left of the "f ", holding down button #1 and moving the cursor across all of the characters in the word. As you do this, the letters are highlighted. This text is now marked and ready for replacement. The text you enter will replace the marked text.

Tip A shortcut for changing text beneath an icon is to select the icon and hold the ALT key while pressing mouse button #1.

Changing Icon Appearance

In the Settings box, you could change the appearance of the icon associated with a folder. If you select **Create another** or **Edit**, you are taken to the Icon Editor, where you either start with a blank icon or edit the existing icon. The icon editor will be discussed more in Chapter 14.

Now that the settings are prepared, close this window by double-clicking on the System icon. The folder now has the new name and the new icon you have assigned, if any. You can open it like any other folder by double-clicking—but the folder is empty! It would be appropriate to move some calendar management functions into this folder.

Copying Objects

Any object on your computer can be put into a folder. Folders that already exist can be opened and some or all of the contents can be moved or copied into a new folder.

Software applications and other utilities that exist on your hard disk can also be placed into any folder you create.

Copying from Other Folders

Open the OS/2 System folder and then open the Productivity folder within it. Your screen should look similar to Figure 4-10. Now you can move a copy of the Monthly Planner from the Productivity folder to your Calendar folder. If you simply drag the Monthly Planner icon from Productivity to Calendar, you merely move that program from one folder to the other.

Instead, by holding the CTRL key down while you drag the icon, you copy the program to the new folder. The Workplace Shell shows this to you visually by making the icon appear the same as the original if you are doing a move, and by showing it in gray if you are making a copy. You can drop the icon anywhere in the Calendar folder and organize the icons later.

Copy the Activities List, the Daily Planner, and the Calendar into the new folder. The Calendar program may not be visible in the Productivity window at first, so use the scroll bar to move to the next set of icons. The new Calendar folder will now look something like Figure 4-11.

FIGURE 4-10

Opening folders for copying ✿

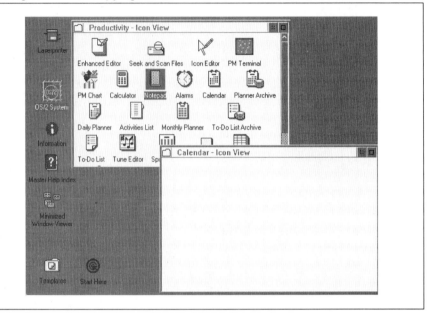

FIGURE 4-11

The new Calendar folder ✿

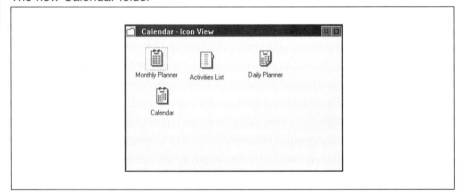

Copying from the Hard Disk

Sometimes the object you want is not contained in a folder. However, everything in your system can be accessed via the Drives windows. Open OS/2 System and then open Drives. You will see an entry in this window for each logical disk in your system, including network drives, as illustrated in Figure 4-12.

The Drives window ✿

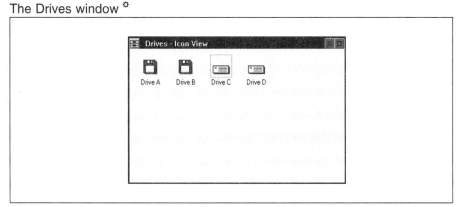

If you open the Drive C icon, you see a directory structure of the drive similar to the one shown in Figure 4-13, which is a map you can use to find the object you want to move into your folder.

If you follow the map through the levels of organization of your hard disk, you will find groups of objects, usually programs and perhaps the

Tree view of a drive ✿

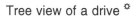

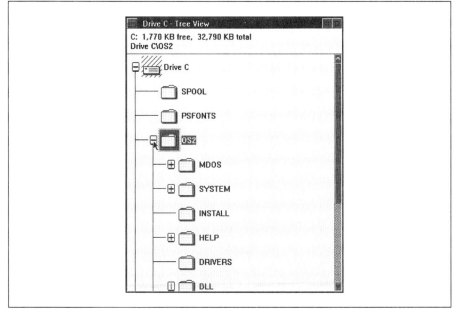

data attached to those programs, depending on how you organize your hard disk.

Figure 4-14 shows the objects contained in a subdirectory a couple of layers down from the root. The organizing of the directories and sub-directories on your hard disk is discussed in more detail in Chapter 5.

Arranging the Icons

Click with mouse button #2 on the System icon of the folder, and select the **Arrange** option. OS/2 rearranges the icons into organized rows automatically, as you can see in Figure 4-15.

The **Arrange** option is sensitive to the size of the window; if you make the window more narrow, **Arrange** wraps the icons to another row.

Customizing the Desktop

There are many things you can do to tailor the desktop to your own particular taste. Open the OS/2 System folder and then the System Setup

FIGURE 4-14 Objects in a subdirectory ✿

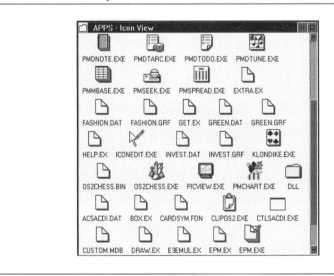

Arranged icons ✵

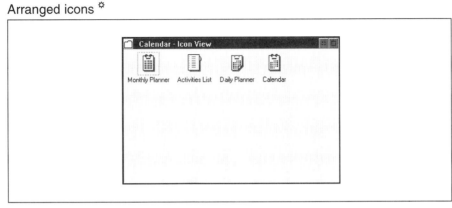

folder to produce a window that looks like Figure 4-16. Each of these objects represents an opportunity for customization of your system.

The Scheme Palette

OS/2 provides a number of pre-established color schemes you can select to make a reasonably coordinated (at least in the eyes of the IBM developers) set of colors for your system. You can select any of these color schemes by dragging the desired scheme onto the desktop. All changes take place automatically.

System Setup folder ✵

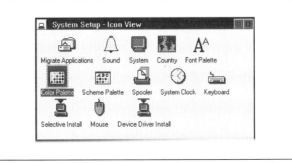

You are not limited to the prepackaged schemes, of course. If you like most aspects of a scheme but want to make a small change, you can choose to edit the scheme. To do so, select the scheme you'd like to change and click on the **Edit scheme** button to produce the window displayed in Figure 4-17. This window shows all aspects of the desktop and their current colors.

Click on the arrow beside the **Window area** drop box and you'll see a list of the desktop components. Select the item for which you want to change the color and click on the **Edit Color** button. You'll see a color wheel that shows the wide range of colors available for the particular video adapter you have. Drag the cross hairs around the wheel to the color that you want for the item being changed. Then just close the window, and you'll see your change take place.

There is an easier way, if you don't want to modify an entire screen. Just open the **Color Palette** from the System Setup menu and you'll see a selection of colors. Drag the color to the area you want changed and drop the paintbrush there. For example, select a color and drag it to an empty spot in the new Calendar window. When you release the button, the background color of the window changes. Title bars and the desktop background color can all be changed just as easily.

FIGURE 4-17   The Edit Scheme window ✧

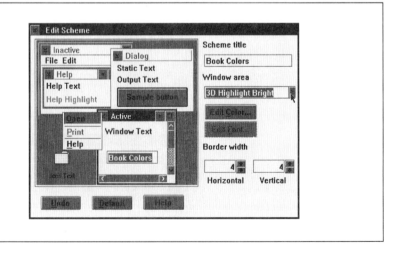

Tip   To change the background color of all windows in the system, hold the ALT key down as you drag and drop the color.

To change the foreground color (the color of the text that appears underneath icons and in the title bar), hold the CTRL key as you drag and drop the color. Holding both the CTRL and ALT keys makes the foreground color change in all windows in the system.

Emulating Other Platforms

Usability studies have shown that computing newcomers enjoy the Workplace Shell immediately and are at ease with its intuitive interface. However, those who have a background with other platforms are taken aback at first by the conceptual change that the object-oriented nature of the Workplace Shell provides. Those people generally grow to appreciate the environment after a week of use.

If you are migrating from another platform, you should work with the default environment for several days before deciding to change its appearance to emulate that of another platform.

Still, a key design point of OS/2 is freedom of choice for users. If you want to change the appearance of the desktop, a straightforward way has been provided. Keep in mind that OS/2's protection mechanism prevents one program from changing key parts of the system that are being used by other programs. Thus, to redo the desktop you must boot OS/2 from diskette. This keeps the desktop files on the fixed disk free for change.

 Caution   These changes may cause certain customizations, such as colors, window size, icon placement, and other features to be removed.

Emulating OS/2 Version 1.3

Part of the OS/2 1.3 look-and-feel can be provided by changing the icon format within folders to Non-flowed. It may be, however, that you wish to emulate the File Manager as well as other aspects of the 1.3 desktop.

To do this, shut down OS/2 and then insert the Installation Disk. Reboot the system, insert Disk 1 when prompted and, at the next prompt, press ESC to get to a command prompt.

Change to the fixed disk by typing

C:

and change to the OS/2 directory by typing

CD\OS2

Change the desktop initialization file with the command

MAKEINI OS2.INI OS2_13.RC

Later, if you wish to return to the 2.0 Workplace Shell, follow the same steps, but change the command to

MAKEINI OS2.INI OS2_20.RC

Emulating Windows 3.0

OS/2 2.0 provides the same free-flow icon structure that Windows users have grown accustomed to. However, there are other aspects of the Windows desktop that differ from the Workplace Shell, such as the default behavior of mouse buttons.

To alter the 2.0 desktop so that it emulates the Windows 3.0 shell, follow the steps documented above for OS/2 1.3, but change the command to

MAKEINI OS2.INI WIN_30.RC

You can change back to the Workplace Shell with the command

MAKEINI OS2.INI OS2_20.RC

Closing the Workplace Shell

It is important at the end of your work session to shut down the Workplace Shell in an orderly fashion before turning off your computer. This allows OS/2 to perform a number of housekeeping functions required to keep things working properly, including the task of clearing any data still in your disk cache, data that otherwise could be lost.

To shut down, move the pointer to an empty spot on the desktop and click mouse button #2. The desktop menu will appear. Click on the **Shutdown** option. You will be asked if you are certain you want to shut the system down: *

Make sure to wait until the message box appears saying that it is safe to turn the computer off.

While shutting down, the Workplace Shell takes note of the windows that are open on the desktop. The next time you start OS/2, those windows are reopened automatically.

Tip If there are certain programs that you are sure you want to start every time you bring up OS/2, you can copy them into the Startup folder in the OS/2 System folder. All programs there are brought up automatically as part of the Workplace Shell startup routine.

CHAPTER

Manipulating Files Through the Workplace Shell

Because of the object-oriented environment of OS/2, manipulating files is easy and hard disk management is uncomplicated. However, you should have an understanding of how the hard disk is arranged. This chapter explains how directories and subdirectories are arranged and how to find files within them, the information provided by file attributes, and ways to associate files with other files or directories.

Directories

The easiest way to understand the hard disk *directory structure* is to envision a traditional organizational chart like the one in Figure 5-1. Below the root (top-level) directory is another level of directories, sections of the hard disk that have been defined and named. There can be several levels of directories (lower-level directories are frequently called *sub-directories*) in the structure of a hard disk.

FIGURE 5-1   Hard disk directory structure

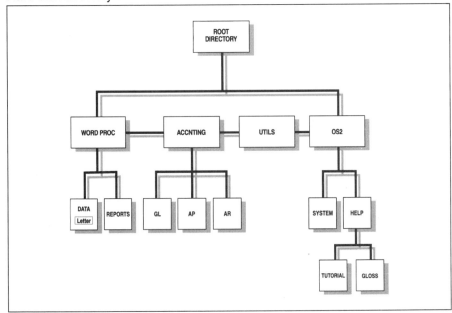

Directories are useful because they put related files in the same place. For hard disk management, the decision about which files belong together is almost always based on specific software packages. Installation of any software should be done with a subdirectory created for that software as the target for transferring the package's files. For example, putting all the files that are part of a particular word processing program in a directory makes sense, as does putting the data produced by the word processor in a connected directory.

In Figure 5-1, the word processing data is one level below the directory that holds the word processor files. If you use more than one word processor, each should have its own directory. Most software installation processes ask you to name a directory before any of the files are transferred, but if you are installing software that doesn't provide this function, it is important to create a directory manually before transferring the files. The designation for the word processing data subdirectory in Figure 5-1 is C:\WORDPROC\DATA. The backward slash identifies how far down in the structure the directory is found. Each backslash indicates another level.

OS/2 Directories

When you installed OS/2, certain directories were created. To avoid interfering with them in any way, do not attempt to create directories with any of the following names:

BOOK	DLL
INSTALL	INTRO
OS2	SPOOL
SYSTEM	

Files

Every file on your hard disk is identified by the operating system. There are two elements in the identification scheme, the *filename* and the *path*.

Filenames

Every file has a name. If it is a data file, you choose the name using some pattern of characters that makes sense to you. If it is a program file, the application programmers named it using a scheme that made sense to them. Both you and the programmers have to follow some rules about naming files. These rules are set by the operating system.

Filename Length

The FAT file system allows filenames and directory names to consist of two parts: a name, which can be from 1 to 8 characters long, and an optional extension, which can be from 1 to 3 characters long. A period separates the name from the extension.

The High Performance File System (HPFS) permits up to 254 characters in filenames and directory names, including punctuation marks and blank spaces. This allows you to write extremely descriptive filenames that may even have multiple sections divided by punctuation marks.

Note   Examples used throughout this book will employ the 8.3 filename convention in order to maintain compatibility with DOS and the FAT file system. If you are using OS/2 exclusively, you can take full advantage of the HPFS file naming facilities.

Forbidden Characters

OS/2 prohibits certain characters from appearing in filenames. The following symbols cannot be used in filenames or directory names:

\ / : * ? " < > | & -

Caution   FAT file system filenames cannot have spaces.

Reserved Names

The following names are reserved by the operating system for indicating devices and cannot be used as filenames or directory names.

KBD$	PRN	NUL
COM1	COM2	COM3
COM4	CLOCK$	LPT1
LPT2	LPT3	CON
SCREEN#	POINTER$	MOUSE$
PIPE	SEM	QUEUE

Note The device names are only reserved by OS/2 if there is no extension to the filename. Once an extension is added, the operating system does not recognize the name as a device; you can have a file named QUEUE.BOB but not a file named QUEUE. This is new with version 2.0 of OS/2.

Case Preservation

In a FAT file system, it does not matter whether you use upper- or lowercase letters when you name a file or directory. The operating system converts the name to uppercase and displays it to you in that form.

With HPFS, *case preservation* is supported, which means that the operating system saves the name of your file or directory exactly as it was typed. If you create a file or directory called TexT, the system saves it and displays it as TexT, not TEXT. However, HPFS is not truly case-sensitive, so you cannot use the same name for multiple files in the same directory. For instance, you cannot create a file named TEXT in the same directory as a file named TexT.

Path

In addition to the filename, a file has a *path*, a guide to where in the directory structure the file is found. In Figure 5-1, the path and filename of the data file called LETTER is C:\WORDPROC\DATA\LETTER.

OS/2, like DOS, does not permit duplicate filenames. You cannot have two files named MYFILE in the same directory. However, since the path is really part of the filename, it is possible to have a file named C:\WORDPROC\DATA\INVOICE in addition to a file named C:\ACCNT-ING\AR\INVOICE.

File Attributes

Characteristics that are attached to files and that further define them are called *file attributes*. The information contained in the attributes can be useful when you are examining or selecting files.

Last Write Date   The *last write date* tells you when the file was last written to disk. It is displayed in other operating sytems as the only date attribute.

Last Write Time   The *last write time* tells you at what time the file was last written to disk. This information is displayed in other operating sytems as the only time attribute.

Extended File Attributes

One of the new features of OS/2 is the capability to supply more information about a file than other operating systems provide, as seen in Figure 5-2.

FIGURE 5-2

Detail view showing file attributes *

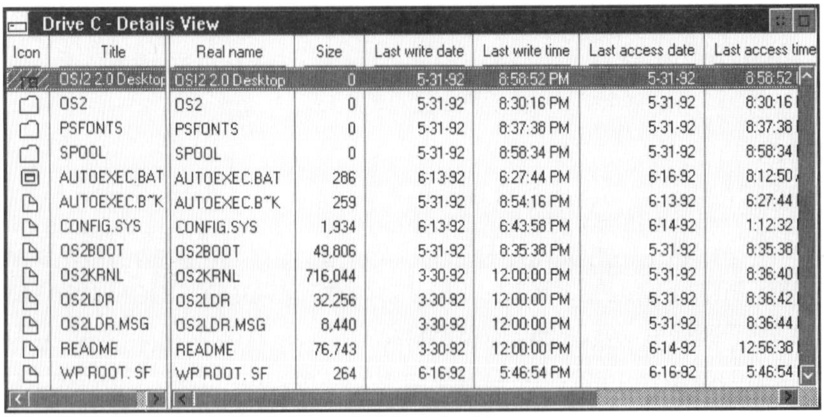

Icon	Title	Real name	Size	Last write date	Last write time	Last access date	Last access time
	OS/2 2.0 Desktop	OS/2 2.0 Desktop	0	5-31-92	8:58:52 PM	5-31-92	8:58:52
	OS2	OS2	0	5-31-92	8:30:16 PM	5-31-92	8:30:16
	PSFONTS	PSFONTS	0	5-31-92	8:37:38 PM	5-31-92	8:37:38
	SPOOL	SPOOL	0	5-31-92	8:58:34 PM	5-31-92	8:58:34
	AUTOEXEC.BAT	AUTOEXEC.BAT	286	6-13-92	6:27:44 PM	6-16-92	8:12:50
	AUTOEXEC.B~K	AUTOEXEC.B~K	259	5-31-92	8:54:16 PM	6-13-92	6:27:44
	CONFIG.SYS	CONFIG.SYS	1,934	6-13-92	6:43:58 PM	6-14-92	1:12:32
	OS2BOOT	OS2BOOT	49,806	5-31-92	8:35:38 PM	5-31-92	8:35:38
	OS2KRNL	OS2KRNL	716,044	3-30-92	12:00:00 PM	5-31-92	8:36:40
	OS2LDR	OS2LDR	32,256	3-30-92	12:00:00 PM	5-31-92	8:36:42
	OS2LDR.MSG	OS2LDR.MSG	8,440	3-30-92	12:00:00 PM	5-31-92	8:36:44
	README	README	76,743	3-30-92	12:00:00 PM	6-14-92	12:56:38
	WP ROOT. SF	WP ROOT. SF	264	6-16-92	5:46:54 PM	6-16-92	5:46:54

Drive C - Details View

Last Access Date   The *last access date* information reports the last time the file was accessed, whether or not changes were made.

Last Access Time   In addition to the date of last access, the time is displayed.

Creation Date   The *creation date* tells you the first time the file was saved. Changing the filename, copying the file to another name or to another place, or moving the file does not change the creation date.

Creation Time   In addition to the creation date, the time is also given.

Additional File Attributes

There is other information that may be attached to files as attributes. It is difficult to define all of the possible extended attributes because they can be determined by the application that creates the file. A word processing program might store information about where to retrieve imbedded graphics within the extended attributes of the file. If an icon is attached to a file, it is stored in the extended attributes. These advanced capabilities give OS/2 software developers enhanced ways to manipulate data.

 Tip   A backup program designed specifically for OS/2 will be aware of extended attributes.

In order to maintain compatibility with DOS, the following four attributes are not maintained in a FAT file system: last access date, last access time, creation date, and creation time.

Flags

Flags, shown in Figure 5-3, are another attribute of files but differ from the others in that they can be altered by the user. There are four available attributes classified as flags.

Read-Only   A *read-only* object can be read but not changed. It also cannot be deleted.

FIGURE
5-3 Detail view showing flags ❉

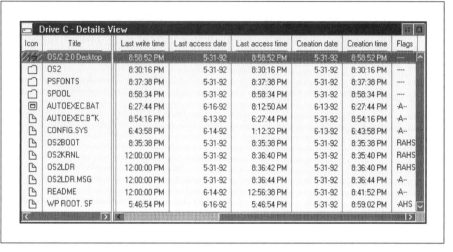

Icon	Title	Last write time	Last access date	Last access time	Creation date	Creation time	Flags
	OS/2 2.0 Desktop	8:58:52 PM	5-31-92	8:58:52 PM	5-31-92	8:58:52 PM	----
	OS2	8:30:16 PM	5-31-92	8:30:16 PM	5-31-92	8:30:16 PM	----
	PSFONTS	8:37:38 PM	5-31-92	8:37:38 PM	5-31-92	8:37:38 PM	----
	SPOOL	8:58:34 PM	5-31-92	8:58:34 PM	5-31-92	8:58:34 PM	----
	AUTOEXEC.BAT	6:27:44 PM	6-16-92	8:12:50 AM	6-13-92	6:27:44 PM	-A--
	AUTOEXEC.B~K	8:54:16 PM	6-13-92	6:27:44 PM	5-31-92	8:54:16 PM	-A--
	CONFIG.SYS	6:43:58 PM	6-14-92	1:12:32 PM	6-13-92	6:43:58 PM	-A--
	OS2BOOT	8:35:38 PM	5-31-92	8:35:38 PM	5-31-92	8:35:38 PM	RAHS
	OS2KRNL	12:00:00 PM	5-31-92	8:36:40 PM	5-31-92	8:35:40 PM	RAHS
	OS2LDR	12:00:00 PM	5-31-92	8:36:42 PM	5-31-92	8:36:40 PM	RAHS
	OS2LDR.MSG	12:00:00 PM	5-31-92	8:36:44 PM	5-31-92	8:36:44 PM	-A--
	README	12:00:00 PM	6-14-92	12:56:38 PM	5-31-92	8:41:52 PM	-A--
	WP ROOT. SF	5:46:54 PM	6-16-92	5:46:54 PM	5-31-92	8:59:02 PM	-AHS

Drive C - Details View

Archive   *Archive* is used for the BACKUP, RESTORE, COPY, and XCOPY commands that use the attribute when performing functions on the files. In addition, backup software application packages use this attribute. A more complete discussion of these commands follows in Chapter 6.

Hidden   A *hidden* object cannot be displayed at the command line with the DIR command and by default is not displayed in the Workplace Shell.

System   An object with the *system* attribute is part of the operating system. System files are not displayed at the command line with the DIR command.

Changing Flags

There are a number of reasons to change the flags on a file. You may want to prevent users from changing files such as boilerplate word processing documents or you may want to protect software files from accidental deletion. Backup software can be configured to manipulate the Archive flag in order to keep track of those files that have been changed since the last backup was performed.

To change the flags through the Workplace Shell, open the pop-up menu for the file from any of the three available views by double-clicking on button #2. Click on the arrow beside **Open** and select **Settings**. Click on **File** and then click on the right arrow in the Settings window to get to the second page, illustrated in Figure 5-4. Click on the appropriate check boxes to make your changes.

The Drives Folder

Every file in every directory in your system can be accessed via the Drives folder. Open OS/2 System and choose **Drives**. The window you see, illustrated in Figure 5-5, has an entry for each drive in your system, including network drives if you are connected to a network.

 Caution The views of the Drives folder that are described in the following paragraphs all contain a Refresh entry in their pop-up menus. After making any changes such as copying, renaming, or otherwise manipulating files, you should close the view and re-open it in order to see the changes, rather than relying on the Refresh function. The function is inconsistent in its ability to redraw the view.

 Changing flags ✿

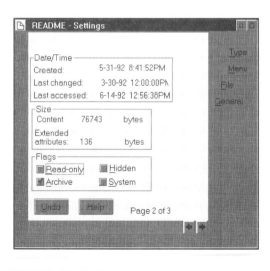

FIGURE 5-5

The Drives folder ✿

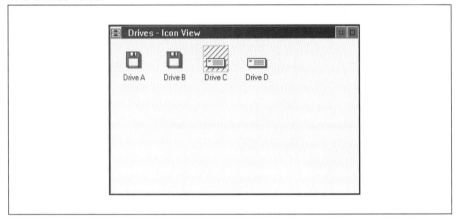

OS/2 offers several viewing modes to survey the information available about your drives.

Tree View

Open drive C and you will see a tree view of the directory structure as seen in Figure 5-6. A tree view shows the drive structure in a form analogous to the limbs of a tree, with some limbs having branches. Some of the directories have a plus sign beside them, indicating that there are subdirectories beneath them. Click on the plus sign to display the component subdirectories. Use the down arrow on the scroll bar or the slider to move down the list. If there are lower levels of subdirectories, there are additional plus signs.

Icon View

Click on the System icon with button #2 to display the pop-up menu. Click on the arrow to the right of **Open** with button #1 and select **Icon view**.

Tree view of a drive ✿

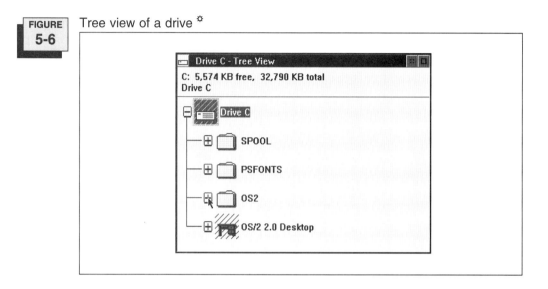

Figure 5-7 illustrates the default icon configuration, in which directories are presented as folders, data files resemble dog-eared sheets of paper, and program files have an icon marked either DOS or OS/2.

Default icon view ✿

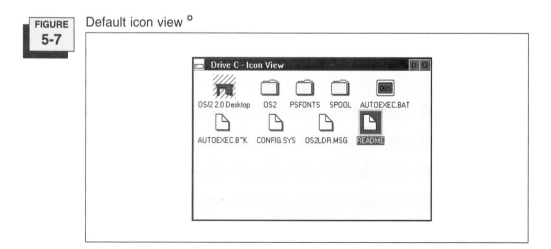

Details View

In the Details view, there are several columns relating to attributes of the objects listed and the icons of any objects that are open are grayed.

Adjusting the Details View

Note the shape of the pointer in Figure 5-8, left-right arrows with two vertical lines between them. This shape indicates that the cursor is on a sizing bar. Much like the sizing border of a window, the sizing bar allows you to change the size of columns within a window. You can drag the sizing bar to the left to get more columns on the screen, or drag it to the right to be able to see the full text of your program titles.

There are two horizontal scroll bars available so you can scroll through the right side of the window horizontally without losing the ability to see the leftmost column where the filename is displayed.

Filtering the View

All views, by default, show all the non-hidden entries in a folder. However, you might want to change the view to look only at the types of

FIGURE 5-8

Using the sizing bar *

Icon	Title	Real name	Size	Last write date	Last write time	Last access date	Last acce
	OS/2 2.0 Desktop	OS/2 2.0 Desktop	0	5-31-92	8:58:52 PM	5-31-92	8:
	OS2	OS2	0	5-31-92	8:30:16 PM	5-31-92	8:
	PSFONTS	PSFONTS	0	5-31-92	8:37:38 PM	5-31-92	8:
	SPOOL	SPOOL	0	5-31-92	8:58:34 PM	5-31-92	8:
	AUTOEXEC.BAT	AUTOEXEC.BAT	286	6-13-92	6:27:44 PM	6-17-92	8:
	AUTOEXEC.B~K	AUTOEXEC.B~K	259	5-31-92	8:54:16 PM	6-13-92	6:
	CONFIG.SYS	CONFIG.SYS	1,934	6-13-92	6:43:58 PM	6-14-92	1:
	OS2LDR.MSG	OS2LDR.MSG	8,440	3-30-92	12:00:00 PM	5-31-92	8:
	README	README	76,743	3-30-92	12:00:00 PM	6-14-92	12:

Drive C - Details View

files in which you are interested, for example your data files. Selecting criteria in this way is called *filtering*.

Pop up the system menu for this window (clicking on the System icon with button #2 always invokes a pop-up menu). Click on the arrow beside **Open** and choose **Settings**. Click on the **Include** tab to get to the Settings section of the notebook (see Figure 5-9).

The entry field at the top allows you to create a set of standards for the filenames you want to appear in the view. Giving the system some parameters, including certain characters, creates a *mask* for your choices.

Using Wildcards

You can use *wildcards*, special characters that indicate that any characters at all will match your choice, in order to select combinations of files. If, for example, you have named all of your word processing files with an extension of .DOC and only want to see those files, you could enter *.DOC in this field, and when you closed this window, only the files that meet that specification would appear.

FIGURE
5-9

The Include selection window ✿

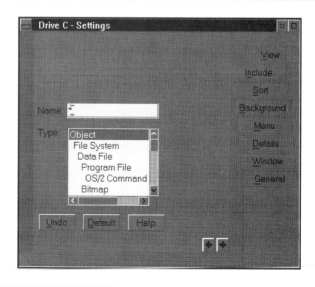

Wildcard An asterisk (*) in the mask means you will accept any character or characters as a match.

? *Wildcard* A question mark means you will accept any single character in that specific position as a match.

BOOK?.WP would match with BOOK1.WP and BOOK2.WP, but not BOOKLIST.WP; BOOK*.WP would match all three.

Note that with the High Performance File System, filenames are not restricted to the 8.3 naming convention, so you must create a mask that matches the protocols you use for filenames. For example, LETTER.*.INQUIRY would match LETTER.SMITH.INQUIRY, LETTER.JONES.INQUIRY, and LETTER.SAM.INQUIRY, while LETTER.S*.INQUIRY would eliminate LETTER.JONES.INQUIRY.

Tip If you plan to run DOS applications, it is wise to use the 8.3 convention for HPFS filenames.

Using Object Types

In the second field on the page shown in Figure 5-9 is a list of object types to be displayed. By changing the type of object, you can restrict the list of files. For example, you can select the **Program file** object to have only the filenames of executable programs appear in the window.

Note Both selection criteria can be used together, so you can select certain file types along with masks for characters.

Filtering Using Flags

You can also select to view files based on their flags. Clicking on the right arrow in the **Include selection** window brings up page two of the Settings notebook, shown in Figure 5-10. The default criteria is that hidden files are not shown.

Note When viewing the contents of a directory via the command line DIR command, the System attribute means that the file will not be displayed even if it is not flagged as Hidden.

FIGURE 5-10   Selecting by flag ✿

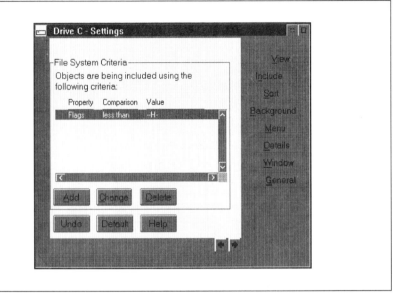

Changing the Flag Filter

When modifying the filter criteria, the term "less than" means filter out all files in which the indicated flag is set. For instance, if you did not want to display (you wanted to filter out) read-only files, you would insert a criterion specifying flags less than R, as shown in Figure 5-11. You would leave the other flag attributes displayed as dashes since you want to ignore the status of the other flags. If, in addition, you do not want to show Hidden files, add the criteria **AND** Flags less than H.

 Note   The order in which flag attributes are displayed is RAHS. However, specifying a single criterion of Flags less than R-H- will not work. Each criterion must be established individually.

It is possible to view Hidden and System files in the Workplace Shell. If you set the criterion flags equal to H and then **Add** Flags equal to S, followed by clicking on the **OR** button, the display will contain only those file types.

FIGURE
5-11

Filtering out read-only files *

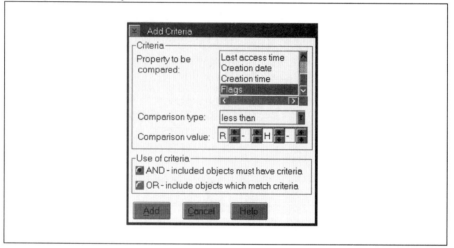

This somewhat convoluted technique for flag criteria was designed so that all the attributes attached to files are filtered in the same manner. For the other attributes, which involve dates and times, the logic of the concept of greater than and less than is more apparent.

Sorting the View

You can change the order in which the objects are displayed in the Icon and Details views.

Setting the Defaults

Clicking on **Sort** while in the Settings notebook provides a way to arrange files according to whatever criteria you need. As shown in Figure 5-12, the initial default sort attribute is **Name**, so if you request a sort of the list of files, they are presented in alphabetical order. Clicking on the arrow beside **Name** drops down the other fields by which the files may be sorted. Select the desired field. When you close the Settings notebook, you have established the default sort scheme.

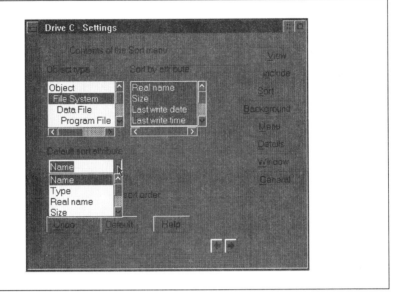

FIGURE
5-12

Setting sort defaults ✿

Tip   There is a check box labeled **Always maintain sort order**   that can be
selected to instruct the system to present that view sorted that way
whenever the view is opened, as well as maintaining the sort sequence
the entire time the view is open.

The available sorting choices are as follows:

Name
Type
Real name
Size
Last write date
Last write time
Last access date
Last access time
Creation date
Creation time

Sorting

To actuate a sort, open the pop-up menu and click on **Sort**, as shown in Figure 5-13.

If you want to view the display in a different sort order without changing the default, you can do so with the Sort choice on the pop-up menu. Click on the arrow to the right of **Sort** to see the choices displayed in Figure 5-14 and click on the option you wish to implement.

 Note   Whatever Sort order you select only affects the listing presented in the Workplace Shell. The listing displayed when using DIR at the command line remains unchanged.

Drag-and-Drop

File management—whether it involves moving, printing, copying, or otherwise manipulating files—can be accomplished by the use of the drag-and-drop technique.

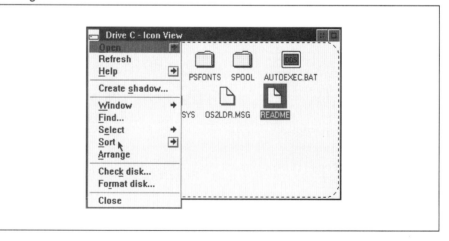

FIGURE 5-13

Sorting the view ✿

Changing the sort key *

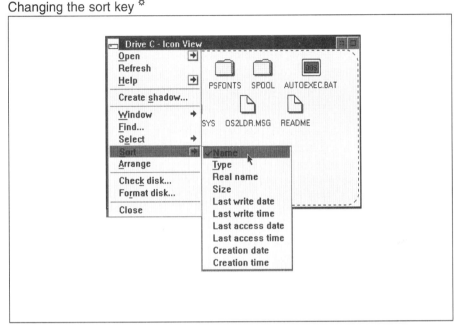

Printing Files

To send a file to the printer, simply drag a file icon to the printer icon and drop it.

Sending Files

As you look through your files, you may find one on which you want to perform some operation. An easy way to send a file to a program is via drag-and-drop.

Look again at the icon view of drive C and double-click on the drive itself to open a view of the files in the root (see Figure 5-7). Suppose you want to look at the file labeled README. Since this is a text file, it needs some type of program to open it and present the contents. The Workplace Shell provides several ways for you to do this.

Open the OS/2 System folder, and from there open the Productivity folder. There you will find the OS/2 System Editor and the Enhanced Editor. These are programs that allow you to look at the README file. Move the pointer to the README icon and drag it to the editor of your choice (see Figure 5-15). The README file is displayed for your review. This activity is so common that OS/2 has established a default association between text files and the OS/2 System Editor.

Sending a file results in opening that file if the object to which it is sent is a program that is Workplace Shell aware. If you drag-and-drop a text file to a word processing program that is not programmed to be responsive to the OS/2 Workplace Shell, the process will not automatically open the program and the text file.

Creating Shadows

There may be occasions when you want the same file to be in more than one place at a time. Perhaps it makes sense to have a file available

FIGURE 5-15

Sending a file ✿

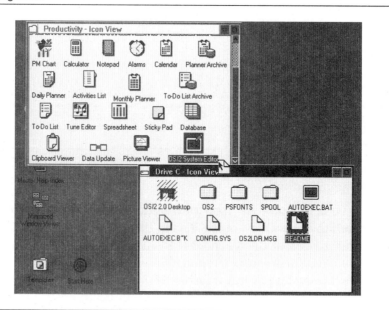

in several different folders in order to enhance your productivity. This could be accomplished by making copies of the file. When you simply copy an object, however, the new copy is a unique object with no attachments to the original. If you change the attributes or contents of the original object, the copy isn't affected.

In contrast, a *shadow* is a copy of an object that is permanently linked to the original object. You can create as many shadows of an object as you need. If you change the settings or the contents of either a shadow or its original, the others are also modified automatically. With shadows, it makes no difference which clone of the file you access.

To create a shadow, open the pop-up menu by clicking on the Drives folder icon with Button #2 and clicking on **Create shadow**. You are then shown a notebook, illustrated in Figure 5-16, that allows you to specify the folder you'd like to hold the shadow.

The first page of the Create Shadow notebook identifies folders that are already open on the desktop. Note that the OS/2 2.0 Desktop itself is considered a folder, allowing you to add shadows on the desktop itself. If the folder to which you would like to add the shadow is not yet open, click on the **Desktop** tab of the notebook to see a list of all folders on the desktop. From there, simply click on the folder where the shadow is going.

The text underneath the shadow's icon is a different color than that below the original object. The Workplace Shell does this to provide a visual reminder that this is a shadow object rather than an original.

 Note If you delete a shadow, any other shadows of the original as well as the original are unaffected. Deleting the original, however, removes all of its shadows.

Associating Files

An *association* means that a file has a default program to which it is related. Once the association is created, opening the file launches the connected application automatically. This means that instead of opening a word processor and then selecting the file you want to work on, you need only open the data file to start the word processor with the file you want already selected. The same result occurs with other types of data

FIGURE
5-16

Creating a shadow ✿

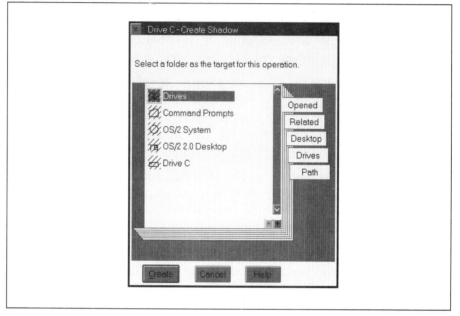

files and software, such as databases, spreadsheets, and productivity software.

In the absence of any other primary association, any text file is associated with the System Editor.

Associating by Type

Sometimes it is advantageous to associate all files of the same type with a single program. If you prefer to work with text files in the Enhanced Editor rather than the OS/2 System Editor, open the Settings notebook for the Enhanced Editor. Click on the arrow beside **Open** and click on **Settings**. Choose the **Association** tab to display the page shown in Figure 5-17.

Use the scroll bar in the **Available types** box to move to **Plain Text**, and then select it. Then click on the **Add** button to move **Plain Text** over to the **Current types** box. That's all there is to it. Once you've closed this window, if you double-click on any file with the type Plain Text, the Enhanced

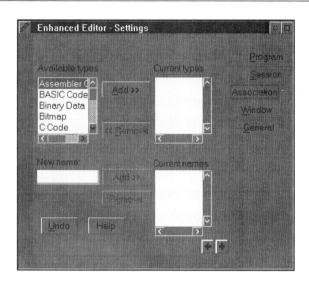

FIGURE
5-17

Associating files by type *

Editor starts and the file is passed to it. Similarly, the Icon Editor can be associated with files of type Icon.

It is possible to have more than one program associated with a file type. Following the steps above causes both the System Editor and the Enhanced Editor to be associated with the type Plain Text. By default, the first program associated with a type will be opened. Pop up the system menu of a file and click on the arrow beside the word **Open**. You will see all programs associated with that file's type listed, as illustrated in Figure 5-18. You can then click on the desired program to start it.

Associating by File Extension

There may be situations in which the association should be by extension rather than a predefined OS/2 file type. For example, you may want to associate all files with the extension .WP with your favorite word processor. Go to the Association page of the Settings notebook of your word processor (see Figure 5-17). In the **New name** field, enter the file extension **WP**. Clicking on the **Add** button moves that mask to the **Current**

FIGURE
5-18

A file with multiple associations

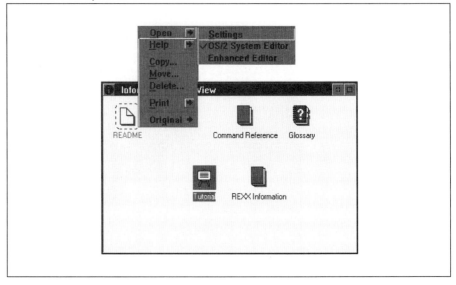

names box. Double-clicking on any file with the .WP extension will now start your word processor and pass it the indicated data file.

Note   The New name field is for extensions, not filenames. You do not use the standard extension protocol of *.WP. There is no way to associate a file with a program by using the filename.

Associating Individual Files

It is also possible to associate individual data-file objects with program objects, regardless of the file's type or extension. Open the file's Settings notebook and click on the **Menu** tab to see the page shown in Figure 5-19. Decide whether you would like to add the program for this file to the pop-up system menu or to the cascaded menu that appears when you click on the arrow beside **Open**. To have the program appear on the Open menu, select **~Open** in the **Available menus** list box. Otherwise, leave the highlight on **Primary pop-up menu**

Next, click on the **Create another** button under **Actions on menu**. Note that this is the button on the lower half of the notebook page. The upper

Menu page of pop-up menu ✿

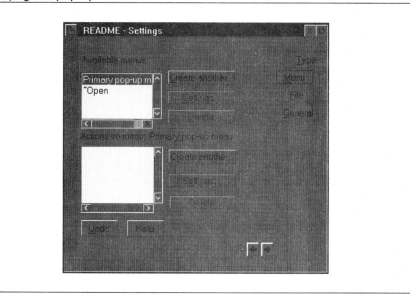

half is for adding entire new menus. You see the Menu Item Settings window shown in Figure 5-20.

Enter the text you want to appear in the **Menu item name** box. You also have to enter the path to the program with which you want this file associated into the **Program Name** box. If you don't know what the path

Menu Item Settings window ✿

is, click on the **Find program** button and then proceed as described in the following paragraphs about finding files. Click on **Ok** in the Menu Item Settings window and close the Settings notebook. The new program appears in the file's pop-up menu.

Finding Files

As files are used, copied, moved, and scattered throughout subdirectories, it can become difficult to remember where to look for them. The Workplace Shell provides a facility to help you locate files.

Open the pop-up menu of any folder and click on **Find** to see the window shown in Figure 5-21. Click on the **Locate** button to see the window shown in Figure 5-22.

This produces a request for a path to the desired object. If you knew the path, of course, you would not be using the Find facility. However, you probably do know which drive you should be searching. Click on the **Drives** tab of the notebook and then click on the appropriate drive.

FIGURE
5-21

The Find notebook ❋

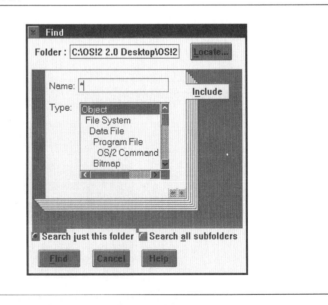

Locating via drive search ✿

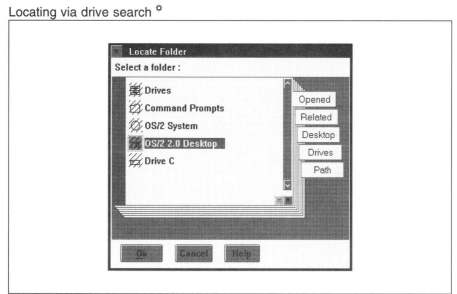

Clicking on **Ok** returns you to page 1 of the notebook. In the **Name** field, enter whatever portion of the filename you are certain of. If you wish to narrow the search further, you can go to the **Type** box and select a specific file type. To search all subfolders on the drive, change the default at the bottom of the dialog box from **Search just this folder** to **Search all subfolders** Clicking on the **Find** button begins the search. A new window containing all the files that match your specification is opened. Select the correct one.

 Note The Find function described is not connected to the FIND utility available at the command line.

CHAPTER

Command-Line
Utilities

W hile the OS/2 graphical interface and the Workplace Shell make tasks less complicated for the user than typing commands and parameters, some experienced computer users feel more comfortable with the familiarity of the command line. Even less experienced users may find some tasks suitable to command-line functions.

A complete reference to all commands is provided in Appendix A. For your convenience, this chapter contains detailed explanations of some of the commands you will probably use frequently.

Accessing the Command Line

Open the OS/2 System folder and then open the folder inside labelled Command Prompts. As you can see in the illustration displayed in Figure 6-1, there are a number of alternative methods available for accessing the command line. You can opt for a command session inside a window on the desktop or a full-screen session.

FIGURE
6-1

Opening a command session ✿

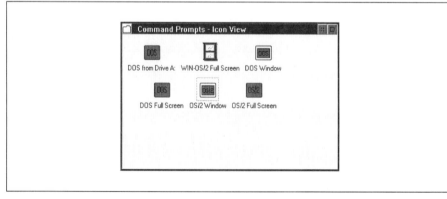

Command-Line Syntax

This is the order of entry for entering commands:

Command Drive:*Path\Filename Target* /*Parameters*

Command is the name of the command you want to process.

Drive is the disk drive that stores the file or directory involved in the command.

Path is the route of subdirectory names the computer must follow to arrive at the file you wish to access.

Filename is the name and extension (if any) of the file you want to access.

Target is a file, path, or device to which the command may be required to send an object. Target is not applicable to all commands but is used for certain processes, for example, COPY or REN (rename).

Parameters are the command parameters that change or enhance the basic function of the command.

To illustrate, look at the following command:

COPY C:\WORDPROC\DATA\LETTER3 A:\WORK /V

This command sends a file named LETTER3—located on drive C with a path of \WORDPROC\DATA—to drive A in a directory called WORK, and it tells the operating system to verify the copy against the original. Since the target includes only the name of a subdirectory, the copied file will retain its name. Had the command been entered this way,

COPY C:\WORDPROC\DATA\LETTER3 A:\WORK\SMITH /V

the file stored on drive A would be named SMITH. The contents of the file would be the same, only the name would be changed.

 Note If there is not a directory named WORK already established on drive A, the file LETTER3 will be named WORK when it is copied and will reside on the root directory of drive A.

DOS Command Session

The DOS command session under OS/2, as displayed in Figure 6-2, looks similar to native DOS. It behaves much the same also. Most of the commands you used with DOS can be issued from this command line.

Remember that you are working in a multitasking environment and you can open more than one DOS command session. In fact, you can have as many DOS command sessions running at one time as you need (the system limit is over 100). Therefore, you can launch software from some command sessions and do command-line hard disk housekeeping from others.

OS/2 Command Session

Looking at Figure 6-3, it isn't easy to distinguish the OS/2 command prompt from that of DOS. OS/2 uses brackets to enclose the path rather than using the "greater than" sign. In case that is a bit too subtle, OS/2 puts either "DOS" or "OS/2" in the upper left corner of the session to help

DOS command line ✿

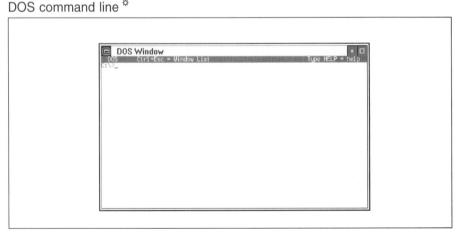

FIGURE
6-3

OS/2 command line *

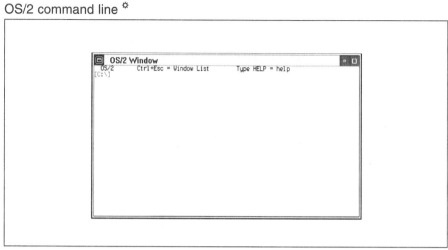

you remember which command session you are employing as well as showing keystrokes needed for basic tasks. Incidentally, if you want to reclaim that line of the screen, you can type **HELP OFF** from the command line. This will not eliminate the help facility.

Disk Management Commands

Disk management commands are those programs and utilities in the operating system that permit manipulation and examination of the structure of the hard disk.

DIR

The DIR command produces a listing of all files and directories contained in the directory from which you issue the command or for any directory you specify. For each file, there is information about the size, the last write date, and the last write time. For each directory, the notation <DIR> appears as well as the creation date and time. At the end of the list, the system reports the following information:

□   *The number of files contained in the directory.*   Subdirectories are included as files for the purpose of counting the entries.

□   *The number of bytes used.*   This number is the total of the bytes used by files in the directory; subdirectory use of space is not counted.

□   *Bytes free.*   This number is the amount of disk space available on the drive in which the directory resides.

DIR Masks

You can create a mask, including wildcards, so that only certain types of files are listed. For example, to see all the command files in a directory, enter the command

DIR *.CMD

DIR /P

The parameter /P displays the directory one screenful at a time instead of letting the file and directory names scroll continuously.

DIR /W

The /W parameter presents the listings in a wide format across five columns. There is no information about the files available, although directory listings are enclosed in brackets so you can distinguish them from files.

MD or MKDIR

This command creates a directory on the hard drive. You may use the full path to create a directory at lower levels or use some shortcuts. For example, to create a directory below the UTILS directory called TAPE, type **MD C:\UTILS\TAPE**

Even if you are on drive D at the time, this directory will be created on drive C. However, the closer you are to the target of the command, the fewer letters you have to type. If you are on drive C, drive letter C does not need to be entered since it is the default.

If you are in the UTILS directory, do not use the backslash; instead, just follow the command with a space and the name of the new directory. If you use the backslash, assuming you are creating a directory one level down from your cursor position, and type **MD \TAPE**, a directory called TAPE is created one level down from the root directory instead of below the UTILS directory. Remember that the operating system uses the backslash to determine the path down from the root.

RD or RMDIR

This command removes directories from the hard drive. The directories must be empty before they can be removed. You cannot remove the current directory (the directory you are in when you issue the command) nor any parent of the current directory. You must be at least one level above the directory you want to remove. If there is any reason that the directory cannot be removed, the system reports back only the fact that the directory cannot be removed; it will not tell you why. In fact, the error message saying simply that a directory cannot be removed will appear regardless of the problem encountered in trying to remove it—including the fact that no such directory exists.

CD or CHDIR

CD is the command used to move around the hard drive. To change to any directory from any other directory, you can either type the entire path at the command line or use shortcuts if you are in the appropriate place on the hard drive. As with MD, movement from one directory to a directory one level below is achieved by using a space instead of a backslash. To move up one level, type the command followed by two periods (CD..).

CHKDSK

This utility analyzes directories and files, determines the file system type, and produces a disk status report. CHKDSK also displays the volume label and the volume serial number of the disk.

You should run CHKDSK occasionally to check for errors. If errors are found, CHKDSK displays the error messages and produces a status report. If you enter a filename after CHKDSK, the OS/2 operating system displays a status report that gives the number of noncontiguous areas occupied by the file.

CHKDSK can detect *lost clusters* on your disk, parts of files taking up space on your disk that the system did not save completely. When CHKDSK finds these, it prompts you with a message asking if you want to convert lost chains to files. If you type   , CHKDSK converts these parts into files that you can examine and then delete to recover the disk space. If you type   , CHKDSK deletes these parts of files from your disk without warning. The files CHKDSK creates from lost chains follow the naming convention FILE*nnnn*.CHK (where *nnnn* is a sequential number starting with 0000).

Note CHKDSK places all files it creates in the root directory of the specified drive.

There are a number of parameters available for CHKDSK. In the discussions following, the syntax will include *x:*, which stands for whatever drive letter is the target of the CHKDSK program.

CHKDSK x: /V

The /V parameter displays all files and their paths on the default or specified drive.

CHKDSK x: /C

The /C parameter is used only with the High Performance File System (HPFS). It specifies that files will be recovered only if the file system was in an inconsistent state when the computer was started. This could happen if the computer had been turned off before all the files were closed or if electrical power to the computer had been interrupted.

Note OS/2 keeps track of whether or not the system was shut down smoothly at the end of the last session. If it was not shut down properly, OS/2 automatically runs CHKDSK on all hard drives the next time you boot. This is controlled by the AUTOCHECK parameter that was put into CONFIG.SYS during the installation of the operating system.

CHKDSK x: /F

Using the parameter /F causes CHKDSK to fix the errors found.

Caution Do not use this parameter in a DOS command session; this level of disk management must be performed in an OS/2 session.

The command CHKDSK /F cannot be run from the hard drive that you want to check. When you use this parameter, the hard drive from which you initiate the command is protected under the OS/2 protected mode and no activity can occur on the disk. Therefore, the drive to be fixed cannot be the one from which you start the operating system, nor can it be the one that contains the CHKDSK program.

To fix the errors found using CHKDSK/F on a system configured with a single partition (drive C), make sure of the following:

☐ If the drive to be searched is a drive formatted for HPFS, the file UHPFS.DLL must exist on the same diskette as CHKDSK.

☐ In order for the system to display error messages, the file OSO001.MSG must be on the same disk as CHKDSK.

Then proceed with the following steps:

1. Insert the system Installation Disk into disk drive A.

2. Restart the system. When the logo panel appears, remove the Installation Disk and insert Disk 1. Press ENTER to continue.

3. At the first text panel that appears ("Welcome to OS/2"), press ESC.

4. Run CHKDSK from drive A, specifying drive C as the drive to be searched:

CHKDSK C: /F

To run CHKDSK /F on a system that has two hard drives or a logical drive in an extended partition, the process can be made a bit easier. Put copies of CHKDSK.COM, OSO001.MSG, and UHPFS.DLL on the other drive (drive D if you are checking drive C or vice versa). Then, to check drive C, boot from diskette, move to drive D, and type **CHKDSK C: /F**. To perform the function on drive D, move to drive C, and type **CHKDSK D: /F**.

CHKDSK x: /F:n

Also used only with the HPFS, the n parameter designates a recovery level (if no number is given, recovery level 2 is the default). The recovery levels are as follows:

☐ CHKDSK x: /F:0   CHKDSK analyzes the file system and reports information about its state, but does not perform any repairs.

☐ CHKDSK x: /F:1   CHKDSK resolves inconsistencies in the file system structures.

☐ CHKDSK x: /F:2   CHKDSK resolves inconsistent file system structure and also scans disk space that is in use but not referred to by the file system. If recognizable file or directory structures are found, they are recovered.

☐ CHKDSK x: /F:3   Includes all level-2 recovery functions and also specifies that CHKDSK is to scan the entire disk partition for recognizable file system structures.

Extended Attributes

CHKDSK attempts to validate the clusters with files or directories that contain extended attributes. If errors occur in any extended attribute chain on the disk, CHKDSK prompts you to recover that chain into a file that follows this naming format: EA*nnnn*.CHK, where *nnnn* is a sequential number starting with 0000.

CHKDSK also recovers the file or directory associated with the extended attribute chain and places it in a file that follows the naming format FILE*nnnn*.CHK. The number in this filename corresponds to the number shown in the EA*nnnn*.CHK filename.

FDISK

FDISK allows you to examine, create, or delete a primary partition or a logical drive in an extended partition. FDISK has a number of parameters available and also has a number of options to limit those parameters.

FDISK /QUERY

FDISK /QUERY displays a list of all partitions and free space on the hard disks. This might be helpful if you are working at a computer that you did not set up yourself or if you are trying to find the best drive in which to install a new software application.

FDISK /SETNAME

This specifies names for primary partitions or logical drives and makes them bootable from the Boot Manager.

Caution If there is no name specified, any existing boot name is removed and the partition is not bootable from the Boot Manager menu.

FDISK /FILE: *filename*

This parameter requires a *filename*, which is a file you create containing FDISK commands you wish to process. It is, in effect, an FDISK batch file. Commas separate each command. Use this option only if you are very comfortable with hard disk management, partitions, and FDISK.

FDISK /NAME: Option

FDISK parameters that indicate action on a particular partition or logical drive can be limited by name. This option can be used with all FDISK parameters except /FILE.

FDISK /DISK: Option

This option specifies the physical hard disk that you want to work with when using FDISK along with parameters. Physical hard disks are referred to by number, beginning with 0. This option can be used with all FDISK parameters except /FILE.

FDISKPM

Supplying the same functions of FDISK, this command invokes the Presentation Manager version of the utility. FDISKPM presents menus and displays to guide you through its tasks. Help is available for all selectable items and entry fields. This is a safer, easier way to deal with the partitions and logical drives on your hard disk.

FORMAT

The FORMAT utility formats a disk in the specified drive to accept OS/2 files by marking the directory and file allocation tables on the disk. FORMAT also checks the disk for defects.

Note You must specify a drive letter followed by a colon (for example, A:). Otherwise, the system displays an error message that you have not specified a target drive.

If you format a drive for HPFS, FORMAT checks the IFS (Installable File Systems) statement in the CONFIG.SYS file to determine whether the drive is listed with the /AUTOCHECK parameter. If the drive is listed, FORMAT does not update the IFS statement. If the drive is not listed, FORMAT adds the drive letter.

Caution   If you format a diskette or hard disk that already contains information, all of the previously stored information is erased.

Be sure to set up an OS/2 partition on all hard disks before formatting them. FORMAT does not recognize a hard disk as being an OS/2 disk if an OS/2 or a DOS partition does not exist. When FORMAT finds such a disk, it skips to the next disk and begins formatting it.

FORMAT x: /ONCE

This command specifies that only one diskette is to be formatted. When the format is complete, the system does not ask if you wish to format another before returning you to the system prompt.

Disk Capacity Parameters

By default, the FORMAT command attempts to format the media to the maximum capacity of the disk drive. To format disks with capacities different from the default size expected for the drive, there are several parameters available.

Caution   Do not attempt to format a disk to an incorrect capacity. A disk formatted in this way will not store your data reliably.

FORMAT x: /F:xxxx   This command specifies the size to which the disk is to be formatted. The parameter can be used for 360K, 1.2MB, 720K, 1.44MB, and 2.88MB disks. For example, FORMAT A:/F:360 formats a double-density 5-1/4-inch disk in a 1.2MB drive.

Note   If you are used to the DOS conventions or you have a need to do things the long way, the old parameters for non-default size disk formatting still work (for example, /T:80 /N:9 to format a 720K disk in a 1.44MB drive).

FORMAT x: /L

This command specifies the Long format procedure, which is the procedure required to install a file system on an IBM read/write optical disc the first time such a disc is formatted. To format and install the file system on an optical disc the first time requires about 20 minutes using the /L parameter. Reformatting a previously formatted optical disc requires only a few minutes because you do not use the /L parameter.

FORMAT x: /V:

This command writes a volume label up to 11 characters long onto the disk. The label is entered after the colon. You may use spaces within a label, but if you do, you must enclose the label within quote marks (for example,"MY WORK").

If you do not use the /V parameter, you are prompted for a label name after the format is completed. Pressing ENTER means no label is to be applied.

 Caution FORMAT does not work on drives that have an ASSIGN, JOIN, or SUBST command in effect (see Appendix A for details on using those commands). Also, FORMAT does not work on network drives.

File Management Commands

All of the familiar DOS commands are available in an OS/2 session and many of them have additional functionality. A quick review of some of the basic utilities may be helpful.

 Note When implementing file management commands, if you are using filenames with embedded blanks, the filename must be enclosed in quotes.

COPY

Probably the command-line utility used most often, COPY allows you to do the following tasks:

❑ Copy files between disk drives

☐   Copy files between directories

☐   Copy files to a printer

☐   Copy a file to another name

☐   Combine files by using a plus sign between source filenames

In addition, the OS/2 COPY command offers some extra services that allow you to manipulate file attributes.

Changing the Date and Time

A plus sign followed by two commas changes the date and time attribute of a file to the current date and time. Wildcards are allowed. The command

COPY *filename* +,,

changes the date and time stamp of the named file.

COPY *.* +,,

changes the date and time stamp of every file in the current directory.

Extended Attributes Checking

If you are working in a directory that supports extended attributes and you want to copy a file to another directory, it may be important to maintain all the extended attributes. The /F parameter allows you to tell the operating system not to let the file copy into a directory that will not retain the extended attributes of that file.

The following command causes the copy to fail if the source file contains extended attributes and the destination file system does not support them:

COPY *filename* C:*subdirectory* /F

Without this parameter, the copy will succeed, but the extended attributes will not be copied.

REN or RENAME

The REN command changes the filename without changing the contents. The file stays in the same directory, so there is no opportunity to move or copy it during a RENAME. In OS/2 this command also works on subdirectories.

DEL or ERASE

DEL or ERASE deletes the specified file. If the target is *.* or a subdirectory, the system will ask for verification.

UNDELETE

The UNDELETE command gives you the ability to recover files that have been deleted or erased.

If you follow the command with a filename, that file will be undeleted. If you do not have a filename, the system presents a list of available deleted files for the designated directory and asks for confirmation of the undelete function for each one.

 Note   UNDELETE can be used in both DOS and OS/2 sessions. Files that are available for recovery are reported as used bytes on the disk.

The Deleted Files Directory

UNDELETE delays the permanent removal of a file, giving you the ability to retrieve the file up until the moment it is permanently discarded. In order to give you the UNDELETE ability, an environment variable called DELDIR was created during installation of the operating system. DELDIR defines the path and maximum size of directories used to store deleted files. One such directory is specified for each logical drive on the system. The DELDIR statement is written in the CONFIG.SYS file as follows:

SET DELDIR = *drive*:*path, maxsize*; *drive2*:*path, maxsize*

The path and maximum size values for each logical drive are separated from each other by a comma, and the logical drive names are separated by a semicolon. When the DEL or ERASE command is issued from any session type, the file is moved to the directory specified in the DELDIR statement for that logical drive.

Note At the time of installation of OS/2, that line in CONFIG.SYS has the word REM in front of it, meaning that the line is a remark, not an instruction. If you want to take advantage of the ability to recover deleted files, you must delete the word REM to turn the line into an instruction to the operating system. You can use the OS/2 system editor to do this; details on this process are found in the following chapter.

If the size of the deleted files exceeds the maximum size of the deleted files directory, files are automatically removed from the directory in first-in, first-out (FIFO) order.

Note To save disk space, there is a way to delete files stored in DELDIR manually. If the scarcity of disk space is severe, you can disable storage of deleted files by removing the directory name from the DELDIR statement in CONFIG.SYS or by REMarking the line (of course, this eliminates the ability to undelete).

Recovering the Deleted Files

If UNDELETE is invoked and the specified file is still recoverable, the file is reclaimed and restored to its specific path. If a duplicate filename exists, you are prompted to rename the file.

UNDELETE /L

UNDELETE/L displays a list of files that are available for recovery without actually recovering the files.

UNDELETE /S

UNDELETE/S tells the system to include all deleted files in the specified directory and all of its subdirectories.

UNDELETE /A

UNDELETE/A recovers all deleted files without prompting for confirmation on each file.

UNDELETE filename /F

The UNDELETE *filename*/F parameter removes the specified file permanently so that it cannot ever be recovered.

TYPE

The TYPE command sends the contents of the file specified to the screen. In OS/2 you may have more than one filename on the command line. For instance,

TYPE MYFILE1 HERFILE2

will type both files to the screen in the order in which they are listed on the command line.

MORE

The MORE command sends the contents of a file to the screen, one screenful at a time. There are two ways to implement this command:

MORE < *filename*

and

TYPE *filename* ¦ MORE

XCOPY

The XCOPY command selectively copies groups of files, which can include lower-level subdirectories. It does not copy Hidden or System files.

The following command copies all the files in the source directory *subdir* to the target directory *newdir*:

XCOPY C:*subdir* c:*newdir*

If *newdir* is not a subdirectory, the system asks if *newdir* is a file or a directory. If you reply with the latter, the system will create the subdirectory for you and then copy the files into it.

To copy all the files in *subdir* to *newdir* and also copy all files in all subdirectories of *subdir* to *newdir*, type this command:

XCOPY C:*subdir* C:*newdir* /S

This will create the appropriate subdirectories in *newdir* as needed.

BACKUP

Use the BACKUP command to back up files to diskettes. After BACKUP fills a diskette, it prompts you to insert a new diskette. Label each diskette in consecutive order, recording the date and diskette number.

BACKUP does not back up the System files (COMMAND.COM and CMD.EXE), hidden System files, or any open dynamic link library files (.DLL).

RESTORE

The RESTORE command is used to restore files that were backed up with the BACKUP command. When RESTORE prompts you to insert the source diskette, make sure that you insert the correct backup diskette. When you restore all your files, RESTORE prompts you to insert the backup diskettes in order. You must restore files to the same directory they were in when BACKUP copied them.

The RESTORE command does not restore COMMAND.COM, CMD.EXE, or the hidden OS/2 and DOS system files on the root directory. Therefore, you cannot use RESTORE to create a startable disk or diskette.

MOVE

New in OS/2, the MOVE command moves a file from one directory to another. The command will not move files across drives. In effect, this command creates the same result as copying a file to another directory and then deleting it from the original directory.

START

This command starts an OS/2 program in another OS/2 session. You can use START to run full-screen applications or applications running in a window such as Presentation Manager programs.

Often when you use this command to start a program, the application will then reside in the background and you can click on its window when you want to work with it. If it opens minimized as well as in the background, you can switch to the application by bringing up the Window List (by pressing CTRL+ESC or clicking on both buttons on the desktop) and selecting it.

This is a useful way to keep your productivity level high when you need to switch to an application that has a lot of introductory screens. Use the START command to invoke the application and continue what you are doing for a few moments. When you are ready for the new application, switch to it and it will be past the introductory parts and ready for you to get some work done.

START filename /F

The /F parameter makes the program the foreground program.

START filename /N

The /N parameter starts a program directly without invoking the command processor (CMD.EXE). It cannot be used on internal commands (see the listing in Appendix A) or on a batch file.

START filename /FS

The /FS parameter indicates that the program is a full-screen DOS or OS/2 application that must run in a separate session, independent of Presentation Manager. This parameter also indicates that the program should start in the foreground.

START filename /WIN

The /WIN parameter indicates that the program is an OS/2 application that runs within an OS/2 window. It starts in the foreground.

START filename /PM

The /PM parameter tells the system that the program is a Presentation Manager application that starts in the foreground. You cannot start a batch file with this parameter.

START filename /MAX

The /MAX parameter is used for any application that usually starts in a window and indicates that the application should open in a maximized state. It has no effect on a full-screen application.

START filename /MIN

The /MIN parameter is the opposite of the /MAX parameter, indicating the application should open in a minimized (icon) state. It, too, has no effect on full-screen applications.

Caution A PM application may choose not to honor the request made by the /MAX or /MIN parameter.

START is frequently used to start programs automatically at system startup. The system startup batch file, STARTUP.CMD, allows you to do this.

Note If you add a START command to STARTUP.CMD, remember to enter the full path for the program. Also remember to put an EXIT at the end in order to avoid keeping open the OS/2 command session that STARTUP.CMD inaugurated.

RUN

Similar to START in its functionality, RUN loads and starts a system program during system initialization. The command is entered in the CONFIG.SYS file with the syntax

RUN=*program*

Be sure the correct path is included.

More than one RUN statement can appear in the CONFIG.SYS file and each statement is processed in the order in which it appears.

Note DEVICE statements in CONFIG.SYS are processed before any RUN statements.

If a program started with a RUN statement requests a window before the user interface is started, it receives a unique error code. The program might respond by delaying its processing until the user interface is started.

Because RUN programs are started before initialization of the user interface and disk error handling, the program must prevent the OS/2 operating system from performing disk handling and perform its own.

Caution You cannot use RUN to start a PM application.

Command-Line Functions

While you are working in an OS/2 command session, the arrow keys give you access to previous commands. Pressing UP ARROW brings up the last command you entered; as you continue to press it, it will loop backward through all the commands you've used. Pressing DOWN ARROW brings up the first command you used and loops through all the commands in the order in which you entered them.

You may wish to use the same facility while in a DOS session. You can do so by modifying AUTOEXEC.BAT. Remove the REM from the beginning of the line that contains the words LOADHIGH DOSKEY and save the file. The next DOS command prompt you open will use the OS/2 command recall keys.

You can change the look of the command line in either DOS or OS/2 by modifying the PROMPT statement. This is in the AUTOEXEC.BAT file for DOS and the CONFIG.SYS file for OS/2.

If you choose a window for your command session, it is easy to switch to another task by clicking on its window. However, if you choose a full-screen command session, you will not be able to see the other windows; you can use CTRL+ESC to switch between tasks. To close a command session, type **EXIT** at the command line.

CHAPTER

The OS/2 Editors

*W*hen you need to compose or change a text file, it is frequently more convenient to take advantage of the editors provided by OS/2 than it is to launch a word processing application. OS/2 provides two editors for this purpose, the System Editor and the Enhanced Editor. Both are located in the Productivity folder in the OS/2 System folder.

Both editors can load and save text files without any need for the user to go through the special keystrokes most word processors require in order to end up with straight ASCII text. They are so easy to use that a high level of productivity is quickly gained.

Both are also Presentation Manager programs. It is worth taking a moment to understand what that means.

Presentation Manager

Presentation Manager, or PM, is the part of OS/2 that allows developers to write graphical applications. It provides many of the graphical elements you encounter in OS/2, such as menu bars, sizing bars, scroll bars, and other graphic functions.

PM programs are *window aware*, meaning that whenever a window changes in size or aspect ratio, PM sends a message to the program so it can adjust to the new dimensions, if the program is written to take advantage of that information. It's important to understand the significance of that. It means that if you enlarge the window you are working in, the amount of data that is displayed will change. If you widen the window, the wrapping function will move to fit the width of the window. The OS/2 System Editor operates in this fashion by default.

PM also allows applications to use the built-in OS/2 graphic functions, including access to the fonts that are included with the operating system.

The System Editor

The OS/2 System Editor is an entry-level, window-aware editor. It has fewer features than some other editors, but it loads faster and is easier to learn.

There are several ways to load the System Editor; the best method varies depending on what you are planning to do with the Editor.

Load by Associated Files

As discussed in Chapter 5, plain text files are associated with the System Editor by default. If you want to examine or edit one of those files, double-clicking on the file itself launches the System Editor automatically, and the text file is in the System Editor window when the program opens.

Load by Dragging

The System Editor also supports drag-and-drop. Using that technique, a text file can be dragged onto the System Editor and dropped, starting the program with the desired file already loaded.

Load with a File from the Command Line

From the command line, the System Editor is loaded by its program name, E along with the name of the file you want to open. The command:

E MYFILE.TXT

opens the System Editor and loads the file MYFILE.TXT into the editor's window.

Load Without a Text File

If you just want to start the program without a file in place, either double-click on its icon in the Productivity folder or use the command line without any filename. Either technique begins the editor with an empty window, as shown in Figure 7-1.

Loading a File

To load a file into the editor window, click on **File** on the menu bar to open the File pull-down menu, shown in the following:✧

Click on **Open**. You are presented with the dialog box shown in Figure 7-2. If you know the complete path and name of the file you wish to edit, enter it into the **Open filename** entry field at the top of the dialog box. Otherwise, use the other fields in the dialog box to search for and select the file.

If the file is on another drive, click on the arrow beside the **Drive** field, and make a selection from the list of drives available. The **File** and **Directory** list boxes are updated automatically.

If the file is not in the current directory of that drive, select the correct directory from the **Directory** list box. Again, this box is updated to show any subdirectories underneath your choice, and the **File** box is updated to show the files in the directory you selected.

The System Editor window ✿

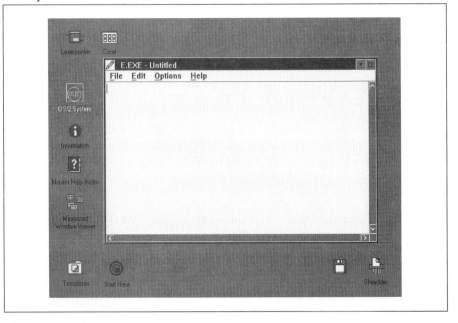

FIGURE 7-2 Open file dialog box [✿]

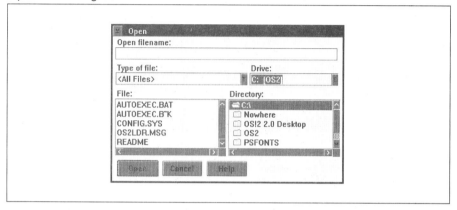

Continue moving down the **Directory** list box until the file you want is shown in the **File** list box. Select it and click on the **Open** button to load it into the editor.

 Tip You can double-click on the filename to open it automatically.

Closing a File

To clear the editor window of an existing file, click on **File** on the menu bar and then click on **New**. If you have made changes to the file in the editor's window before clicking on **New**, you are reminded that the file has been changed and asked if you would like to save those changes:[✿]

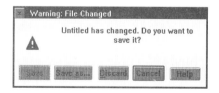

 Note There is no **Close** choice on the File menu.

Customizing the System Editor

There are several ways in which the appearance of text in the editor can be tailored to suit your tastes.

Changing Fonts

By default, the System Editor uses the OS/2 System Proportional font. You may prefer to see your data in some other font or some other form of the font. Click on **Options** on the menu bar to see the pull-down menu shown here:*

Selecting **Set font** from that menu produces the Font dialog box shown here:*

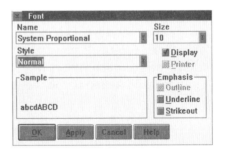

The first thing that can be changed is the font itself. Clicking on the arrow beside the **Name** field presents a list of fonts from which you can select. The actual contents of this list will depend upon the fonts you selected during system installation and what other fonts you might have added since then. You'll find a more detailed discussion of fonts in Chapter 10, but you should note here that the Courier and System

Monospaced fonts align characters in straight columns like a typewriter. The other available fonts are proportional, meaning that the character width varies and the characters don't always align vertically. As you change the font selected, the **Sample** field in the dialog box displays an example of the new font.

You can also modify the size of the font. Clicking on the arrow beside the **Size** box displays a list of the sizes available for the font you have selected. If you have installed outline fonts, you can select any size you wish.

If you want to change the appearance of a font, click on the arrow beside the **Style** box to show a list of font characteristics, including Normal, Bold, Italic, and Bold Italic.

 Note The System Editor is an entry-level product. As such, the font changes made here are not stored in the file when it is saved. However, the choices become the new default for the appearance of the data while you work.

Changing Colors

The second entry on the Options pull-down menu is **Set colors**. Clicking on this option displays the dialog box shown here:*

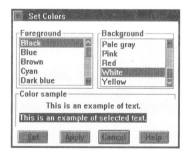

The foreground and background colors may be changed independently, and the **Color sample** window always previews the appearance of the choices made.

Note As you work in the System Editor, if you mark text for some action such as deletion or copying, that text will be highlighted in the inverse colors of the color scheme you select.

Word Wrap

Being a Presentation Manager program, the System Editor is sensitive to the size of the window. If the length of a line of text exceeds the width of the window, by default the editor will wrap the text around to the next line on the screen.

While this allows all text to be seen, it can also cause you confusion about what text is on which line in the physical file. To turn word wrap off, click on **Word wrap** on the Options menu to show the cascaded menu shown here:✿

When you select **Off**, the text beyond the width of the window is truncated so that each line on the display matches the physical lines in the file.

Creating a File in the System Editor

Typing text into a blank window begins the creation of a file. If you have been working on a file, select **New** from the File pull-down menu to get a blank window.

Editing Text

The System Editor is by default in *Insert mode.* If you move the cursor between two characters, anything entered at that point is inserted, and the characters to the right are moved over to make space. Pressing the INS key switches the editor to *Typeover mode*, in which characters replace those to the right.

To manipulate sections of text, the System Editor uses the *clipboard*, a device in OS/2 that acts as an area of memory to hold data being passed from one place to another. The memory is temporary and data is not retained after system shutdown. The clipboard automatically accepts text that has been cut or copied (see the following paragraphs on cutting text) and holds one section of data at a time.

 Note In addition to allowing you to move sections of text around within a file, the clipboard permits the exchange of text between programs.

Marking Blocks of Text

It is often necessary to work with a section of text, perhaps for cutting or pasting. To mark a block of text, move the cursor to the beginning of the block of text you wish to manipulate. Holding down mouse button #1, drag the cursor to the end of the block.

If your cursor reaches the border of the window, the editor will scroll past it. This means you can select more text than you actually see displayed in the window.

As shown in Figure 7-3, the marked area reverses color as a visual indication of your progress. To unmark an area, simply click button #1 anywhere within the editor's window.

Cutting Text

Eliminate text either by deleting it or cutting it. To delete, press the DEL key after marking the section of text, or select **Clear** from the Edit menu. If you change your mind and want to put the text back where it was, restore it by selecting **Undo** from the Edit pull-down menu, shown in the following:*

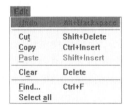

Selecting Cut from the Edit pull-down menu is similar to deleting the text, but the removed information is copied to the OS/2 clipboard. From there, it can be pasted somewhere else in the same file or into any OS/2 program that works with the clipboard.

Copying Text

The **Copy** option on the Edit pull-down menu also moves the marked information to the clipboard, but it does so without removing the text from its current location.

Marking text *

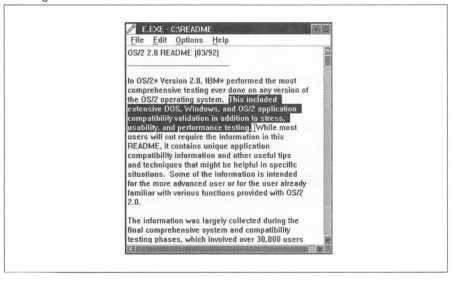

Pasting Text

Use **Paste** to copy the current contents of the clipboard into the file at the current cursor location. This text can be brought from any OS/2 program, not just the editor.

As with deletion, **Undo** also works on cut, copy, and paste operations.

Finding Text

In a large file, finding a specific string of text can sometimes take a long time. The System Editor provides a search capability to locate text quickly.

Click on the **Find** option of the Edit pull-down menu to display the dialog box shown here:✿

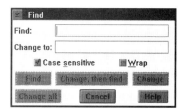

To move the cursor to the next occurrence of a string, enter the string in the **Find** entry field and click on the **Find** button. The search begins at the current location of your cursor and moves forward through the file. Selecting the **Wrap** check box instructs the editor to wrap around to the beginning of the file and continue the search if it has not located the string when it reaches the end of the file.

To locate the next occurrence regardless of capitalization, remove the check from the **Case sensitive** box by clicking on it before clicking on the **Find** button.

Replacing Text

While you are editing, if you highlight text and then begin to type, the highlighted text disappears and the characters you type appear in its place.

You can also replace existing text automatically.   **Find** option allows you to replace text that isn't at the cursor position, the same way the search-and-replace function works in your favorite word processor. Looking again at the Find dialog box, notice the **Change to** entry field. Specify a string of text in that field to replace the string in the **Find** field. Clicking on the **Change** button instructs the editor to find the next occurrence of the text in the first field and replace it with the contents of the second field.

There may be situations in which you want to make the same changes multiple times in a file. If you are certain that you want to change every occurrence of a string, click on the **Change all** button.

If you are uncertain or if you only want to make the change at some specific places, use the **Change, then find** button. This finds the next occurrence of the string, changes it, and then finds the next occurrence and stops. You can review the file at that point and determine whether or not you want to make the change.

Saving the File in the System Editor

When you are finished editing the file, use the **Save** option in the File pull-down menu to store the updated file.

If you began the session by loading a file, it is saved under the same name. If you want to change the name, use the **Save as** option. The editor prompts you for the name and directory you wish to use, as shown in the following:[*]

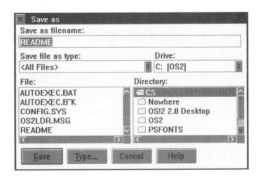

If you are saving a new file, selecting **Save** produces the **Save as** dialog box.

Autosave

The **Autosave** option of the File pull-down menu, shown in the following illustration, allows you to request that the System Editor perform an automatic save of the file periodically. The frequency of saving is based on the number of changes you make to the file.[*]

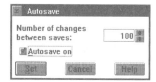

Click on the check box to turn Autosave on, and then click on the arrows beside the **Number of changes between saves** field to choose the number of modifications to a file that will activate the Autosave function.

Autosave only works on named files. If you are creating a new file, you must first use **Save** to assign the file a name before activating Autosave.

Closing the System Editor

Close the System Editor by double-clicking on the System icon. If you have made changes since you last saved your work, the **Warning: File Changed** dialog box is presented. You have the option of saving the file, discarding the changes made since the last time you saved the file, or canceling the command to close the System Editor.

The Enhanced Editor

New with OS/2 version 2.0, the Enhanced Editor for Presentation Manager (EPM) is an outgrowth of an editor that has been used internally at IBM for many years. Over the years, it has developed a rich set of features for end-users and developers alike so that it can be used as a full-function word processor for many tasks.

Starting the Enhanced Editor

The Enhanced Editor is in the Productivity folder of the OS/2 System folder, and it can be started from there by double-clicking on its icon. It will also open by using drag-and-drop with a text file or by opening a command session and typing **EPM** at the command line. If you add a filename after the command, that file will be loaded when the program opens.

Once opened, EPM presents the user with the window shown in Figure 7-4. (Of course, had you dropped a file onto the editor or specified a filename on the command line, the desired file would already be loaded into the window.)

Operating Modes

An understanding of the operating modes of EPM is required to appreciate how portions of the editor change to reflect the current mode.

Text in Stream Mode

Stream mode means that the file is viewed as a long stream of characters that wrap around from line to line. In this mode, when you press ENTER, EPM inserts the CR/LF (a carriage return and a line feed to force the beginning of a new line) into the stream at the current cursor position. In other words, if the cursor is in the middle of a line, the line is split at that spot. Stream mode also means that if you backspace past the beginning of a line, the cursor moves to the end of the preceding line and continues. Stream mode is the norm for word processors.

Text in Line Mode

Some situations, such as programming development, lend themselves more to *line mode*. In line mode, pressing ENTER will not split the current

The Enhanced Editor window ✿

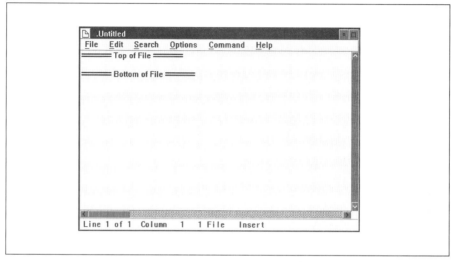

line. Further, the cursor will stop at the beginning or end of a line until an up or down cursor movement key is used.

Changing Text Modes

Stream mode is the default for EPM, but this can be changed readily. Click on **Options** on the menu bar to get to its pull-down menu. Select **Preferences** to show the cascaded menu seen here:✿

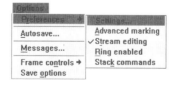

The **Stream editing** mode selection is a toggle; there is no specific menu item for line mode. The check beside **Stream editing** indicates that it is currently active. Clicking on the option removes the check and disables stream mode. Just click again to return to stream editing.

Ring Mode

There may be times when you would like to edit more than one file at a time, especially if you are moving text between files. To facilitate that, EPM provides *ring mode*.

To activate ring mode, click on **Ring enabled** on the **Preferences** cascaded menu. When ring mode is active, two new icons appear in the title bar, as shown in Figure 7-5. These allow you to move quickly among the files being edited in a circular manner.

Clicking on the counterclockwise arrow takes you to the previous file in the ring. Clicking on the clockwise arrow takes you to the next file in the ring. Of course, if you're editing a large number of files, it can take awhile to move through all the files in the ring this way, so EPM provides another method.

In Figure 7-5, one of the menu items is **List ring**. Clicking on that item pops up the list of files in the ring, as shown in the following:*

From here, you can quickly select the desired file.

Adding Files to the Ring   Click on **File** on the menu bar to see its pull-down menu, as shown here:*

Activating ring mode *

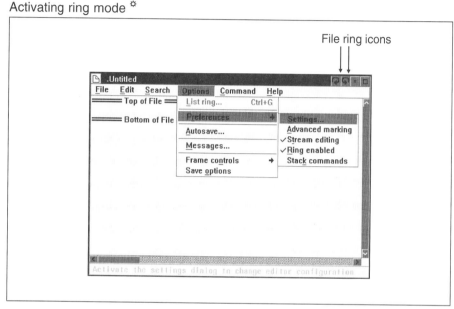

The **Add file** option only appears if ring mode is active. Clicking on that option results in a prompt for the file to be inserted into the ring.

Opening Files

Once the EPM window is open, you can begin entering text. When you are ready to save the text, click on **Save as** in the File menu to enter the filename.

File New

The **New** option in the File menu causes any existing file to be removed from memory, allowing you to start a new file in the blank window. If you have made changes to the file currently in memory, you will receive the warning shown in the following, allowing you to save those changes or discard them:*

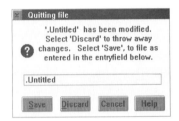

Running Multiple EPM Sessions

Sometimes it is more productive to open additional sessions of EPM instead of moving between files via ring mode. Multiple sessions permit simultaneous viewing of the various files you are working on.

Note   The decision regarding the use of ring mode versus multiple EPM sessions is frequently a matter of desktop real estate availability. If you have a number of applications open on the desktop, you may not have room to see most or all of them at once. If you need to move windows around and hunt for hidden windows in order to move between multiple EPM sessions, opt for ring mode.

Open .Untitled

This File menu option causes a second EPM session to be started, with no file loaded in the window. If, for example, you want to create a new file based on information in an existing file, you might open the original file and then use the **Open .Untitled** option to bring up a second window into which you could copy the information you want from the first file.

Open

This File menu option causes a second EPM session to be started with the desired file in the additional window. You will see the prompt shown in the following, allowing you to select the file you would like to edit:✥

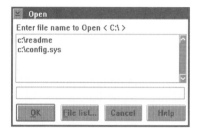

Note that EPM remembers the last files you've edited and puts them in a list box. You can select any one of these either by double-clicking on it or by clicking on it and then clicking on **OK**. If the file doesn't appear in the list box, you can enter its path and name into the entry field at the bottom of the dialog box.

If the desired file isn't listed, and you are uncertain of the path or name of the file, EPM offers a third option. Clicking on the **File list** button brings up the dialog box shown in Figure 7-6. You can move through the directory tree and the files in those directories to locate the one you wish to edit.

Editing Text

EPM provides enough text manipulation options that are usually absent in text editors to make it very effective as a word processor. To mark sections of text, EPM provides a number of alternatives.

Character Marking

Character marking treats data as streams. Pressing mouse button #1 and dragging the cursor causes text to be marked from the original cursor position to the new position, with the marked area wrapping around line boundaries. The marked block can then be manipulated via the Edit menu. The clipboard functions—Cut, Copy, and Paste—work just as they do with the System Editor. They provide straightforward techniques for moving marked blocks within the file. If you change your mind about text that was cut, the **Undo** option in the Edit menu puts it back where it was.

FIGURE 7-6

File list ✿

Advanced Marking Mode

The character marking mode isn't appropriate for all situations, and EPM provides two other ways to mark blocks. Look again at the Options/Preferences cascade menu shown in Figure 7-5. The **Advanced marking** option activates these additional techniques.

Dragging the pointer with mouse button #2 marks entire lines; you don't have to worry about dragging the mouse over every character in the line. The same effect can be accomplished by pressing ALT+L on the first line to be marked and then again on the last. All lines between the first and last line are also marked.

Any arbitrary rectangular region in the file can be marked by dragging the pointer with mouse button #1. The same effect can be accomplished by pressing ALT+B on one corner of the region and then again on the opposite corner. This is especially useful if you have embedded diagrams in your document. See the section "Drawing Line Graphics" later in this chapter for more information on creating diagrams.

Note The ALT+L and ALT+B keystrokes mentioned here are just two of a great many accelerator keys implemented by EPM. If you are more comfortable using keystrokes than mouse actions, explore the **Keys help** and **Quick Reference** options found in the pull-down menu under Help on the menu bar.

Undo

As you mark text and edit it by cutting or pasting into different parts of the document, an occasional mistake is inevitable. While it is possible to go back to the appropriate point and enter or delete information again, EPM provides a more efficient way.

In the Edit pull-down menu, selecting **Undo** returns the current line to the condition it was in before changes were made. This works as long as the cursor hasn't been moved to a different line.

The **Undo** option also provides access to a buffer EPM maintains in which are stored the most recent changes made to the file. The number of changes stored varies because the buffer is of finite size and the changes are of varying sizes, but generally you should be able to count on about 50 changes being stored.

Selecting **Undo** brings up the following dialog box, which allows you to cursor through your recent editing actions:[*]

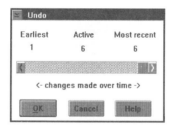

The scroll bar allows you to move back and forth through the changes you made to the file. EPM stores any discrete action as a change; typing a word is an action, and cutting or copying or pasting a block is also an action. Repeated clicking on the left arrow will step back through the changes. When the correct text is found, click on the **OK** button and you are returned to the edit window.

Note Like any window, the Undo dialog box can be moved to a different part of the screen so that you can see the changes to the file as they take place.

File Import

When you have to include an entire file in your document, import the file using the **Import text file** option in the File menu. After clicking on that option, you see a dialog box asking for the file you wish to import, as shown in Figure 7-7.

The Import text file dialog box lists the last files you've edited. You can select from them or enter a new filename, remembering to include the path. You can also click on the **File list** button to search through the directory tree for the desired file.

The file is imported into the existing document at the current cursor position.

Locating Text

As files get large, finding a precise point in the file to edit or view can become time-consuming. EPM provides simple methods for moving to specific areas of files.

FIGURE 7-7   Importing a file ✿

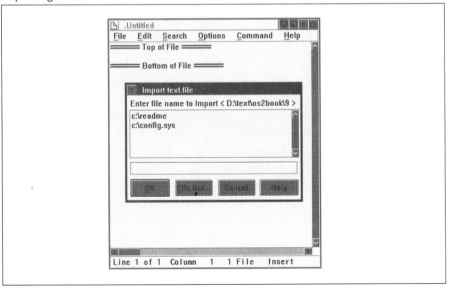

Search

The **Search** option under the pull-down menu of the same name produces the following dialog box:[*]

Enter the text you are searching for into the first entry field, and then either press ENTER or click on the **Find** button.

EPM will move to the next occurrence of the desired string and highlight it as shown in Figure 7-8. You can see that the Search dialog box is still on the screen. To move to the next occurrence of the string, click again on the **Find** button. To move to the next occurrence, highlight it, and automatically remove the dialog box, and click on the **Find, cancel** button.

The default for Search is to find the next occurrence of the string regardless of capitalization. In other words, searching for the string "OS" to locate the word "OS/2" would also cause EPM to stop at "osmosis". Change the **Ignore case** check box by clicking on it to toggle the function. When the check mark is removed, the Search function will only locate the occurrences of the string that match the capitalization you have indicated.

You can also move backward through the file to previous occurrences of the string by clicking on the **Reverse search** check box in the dialog box. By default, EPM moves from the current cursor position either forward to the end of the file or backward to the beginning of the file. You can narrow the search by clicking on **Marked area** to activate that check box. EPM will then only search through the block of the file that has been marked with one of the techniques described earlier.

FIGURE
7-8

Finding the search string *

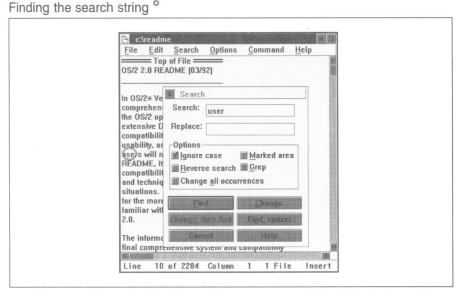

Grep

The **Grep** option is named after a utility made popular on UNIX systems. Clicking on this check box activates the ability to use special substitution characters in the search string. Those who need to do complex searches will find a good description of the wildcard search possibilities in the online help.

Replace

Looking again at Figure 7-8, you can see that after the **Search** entry field is a **Replace** entry field. If, for instance, you have a document full of references to someone named "Jean" and you discover she spells her name "Jeanne", you can type **Jean** in the **Search** field and **Jeanne** in the **Replace** field. Clicking on the **Change** button will cause EPM to find the first occurrence of "Jean" and change it to "Jeanne". The cursor is left at the substitution location and the search dialog box is left on the screen.

Note that the **Find, cancel** button becomes a **Change, cancel** button as soon as text is entered in the **Replace** field. Clicking on that button will change the string and then close the dialog box.

If you have to make a number of replacements throughout the document, click on **Change all occurrences**. A caveat, however, on performing automatic replacements is that sometimes you may not be aware of certain occurrences of the string. For example, if "Jean-Jacques" is mentioned in your document, the spelling of his name will change also.

To approve of each change as it is made, click on **Change, then find** to have each occurrence of the Find string shown to you. After approving it (or not), click again on **Change, then find** to move to the next occurrence.

Bookmarks

As with a physical book, EPM lets you set bookmarks, or placeholders in your file. Particularly with large files, this can make it much easier to move to sections that you access frequently. Bookmarks are accessed via the **Search** entry on the menu bar. Clicking on **Search** reveals the **Bookmarks** entry. Clicking on **Bookmarks** reveals its cascaded menu, shown in the following:*

Setting Bookmarks

Select **Set** to bring up the following dialog box, which permits you to name the bookmark that is placed at the current cursor location:*

Enter the name you would like to assign to this bookmark, using whatever text will act as a memory-jogger for you. Clicking on **Set** causes this bookmark to be placed for the rest of the current editing session. Clicking on **Set permanent** causes the bookmark to be saved with the file so that it exists in future editing sessions.

Moving to a Bookmark Location

There are two ways to move to a bookmark. The **Next** and **Previous** entries in the Bookmark cascade menu move you forward or backward through all your bookmarks.

You can also choose to move directly to a specific bookmark. Select **List** from the Bookmark cascade menu to see the following dialog box, which lists the bookmarks that have been set in this file:[*]

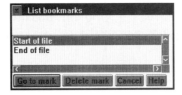

Use the scroll bar to move through the list of bookmarks. You can move to a bookmark either by clicking on its name and then clicking on the **Go to mark** button, or by double-clicking on the bookmark name.

Bookmarks can be removed from this list by clicking on the name and then clicking on the **Delete mark** button.

Defining Styles

You can define specific styles for parts of a document—for example, headings, sub-headings, and body text. Then, when you want to change to a new heading, you can select a predefined heading style and have the typeface, point size, color, and other attributes all changed automatically.

To create a style, select **Style** from the Edit menu and make the appropriate font and color selections (see Figure 7-9). Type a descriptive

The Style dialog box ✿

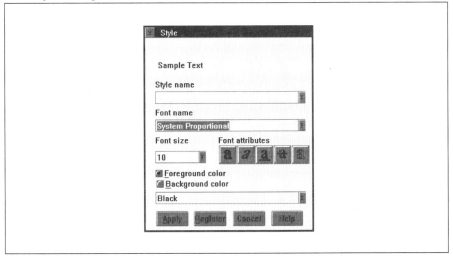

title in the **Style name** entry field and click on the **Register** button to tell EPM to remember the new style.

To use styles, click on the down arrow to the right of the **Style name** field, find the name of the style you want, and then click on the **Apply** button.

Using Macros

Macros simplify common tasks by automating frequently used keystrokes. EPM provides two types of macros.

Keystroke Macros

Keystroke macros act like a tape recorder, allowing the user to record a series of keys and then replaying those keystrokes on demand. To record a macro, press CTRL+R. Each key you press from then on will be remembered until you press CTRL+R again to stop recording. From then on, each time you press CTRL+T, the remembered keystrokes will be replayed just as if you had typed them again.

Program Macros

For more complex text manipulation functions, EPM allows you to write actual programs that can be executed as macros. EPM macros are written using REXX, which is described in more detail in Chapter 19. EPM provides several interfaces to a REXX program, such as cursor location functions, to allow very sophisticated programming. Details on these interfaces are given in section 9 of the Quick Reference in EPM's online help.

Formatting Text

EPM provides several additional functions that make it useful as a word processor.

Setting Tabs

From the Options pull-down menu, select **Preferences** and then **Settings** to bring up the Tabs setting dialog box shown in Figure 7-10.

The EPM default is a tab every eight columns. Entering a single number sets tabs at that interval all the way across the document horizontally. Enter specific numbers to set tabs at those column positions. For example, enter **5 8 18** to set tabs at the fifth, eighth, and eighteenth columns.

Note Tabs work by measuring spaces between characters rather than fixed horizontal positions. Therefore, using tabs with proportional fonts may cause columns to line up improperly, unlike the straight vertical lines that would be formed with fixed-size fonts such as Courier or System Monospaced.

FIGURE
7-10
Setting tabs ✿

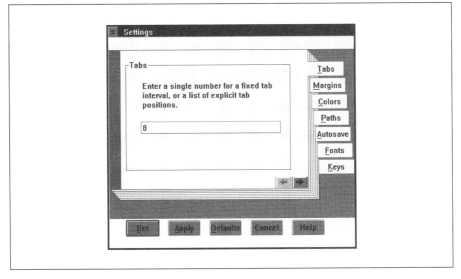

Setting Margins

Clicking on **Margins** brings up the window shown in Figure 7-11, where you fill in the **Left** and **Right** margin settings boxes. Those settings are based on column positions. The field for **Paragraph** is where you tell EPM how many column positions to indent each paragraph. Once the margins are set, pressing ALT-P automatically reflows the current paragraph to fit within the selected parameters.

Drawing Line Graphics

When putting lines around text or having material enclosed within a box can help emphasize the information you are presenting in a file, EPM makes it quite easy to insert the graphics. Press F6 to bring up the command prompt, with a list of the valid drawing line styles as shown in Figure 7-12. The Command dialog box is open, with the Draw command

FIGURE 7-11   Setting margins *

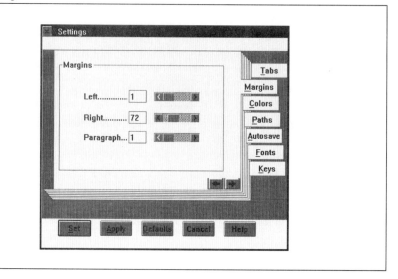

FIGURE 7-12   Drawing lines *

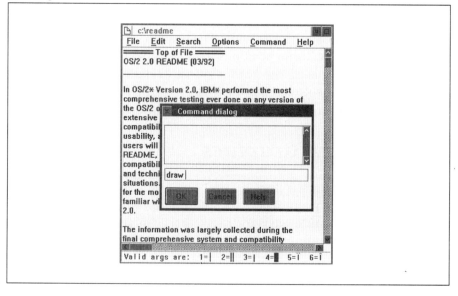

already inserted. Type the number from the prompt at the bottom of the window that corresponds to the style of line you wish to draw, and press ENTER to activate drawing mode.

Press the arrow keys to draw lines in the direction indicated on each arrow key. If lines cross, an intersection graphic is used automatically. If you change direction, a corner graphic is applied. These graphic features can be seen in Figure 7-13.

To exit drawing mode, press ENTER.

 Note Accurate positioning of line graphics is extremely difficult with proportional fonts. You should always use a monospaced font to ensure that your graphics align properly.

| FIGURE 7-13 | Example of the graphic feature ✿ |

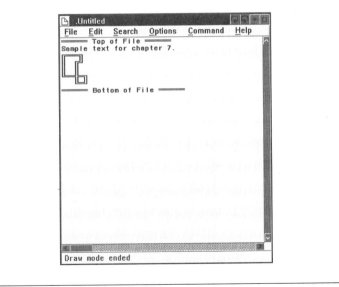

Changing File Fonts

Unlike the System Editor, EPM allows multiple fonts within a file. Mark the section of the file you would like to change, click on **Edit**, and then click on **Style** to see the dialog box shown in Figure 7-9. Use the pull-down menus and icon buttons to change the typeface, size, and attributes of the font for the marked text. Click on the **Apply** button to make the changes.

 Caution   At the time of this writing, there were some inconsistencies in the ability to change the appearance of a block within a file, which IBM was working to correct. In the meanwhile, you may have to try more than once to get EPM to accept the requested changes.

Printing

You can print all or part of your file directly from within EPM. To print a portion of the file, mark the area to be printed. Click on **Edit** and then choose **Print mark** from the pull-down menu.

To print the entire file, click on **File** and then click on **Print file** from the pull-down menu. Either way, you will be presented with the Print dialog box shown in Figure 7-14.

FIGURE
7-14

Choosing the print settings *

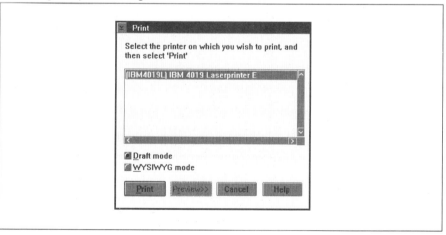

If you have more than one printer installed, select the desired printer from the list box.

Next, select the print mode. In draft mode, the output is printed using the default printer font, the font that is internal to the printer, thereby giving very quick output. Any formatting you did in the file for fonts or sizes that are not internal to your printer will not be shown.

In WYSIWYG (What You See Is What You Get) mode, the printed output reflects the specific font choices used in the file's creation. The fonts you see on the screen are matched in the printed document.

Saving Files

The **Save** and **Save as** entries in the File pull-down menu work the same way they do in the System Editor, allowing the file to be saved either with its current name or with a new name. Choosing **Save** for a new, unnamed file brings up the Save as dialog box.

EPM, like the System Editor, provides an additional option to allow periodic saves to take place automatically in the background, so that in case of problems like a power failure, not all of your work will be lost. The Autosave settings are found under **Options Preferences**.

 Note Setting Autosave with a small number causes backups to take place frequently, minimizing the amount of information that can be lost. However, this uses a lot of system resources and you may see the results of this additional overhead, especially if you are using a laptop computer where each disk access shortens battery life. Setting Autosave with a higher number minimizes the system resources used for backups, but leaves more information potentially unsaved. For most people, the default value of 100 is a good compromise.

Customizing Appearance

EPM exploits the Adobe Type Manager and Presentation Manager, providing support for a variety of typefaces, sizes, and colors. This can be used to dress up a document and, like a word processor, EPM can print files with varying fonts.

Changing the Default Settings

The default font is System Proportional 10 point, with black text on a white background. You can change the default settings of EPM by selecting **Options** from the menu bar, then **Preferences**, and then **Settings**.

Setting Colors

Click on **Colors** in the Settings menu to move to the page shown in Figure 7-15. You can change the color for four separate areas of the edit window:

Text   The color of the text
Mark   The colors used when text is marked

Setting colors ✿

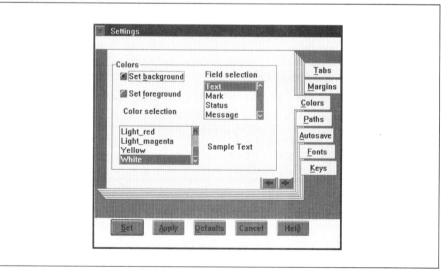

Status   The color of the line at the top of the window that identifies
            the cursor position and other information about the file
            being edited

Message   The color used for messages from EPM

Status Line

The status line is the line at the top of the document window that
identifies the line and column position of the cursor, whether you are in
Insert or Typeover mode, and whether or not the file has been modified
since last being saved.

When EPM sends a message, it is placed on the status line and the
status information is removed from view. You can configure EPM to
reserve a line for messages so that status line information is always
visible. Click on **Options** and then on **Frame controls**. Selecting **Message
line** inserts an additional line at the top of the window for messages.

Setting fonts ✿

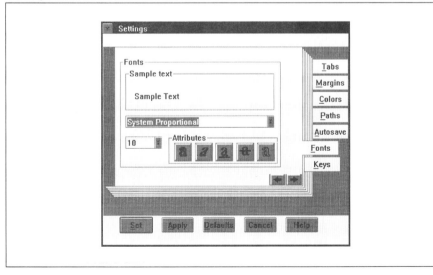

FIGURE
7-17
List of available fonts ✿

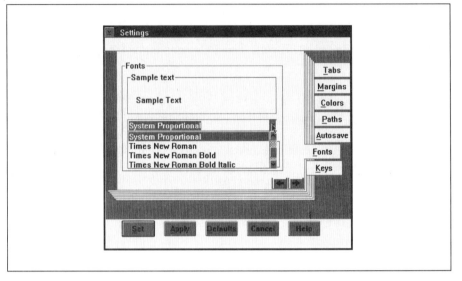

Setting Fonts

Also in the Settings notebook is a page for modifying the default font. Click on the **Fonts** tab to get to the screen displayed in Figure 7-16.

EPM can access all Adobe Type Manager (ATM) fonts installed in your system. Click on the arrow to the right of the font name to see the list of available fonts, as shown in Figure 7-17.

Scroll through the list of fonts to find the desired one. As you select fonts, a sample will appear in the box at the top of the window.

To change the size of the font, click on the arrow beside the current point size. Again, as you change size, the sample text will reflect the change.

You can choose other attributes—such as bold, italic, underline, strikeout, and outline—by clicking on the appropriate icon.

Exiting EPM

There are several ways to exit EPM. Select **Quit** from the File menu or double-click on the System icon. If you have not made any modifications to the current file since you last saved it, EPM will close and return you to where you were when you launched it, either to the command line or the Productivity folder. If you have made changes, you are presented with the warning that changes have been made but not saved and you may either discard the changes or save the document again before exiting.

There is also a **Save and close** option on the File menu, which saves any changes and exits EPM.

CHAPTER

Batch Files

A *batch file* is a text file containing a series of OS/2 commands, one to a line, which the system processes one line (or one command) at a time. Using batch files is an easy way to perform a task that involves several OS/2 commands, such as changing directories and then launching a program. A batch file can be created with any text editor or word processor that is capable of saving files as ASCII or DOS text.

Writing Batch Files

The procedures and rules involved in writing a batch file are short and simple: any legal operating system command can be included and there is no limit to the number of lines you can have in the file. Remember, the reason for using batch files is to automate those functions you perform at the command line, particularly if the process involves the entry of several commands to complete a task. For most of your work, the Workplace Shell provides the tools and programs you need.

For example, if you frequently use the command line to look at a list of the word processing documents you have been saving in your personal data directory, you could write a batch file that changes to the proper directory and copies a list of the filenames to the printer. Once the batch file exists, you can press one or two keys instead of entering all the individual keystrokes ordinarily needed to complete the task. The following is an example of the keystrokes required to execute this chore:

```
CD\WORDPROC\MYDATA
DIR > PRN
```

Or, if you want to copy your personal letters to a diskette, and you always give those letters a filename with the extension .LTR, you can write a batch file that has these commands:

```
CD\WORDPROC\MYDATA
COPY *.LTR A:
```

Naming Batch Files

You are free to call a batch file by almost any filename that will remind you of the task it performs. The exceptions are any internal system filenames, such as COPY, DIR, and CLS. While technically you can use the same name as an OS/2 external command or software application filename, it is not a good idea to do so because you may not be able to control which of the two similarly named files will execute first.

 Note There is a standard order for the execution of commands; the operating system searches file extensions in the following order: COM, EXE, CMD, BAT.

Throughout the OS/2 online help for commands, these files you create to automate commands are referred to as batch files, and that terminology is used in this chapter. However, in OS/2, batch files are really called command files, and there is a difference. OS/2 batch files have an extension of .CMD. When you execute a .CMD file, the command session that opens is an OS/2 session.

Executing Batch Files

To execute a batch file, you can either open a command session and type the filename and any necessary variables and parameters, or you can click on an icon that you create to represent the batch file. (Creating an icon to represent the batch file is discussed in the following section.)

Each batch file is automatically started in a separate command session. When you execute a batch file, OS/2 opens a new command session to run it.

Although OS/2 batch files have a .CMD extension, OS/2 also recognizes the .BAT extension. Any batch file created to run under DOS can be started from an OS/2 session. When the OS/2 command processor sees the .BAT extension, a DOS command processor is opened, and when the batch file procedures are complete, the DOS command session is closed.

 Note If there are .BAT files on your system that do not require a DOS command session but will run perfectly well in an OS/2 command session, change the extension of the file to .CMD in order to stay in an OS/2 command session for the execution of the file.

Creating Icons for Batch Files

Once you haved created a batch file, you can view it as an icon by opening the directory where it resides. The icon is a representation of a screen with "OS/2" on it.

It is easier to find and use batch files if they have a unique icon. It is not terribly difficult to create a special icon for batch files or even individual icons for individual batch files.

To create an icon, click on the generic batch file icon with mouse button #2. Click on **Settings** with button #1 and select the **General** page. Choose **Edit** to edit the icon. Then, using your creativity, the color palette, and the ability to create small or large sections of color, design something you like. You can choose colors, shapes, and design elements from the onscreen palettes.

Keeping Batch Files Together

It is usually productive and convenient to create a folder for batch files or to put your batch files into an appropriate folder already on the desktop. If you have a folder for OS/2 programs, it might be helpful to keep your OS/2 batch files there. If you use a particular batch file frequently, consider moving it to the desktop.

Linked Commands

There are a number of commands in OS/2 that are used within batch files. They expand and refine the processes executed in the batch file, as described in the following sections.

ECHO

ECHO permits or prevents the display of commands as they are processed in a batch file. If you want to display each command on the screen as it is processed, add the following line to your batch file:

ECHO ON

If you want to prevent the commands from displaying as they are processed, put the following line in your batch file:

ECHO OFF

You can use the ECHO command more than once within a batch file. You can put ECHO in one stage of your batch file, and ECHO OFF in another, if necessary.

If you are using ECHO OFF, you can still display a command on the screen without permitting any following commands to display by entering the following line in your batch file:

ECHO *insert a message here*

If ECHO is on, you can prevent any command from displaying by preceding the command with the symbol @. Since the default state of ECHO is that it is *on*, even if a batch file has ECHO OFF as the first line, that line will display to the screen because ECHO is not turned off until after that line has been processed. Putting @ before the line will prevent the command from displaying.

 Note   The ECHO command acts on the commands in the batch file only. If there are system messages, they will display regardless of the state of ECHO.

You can use ECHO to display user messages on the screen. For example, if ECHO is off but you want to send an onscreen message to the user, add the following line to your batch file:

```
ECHO Performing the process, please wait
```

"Performing the process, please wait" will display onscreen so the user does not have to stare at a blank screen while the batch file goes through its processes.

If you want to send a longer message, be sure to put ECHO in front of each line, as shown in the following:

```
ECHO Performing the process
ECHO This could take a minute
ECHO Please wait...
```

When the batch file containing these lines is run, the following messages appear on the screen:

```
Performing the process
This could take a minute
Please wait...
```

 Tip If you ECHO multiline messages, they are easier to read if you create a blank line between each line of the message. You can accomplished this by following the ECHO command with a space and ALT+**255** (hold down the ALT key while typing **255** from the numeric keypad). Merely typing **ECHO** followed by a space will not work.

REM

REM adds remarks to the batch file. It is entered as the first word in a line to indicate either that the line does not contain an OS/2 command or that the command on that line should not be executed. When the operating system sees the REM command, it ignores anything else on the line.

REM has a number of practical uses. It gives you an opportunity to explain what you are doing with the various steps in your batch file, much as a programmer puts comments in programming code to reveal the nature and purpose of specific parts of the code.

Note If ECHO is on, any lines beginning with REM will display to the screen unless they are preceded by @.

Anyone, for instance, who looks at the following batch file, either by typing it to the screen or loading it into a text editor, will know what the originator was doing in the file:

```
@ECHO OFF
CLS
REM Change to the accounting program subdirectory
CD\ACCTNG
REM Invoke the general ledger module
GL
REM Return to the root directory after exiting GL
CD\
```

Note It's always a good idea to add the internal command CLS, shown in line 2 of the preceding batch file listing. It creates a blank screen before any messages or data appear as a result of the batch file.

If a batch file is lengthy and filled with many commands and explanations, REM can be used to make the line-by-line commands easier to read, as shown in the following (a line that has only REM on it is, in effect, a blank line):

```
@ECHO OFF
CLS
REM
REM Change to the accounting
REM program subdirectory
CD\ACCTNG
REM
REM Invoke the general ledger module
GL
REM
REM Return to the root directory after exiting GL
CD\
```

In the preceding example, note the fact that the explanation of the change to the accounting program subdirectory is split between two lines. Even though REM lines are text, the one-line-at-a-time rule for batch files means that if you split a long sentence, you must begin each individual line with REM. Remember that this is not text and there is no word-wrapping available. It is best to keep each line short and to split up sentences.

CALL

CALL provides a way to execute another batch file without ending the original one. If, for example, you want a batch file called SHOWME.CMD that displays the directory of your word processing data directory, and you already have a batch file named LETTERS.CMD that displays all the filenames with the extension .LTR in the same directory, you can write a batch file that does both things.

The following is SHOWME.CMD:

```
@ECHO OFF
CLS
REM Change to the word
REM processing data directory
CD\WORDPROC\DATA
DIR
CALL LETTERS
REM Return to the root directory
CD\
```

The following is LETTERS.CMD:

```
DIR *.LTR
```

Using CALL means you tell the operating system that once the batch file named after the CALL command has finished executing, control is to be returned to the original batch file. The commands continue to execute beginning with the line following the CALL command. You can have multiple CALL statements in a batch file.

If the batch file had been written without the word CALL in front of the word LETTERS, once the display of extension .LTR filenames was shown on the screen, the batch file would end; the rest of the SHOWME batch file would not execute and you would not be returned to the root directory. Unless you use a CALL statement, once a batch file passes control to another batch file, control cannot be passed back.

PAUSE

The PAUSE command suspends the processing of the batch file. When PAUSE is invoked, the system displays the following message:

```
Press any key when ready . . .
```

PAUSE is useful in any situation where you must take some action before the rest of the batch file can execute. For example, a batch file that copies all the files about the SMITH account to a disk created for that account might read like the following:

```
@ECHO OFF
CLS
CD\WORDPROC\DATA
ECHO Put the Smith Diskette into Drive A:
PAUSE
COPY *.SMI A:
```

The copying will not commence until the user, who has received the message to "press any key when ready", presses any key.

If ECHO is on, you can place the PAUSE message on the same line as the PAUSE command, as shown in the following:

```
PAUSE Put the Smith Diskette into Drive A:
```

You can also use PAUSE to indicate strategic places where a batch file might be stopped and abandoned. An interruption in the batch file provides an opportunity to stop the batch file process by pressing CTRL+C or CTRL+BREAK from the command line.

 Note In an OS/2 session, stopping the batch file is absolute. In a DOS session, the user is presented with the option "Terminate Batch File Y/N". Typing **N** continues the execution of the batch file and typing **Y** terminates it.

Substitution Variables

Substitution variables are placeholders for items that are specified at the time the batch filename is entered on the command line. The variable that is replaced by the data entered is preceded by the % character.

The substitution variable characters available are %0 through %9. The system assigns %0 to the command so that %1 through %9 are available for specific data at the time of execution.

If individual users regularly copy certain groups of files to disks, for example, it is easiest to write one batch file and have each user enter the parameter, which is the name of the user's subdirectory. This batch file, shown in the following, is called BU.CMD:

```
@ECHO OFF
CLS
REM Copy user documents
REM to a backup diskette
ECHO Insert your disk in A:
PAUSE
XCOPY C:\WORDPROC\%1\*.* A:
```

At the command line, user #1 would type **BU USER1** and user #2 would type **BU USER2**.

For comparison, the following is user #1's individual safety backup batch file, called USER1.CMD. Without substitution variables, you would have to write a separate batch file like this for each user:

```
@ECHO OFF
CLS
REM Copy User1 documents
REM to a backup diskette
ECHO Insert your disk in A:
PAUSE
XCOPY C:\WORDPROC\USER1\*.* A:
```

The parameters are read from left to right in the order in which they are entered. For example, the following is a batch file called C.CMD:

```
@ECHO OFF
CLS
COPY %1 %2
```

At the command line, enter

C FILEONE FILETWO

or

C FILEONE C:\WORDPROC\USER1\FILETWO

The second example copies the file into a different directory. If you eliminate the filename FILETWO in the second example, only FILEONE is copied to the appropriate directory.

SHIFT If you need more than 10 substitution variables in a batch file, the command SHIFT permits you to move the parameters on the command line one position to the left. The %0 variable is replaced by the %1 parameter, the %4 parameter is replaced by the %5 parameter, and so on.

SHIFT also works to make things easier even if you have less than 10 substitution variables.

For example, suppose you wanted to copy 4 specific files to a disk. The following batch file, called CO.CMD (which would also work for more than 10 substitution variables), performs the action:

```
COPY %1 A:
SHIFT
COPY %1 A:
SHIFT
COPY %1 A:
SHIFT
COPY %1 A:
```

At the command line, enter

CO FILE1 FILE2 FILE3 FILE4

Note Once you have mastered some of the other functions available for batch files, such as IF and subroutines, you could write this batch file to keep repeating the copy command until %1 doesn't exist (IF "%1" == " " GOTO DONE) instead of repeating the command over and over again in the batch file.

IF

Using IF creates the capability to execute a command only when a stated condition is true. One of the IF conditions you can test for is EXIST, as well as NOT EXIST.

If you enter the command

COPY MYFILE C:\WORDPROC\USER1

and MYFILE does not exist in the current directory, OS/2 sends the error message "The system cannot find the file specified". (In a DOS command session, the message would be "File not found".)

No system error messages would be forthcoming under the same conditions if the command were written this way:

IF EXIST MYFILE COPY MYFILE C:\WORDPROC\USER1

Under these circumstances, the file is copied if it exists in the current directory. If the file does not exist, nothing happens.

One extremely useful application of the EXIST and NOT EXIST conditions is the ability to prevent copying a filename into a directory that already contains a file by that name. That, of course, causes the original file in the target directory to be overwritten. If it was an important file, you suffer a loss. Neither OS/2 nor DOS warns you that you are about to overwrite an existing filename. Almost everybody has made this error and realized it too late, screaming "Oh, no" as the familiar message "1 file(s) copied" appears on the screen.

Writing a batch file to control copying and making sure there is a NOT EXIST statement can prevent accidental overwriting of a file. For example, a batch file for copying files called C.CMD would prevent overwriting if it contained the following commands:

```
@ECHO OFF
CLS
IF NOT EXIST %2 COPY %1 %2
```

To execute the batch file, enter

C MYFILE C:\WORDPROC\USER1

which copies MYFILE to the USER1 word processing subdirectory unless a file named MYFILE already exists. In that case, the response "1 file(s) copied" would not appear and user #1 would know that she either has to change the name of MYFILE in the current directory or add another backslash and a different filename to the second substitution variable.

Redirection

Just as at the command line, within a batch file you can redirect the results or output of certain commands. The redirection applies only to the individual lines in the batch file; you cannot redirect an entire batch file.

The greater than symbol (>) redirects output to a device or a file. One of the most common uses of this is the redirection of a directory listing, shown in the following:

```
DIR > PRN
```

This command sends the directory listing to the printer instead of to the screen. The following command sends the directory listing to a file named LISTDIR:

```
DIR > LISTDIR
```

The directory listing LISTDIR is created by the operating system as a result of this command. If a file named LISTDIR already exists, the new contents will replace the existing file.

Two greater than symbols (>>) append the output to an existing file. For example, the following adds a subdirectory's file list to the contents of LISTDIR:

```
DIR C:\WORDPROC\USER1 >> LISTDIR
```

The following command appends the contents of MYFILE to the directory listings already contained in the file LISTDIR:

```
TYPE MYFILE >> LISTDIR
```

& (Ampersand)

The & (ampersand) permits two actions to be performed with the execution of only one line; it means "and then do this next task." If the current directory is on drive C, the following line moves MYFILE to drive D and erases it from the current directory:

```
COPY MYFILE D: & ERASE MYFILE
```

Incidentally, since the MOVE command does not cross drives, building a batch file with substitution variables is a good substitute. Rather than going through a series of entries at the command line to copy each file to a different drive and then delete the file from the original drive, a batch file called MOVEIT.CMD could be written as follows:

```
@ECHO OFF
CLS
COPY %1 %2
DEL %1
```

At the command line, enter

```
MOVEIT FILE1 D:\
```

Other Batch File Commands

There are a number of commands specifically used in batch file processing. While a complete explanation of all of them is beyond the scope of this book, OS/2 online help is available for each command if you wish to experiment. A brief description of each is given here.

CMD	Starts another command processor
SETLOCAL	Sets the drive, directory, and variables that are local to the current batch file
ENDLOCAL	Restores the drive, directory, and variables that were extant before SETLOCAL was invoked
EXIT	Ends the current command session and returns to the previous one (if one existed)
EXTPROC	Defines an external batch file processor
FOR	Allows repetitive processing of commands in a batch file
GOTO	Transfers batch processing to a label (a section of commands preceded by a name and a colon) specified in the batch file

CHAPTER

Printing

*O*rdinarily, you will be accessing the printer through your application software, using whatever keystrokes the program requires. However, there may be occasions to print from the command line or from the Workplace Shell. For example, if there is a text file you want to read, you may want to send it to the printer without having to open a word processor or editor and go through all the keystrokes required to invoke printing. Before discussing printing from either the command line or the Workplace Shell, however, an understanding of spooling is helpful.

The Spooler

With multitasking, it is quite possible that several programs will be trying to print documents simultaneously. Imagine the confusion if the system printed a line from your word processor, followed by a line from your spreadsheet, and then a line from your database. It would be unintelligible.

One way to prevent mixing data from different print jobs would be to send print jobs one at a time. You would have to wait for your word processor document to print before sending a database print job, and then wait for the database document to print before sending your spreadsheet print job. Data would not be mixed, but you would do a lot of waiting, and the advantages of multitasking would be lost.

OS/2 resolves this problem with *spooling*. When a program sends output to the printer, the OS/2 spooler intercepts the output and writes it to disk, keeping it in a file called a *queue*. Your queued print jobs are held in an area of your hard disk called the *spooler path*. The spooler can receive output from multiple programs at the same time, keeping each print job in its own separate file on the disk. Each program, having been fooled into believing the output has reached the printer, continues running at full speed, unconcerned with whether other programs are attempting to print. It is the spooler that sends the files to the printer, dispatching them one at a time. Each file that is sent is called a *print job*.

The spooler, however, does not permit the printing process to begin until the entire file has been spooled, in order to make sure that files from separate applications are not mixed. Different software applications may require different formats or job properties, such as the paper size expected (perhaps your spreadsheet is printing on wide paper) or any fonts that might be accessed or downloaded (if you are preparing a document in your word processor and want to take advantage of any fonts you've added to your printer definition).

Disabling the Spooler

If you are printing from only one program and you want to begin printing as soon as the document is ready, you do not have to wait until all the pages of your document have been sent to the spooler. Instead, you can stop the spooling process.

From the OS/2 System folder, open the System Setup folder, shown in the following, and find the Spooler icon: ❂

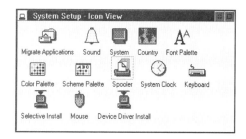

Clicking on the Spooler icon with mouse button #2 reveals the following pop-up menu: ❂

To stop spooling, click on **Disable spooler**. To restart it, bring up the same menu and click on **Enable spooler**. If you haven't enabled the spooler and you begin sending multiple jobs from different applications (or even the same application), OS/2 will not be able to separate the jobs.

Printing from the Command Line

OS/2 provides a straightforward command for printing files from the command line: PRINT.

To print a file named README, type **PRINT README**. By default, this sends output to the printer attached to the first parallel port, LPT1.

To send the output to a different location, use the /D: (Device) parameter by typing **PRINT /D:LPT2 README**. The valid device names are PRN, LPT1, LPT2, and LPT3. If you are printing to a network printer, devices LPT4 through LPT9 are supported for networks only.

If you want to print more than one file, it's not necessary to have separate entries of the command; instead, list the filenames after the PRINT command. For example, typing the command **PRINT FILE1 FILE2 FILE3** will send all three files to the printer. Repeated PRINT commands continue to add files to the spool queue.

 Note Wildcards are permitted for multiple-file printing. The files are queued for printing in the order in which the filenames were entered on the command line.

Canceling Queued Print Jobs

In an OS/2 command session (but not in a DOS command session), there are parameters of the PRINT command that can be used to manipulate the spooler. If you decide you don't need the rest of the output from the job currently being printed, use the /C (Cancel Job) parameter and enter the command **PRINT /C**, which cancels this job immediately. You do not need to enter a filename when using this parameter because the command works on the job currently being printed.

 Note Printers have internal memory, called a *print buffer*, and any data already transferred to the buffer will continue to print after a job is canceled, even though the spooler stops sending information to the printer immediately. If the buffer is large and you don't want to wait for it to empty (or waste any more paper), turn off the printer to clear its memory.

You can cancel the current print job and all files waiting in the queue to be printed by using the /T parameter (Cancel All Jobs) and typing **PRINT /T**. Do not enter any filenames when using this parameter; the command directs itself to the files in the queue.

It is possible to see what jobs are in the queue before canceling all of them. The procedure is explained later in this chapter.

Note   Either of the commands that cancel printing may be modified with the /D parameter.

Printing from the Workplace Shell

As with other parts of the Workplace Shell, the printer supports drag-and-drop. To print a text file, simply drag its icon to the printer icon, as shown in Figure 9-1. If you have installed more than one printer, drag the icon to the appropriate printer icon.

Drag-and-drop a file *

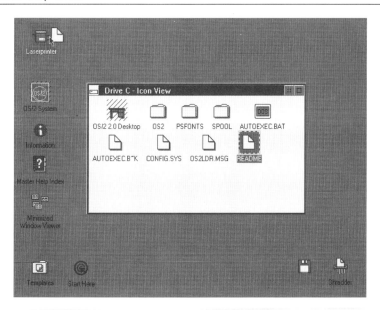

Viewing the Spool Queue

To view the spool queue for any printer, double-click on the printer icon to open its window, as shown in the following illustration: ✿

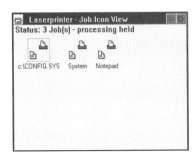

All files waiting to be printed are shown in this window.

For a reminder of what the contents are of any of the files in the queue, double-click on the file icon. If it is a text file, it will be opened in the System Editor, as shown in Figure 9-2. Spooled jobs that are graphical are opened in the Picture Viewer, one of the utilities provided in OS/2.

FIGURE 9-2

Viewing print job contents ✿

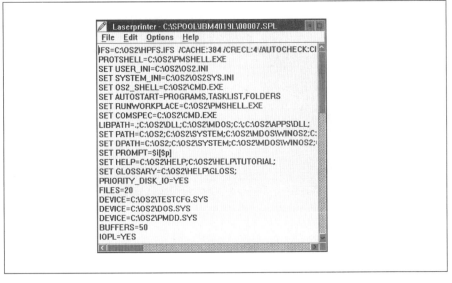

Manipulating the Spool Queue

Murphy's Law dictates that there will be times when the next file in the queue is a 100-page report, but what you desperately need printed is the file that is in the queue *behind* that report. There may be times when you have sent some output to the spool queue, but want to delay printing it. OS/2 allows you to place specific jobs, or the entire queue, on hold.

To hold the entire queue for a printer, click on the printer icon with mouse button #2. Clicking on **Change status** brings up the cascaded menu shown in the following, which allows you to hold or release the entire queue. ✿

As you can see, OS/2 shows you the hold status of the queue at the top of the printer's window.

It is also possible to hold and release individual jobs in the queue. Click mouse button #2 on the icon of the job you want to hold. This opens its pop-up menu, as shown in the following: ✿

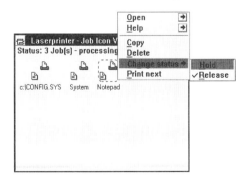

Both pop-up menus for placing jobs on hold also allow you to delete a job from the queue. The queue's pop-up menu also has an entry to delete all jobs from the queue.

Print Job Status

OS/2 uses graphical cues to let you know the status of each job in the queue. In the following illustration, you see that the queue itself is not on hold: *

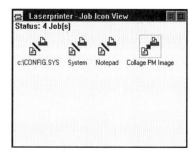

The first three jobs, however, are on hold, indicated by the slanted bar separating the file from the printer. The fourth job is in the process of being printed, indicated by the arrow between the file and the printer.

Printer Problems

If OS/2 can't print your output, it will notify you with the following message: *

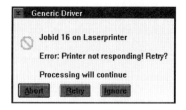

The first thing to check is whether or not the printer is connected to your computer and turned on. Any other problem that causes the printer to send a "not ready" message back to the system—such as having run out of paper—will also yield this error message. If nothing is apparent, you may want to check the cable connection to make sure it is tight, or change the cable in case it is bad. Correct the problem and retry the output or abort the printing process.

Of course, as a multitasking operating system, OS/2 continues processing all other tasks while waiting for the printer.

CHAPTER

Adobe Type Manager

Not so long ago, the only display available on computer terminals was 25 rows of 80-column text. With the Computer Graphics Adapter (CGA), direct screen point addressing became possible, creating the ability to draw graphics and display text that did not look like a series of dots. CGA was soon followed by the Enhanced Graphics Adapter (EGA) and the Video Graphics Adapter (VGA), enhancing the look even further.

Today's graphic adapters and displays provide much more than the graphics capabilities that allow us to play video games on personal computers. They make possible the type of interactive user environment typified by the Workplace Shell, where the operating system can keep the display in graphics mode and provide an unlimited range of fonts.

This poses some problems as well. The operating system must provide an easy way for programs and users to access these fonts and add new ones. The key is standardization.

OS/2 Fonts

Some font programs have emerged as standards for graphical operating systems. OS/2 2.0 has chosen to support Adobe Type Manager (ATM). This product, like some other similar products, appears to have long-term support and will continue to be enhanced. OS/2 2.0 comes with a Windows version of ATM, so all OS/2 fonts can be used by your Windows applications as well. ATM fonts work with all OS/2 programs that use Presentation Manager.

A *font* is an aggregation of characters in a particular size and style. Size, in ATM, is measured in *points*, a typesetting measurement of height. Style is a characterization of the way the font is displayed or printed, such as bold, italic, underlined, and so forth. These styles are usually referred to as *attributes*.

There are two kinds of fonts, *monospaced* and *proportional*. A monospaced font is one in which each character, the letters *m* and *i*, for example, occupies the same amount of space. A proportional font causes each character to occupy the space needed to print the character; the letter *m*, for example, occupies more space than the letter *i*.

In addition to 13 ATM fonts, the fonts included with OS/2 include IBM core fonts. IBM core fonts are *bitmap* fonts, meaning that each character is treated as a graphic image. The ATM fonts are not bitmap fonts, and therefore each character is treated as a regular letter or symbol, depending on the character.

IBM core fonts are Courier, which is monospaced, and Helv and Tms Rmn, which are proportional. There is also a System Monospace font in the Helv family of fonts. (For copyright reasons, IBM refers to *Helvetica* as *Helv*, and *Times Roman* as *Tms Rmn*.)

The ATM fonts are Times New Roman, Helvetica, Courier, and Symbol. Except for Symbol, all the fonts can be displayed and printed with the bold, italic, bold italic, and underline attributes.

Workplace Shell Fonts

The Workplace Shell, by default, uses mostly the System Proportional and Helvetica fonts. Fonts represent another area in which you can customize the system to your taste. Computers don't have to look dull—use your creativity to liven things up.

Changing Fonts

The first step is to understand the Font Palette. Open the OS/2 System folder and then open the System Setup folder. Open the Font Palette by double-clicking on its icon. As shown in the following, a variety of fonts and attributes is available for your use: ✿

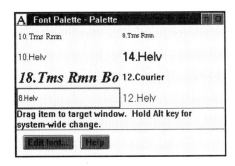

Changing fonts is as easy as dragging-and-dropping. To change the font in the title bar of the Font Palette window, move the pointer to the font you want and then drag it with mouse button #2 to the title bar.

As you can see, the icon changes to a pencil point so that you can pinpoint the area to be changed. In this case, the font of the title bar has been changed to 18-point Times Roman Bold Italic, as seen in the following: ✿

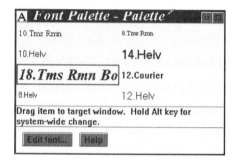

If you hold the ALT key down while making this change, all similar areas will be changed to the new font. In other words, holding the ALT key while changing the title bar of this window would cause the title bar of *all* open windows in the system to change. Similarly, holding the ALT key while you change the text under an icon would cause the text under all icons to change.

Changing the Font Palette

The fonts shown in the Font Palette are the eight fonts automatically set during installation; they are only a subset of all the choices available to you. The palette does *not* provide a complete selection of every font in your system, only a selection of fonts to which you have easy access. You can change the Font Palette selection to suit your needs by adding and deleting fonts from the palette. Applications can access all the fonts you have, not just the ones shown on the palette; when a font selection needs to be made in a document, the complete list of system fonts will be displayed.

Note, for example, that there is no 12-point Times Roman shown. To be able to access 12-point Times Roman, you need to replace one of the existing fonts in the palette. (Don't worry, it's easy to add it back if you change your mind later.)

Adding and Deleting Fonts on the Font Palette

Select the font you want to replace by clicking on it with mouse button #1. Then click on **Edit font** to see the following dialog box: ✿

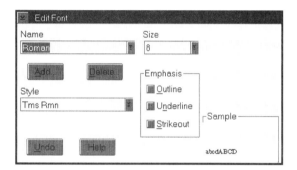

Click on the down arrow beside the **Name** field to see a list of the fonts you've installed. Then click on the down arrow beside **Style** to select among the variations available, such as italics and boldface. The down arrow beside **Size** allows you to select the point size of the font and the **Emphasis** checkboxes allow you to select highlight techniques, such as outline, underline, and strikeout. Closing this window causes the requested font to be added to the palette. As shown in the following, 8-point Times Roman has been replaced with 12-point Times Roman: ✿

Installing New Fonts

The real fun begins when you install new fonts on your system. There are hundreds of ATM fonts available. Some can be purchased in font libraries, and many are available for free or for a small charge from electronic bulletin board systems (BBS) or shareware catalogs. Several fonts are available for downloading from the IBMOS2 forum on CompuServe.

Installing new fonts is accomplished through the Font Palette. Select the font you want to replace and click on the **Edit** button to see the Edit Font dialog box. Since you want to install a new font, click on the **Add** button. You will be prompted for the path to the fonts you want to install, as seen in the following: ✿

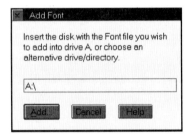

Enter the path to the new fonts and click on the **Add** button. OS/2 scans the directory specified for valid ATM fonts. The fonts found will be displayed, as seen in Figure 10-1.

As you select fonts by clicking on them, the font name will show up in the box to the right, as seen in Figure 10-2. After selecting the fonts you wish to install, click on **Add**. The entry field asking for the path in which to install the fonts defaults to an OS/2 subdirectory. It is not recommended that you change this path, since any program or function that needs to use the fonts will have to be told about the change.

After the fonts are installed, you are returned to the Edit Font dialog box. You can then replace any of the existing fonts on the Font Palette with one of the newly installed fonts, and you can drag-and-drop those new fonts as desired.

List of newly-installed fonts ✿

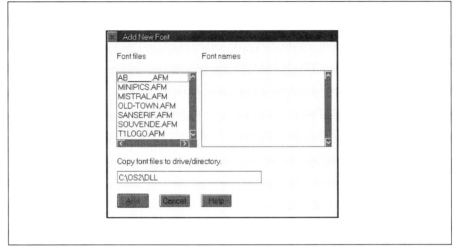

Note   Applications that were open when you added the new fonts may not be able to access those typefaces until the application is closed and reopened.

Selecting newly-installed fonts ✿

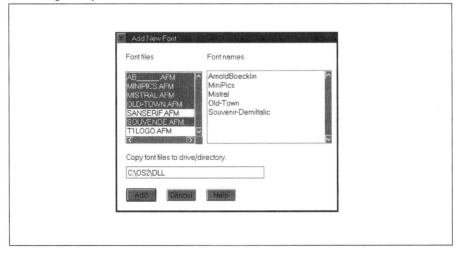

Printing with Fonts

Applications written for OS/2 can display and print any ATM font installed in your system. Windows applications also can take advantage of these fonts. There is nothing special you have to do to make that happen, since programs written for OS/2 utilize the OS/2 interfaces and functions automatically.

For DOS applications, software developers have to work within the limitations of the operating system and manually download fonts that have been purchased specifically for DOS. This procedure does not translate properly to OS/2, so DOS software must be run with whatever steps are necessary to access the fonts designed for that software. Your OS/2 ATM fonts will not be available for DOS applications.

CHAPTER

Running DOS
Applications

Whether you run your DOS programs from a command line or the Workplace Shell, you will sometimes need to modify the default DOS settings to run these programs more efficiently, or indeed to be able to run them at all. These settings should be manipulated before opening the DOS session. Once the session is established, changing the value has no effect on most of these settings. The exceptions will be noted in this chapter.

Changing DOS Settings

To modify the settings of a DOS session, open the System folder and the Command Prompts folder to see the window shown in Figure 11-1. Choose the icon you use to implement DOS from the command line and click on it with button #2.

Open **Settings** and then click on **Session** to bring up a window like the one shown in Figure 11-2.

Click on **DOS settings** to display a list of the current values for the settings for the type of DOS session you selected, as shown in Figure 11-3.

COM_HOLD (default OFF)

In order to maximize shareability of resources and minimize the effect of DOS applications on the system, OS/2 releases communications ports

FIGURE
11-1

The Command Prompts window ✿

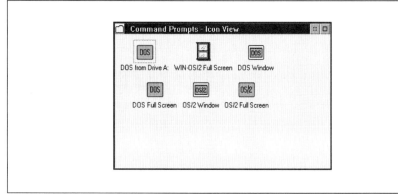

Session settings ✿

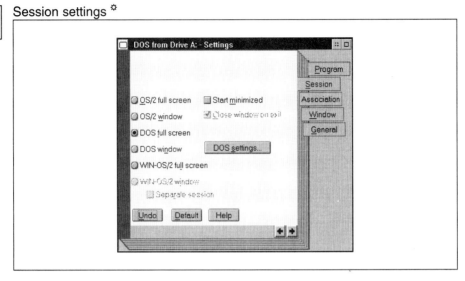

as soon as a DOS program is finished with them. This can cause difficulties with some DOS communications software, particularly if it uses several programs in succession such as might be found in a batch file that sets communications parameters before starting the communi-

DOS settings ✿

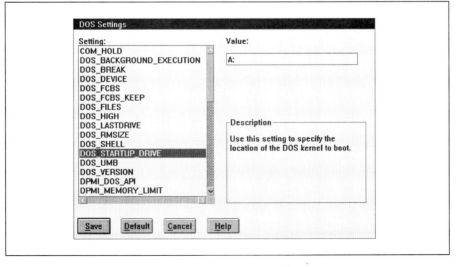

cations program. Changing this parameter to ON instructs OS/2 to keep the communications port attached as long as the DOS session is open.

DOS_BACKGROUND_EXECUTION (default ON)

Since OS/2 is a multitasking operating system, while you are working with one program, others in the background continue running. In most cases, that is exactly how the operating system should work.

DOS programs, however, are generally written with the assumption that they are the only program in the system. This is fine for things like communications programs, for which you want operations such as file transfers to continue in the background. With some programs, though, this can cause problems.

One of the best examples is game software. If you switch out of a car race simulation, and the car continues running without a driver, chances are good that it will crash. Changing this setting to OFF tells OS/2 to suspend execution of the session when it is not running in the foreground.

 Note   This setting is an exception to the rule that changes must be made before the session is opened. Any change in this setting is effective immediately.

DOS_BREAK (default OFF)

In general, applications provide a straightforward way for the user to terminate them. At least that's true when they're working properly. Suppose, however, that the program isn't working correctly, or appears to be "hung" or frozen. Pressing CTRL+BREAK (or CTRL+C) is one way to force the program to end. This setting determines when the operating system checks to see if the user has pressed CTRL+BREAK.

If this setting is on, OS/2 checks regularly for a break request. This makes it easy for you to cancel a program at any time. On the other hand, this adds a lot of overhead, since OS/2 is constantly checking for breaks, which affects the program's performance. Turning this setting off causes OS/2 to check for a break request only during keyboard input or display output operations. Performance is not adversely affected, but if the program is caught in a tight processing loop in which no input or output is taking place, the BREAK key will not work. This is less troublesome when running DOS applications on OS/2, since you can always close the session in which the program is running.

 Note   OS/2 puts the command BREAK=OFF in the CONFIG.SYS during installation. If you change that to BREAK=ON, you have changed the default. Remember that changes in CONFIG.SYS do not take effect until the next time you boot the system.

DOS_DEVICE

In order to run DOS applications properly, OS/2 also runs DOS device drivers. Device drivers are specialized programs that act as an interface between general-purpose programs and specific hardware devices, such as printers and communications ports.

Most standard devices are taken care of by OS/2 device drivers, but some special-purpose hardware devices, such as sound adapters, for example, may not have an OS/2 device driver. DOS device drivers can be loaded in the CONFIG.SYS file just as if they were OS/2 drivers.

Device drivers that are loaded in CONFIG.SYS will be present in each DOS session. While OS/2 makes more standard memory available to DOS applications than DOS does, you still may not want to use that memory for device drivers in sessions that don't access the device.

Clicking on **DOS_DEVICE** brings up the window shown in Figure 11-4. You can enter into the **Value** field the path and filename of a device driver you want loaded into this specific DOS session, but not automatically into all others.

DOS_FCBS (default 16)

DOS_FCBS establishes the maximum number of file control blocks (FCBs) the DOS session can have open. FCBs are used to keep track of information when files are being shared, for example across a network. If the session attempts to open another FCB after the maximum specified here is reached, the least recently used FCB will be closed first.

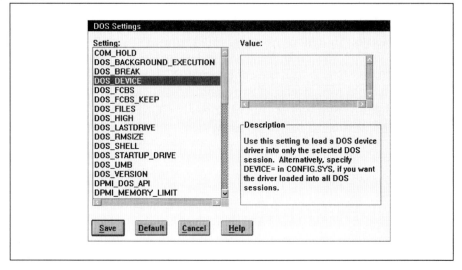

FIGURE
11-4

DOS_DEVICE value *

DOS_FCBS_KEEP (default 16)

The DOS_FCBS_KEEP parameter allows you to specify a number of FCBs that will be kept and not closed automatically. It is quite unusual for the average user to modify these settings. The installation instructions for your software should tell you if the number of FCBs needs to be changed.

Note   Changing the FCBS parameter in the CONFIG.SYS file also changes the default value of this setting.

DOS_FILES (default 20)

The DOS_FILES parameter specifies the number of files a program can have open at one time. Since memory is reserved for tracking information on each open file, it is wasteful to set this parameter much larger than necessary. Unless you are running Windows applications, you probably don't need to set this value larger than 32.

Note The default for this parameter can be set by a FILES= statement in CONFIG.SYS. This setting can be changed after the session is open and will take effect immediately.

DOS_HIGH (default ON)

One of the key reasons that DOS applications run out of memory is the amount of space taken by DOS itself. This setting allows OS/2 to load its DOS emulation into *high memory,* memory above the normal DOS boundary of 640K. This leaves much more storage available for the DOS program. If you have a program that requires DOS to be loaded in conventional memory below 640K, change this setting to OFF.

DOS_LASTDRIVE (default Z)

The DOS_LASTDRIVE setting allows you to specify the highest drive letter that can be accessed from the DOS session. Since the default is Z, the only reason to change this setting is to prevent DOS sessions from accessing certain drives, such as network drives.

DOS_RMSIZE (default 640)

The DOS_RMSIZE setting allows you to specify how much conventional memory should be made available to the DOS session. OS/2 allocates storage for the full 640K for the DOS session. If you plan to run several DOS sessions, there is some benefit to reducing this number in resource-constrained situations in order to minimize swapping and the size of the swap file. It may also be necessary to lower this number with some video adapters, which require memory below the 640K boundary for their own use. While this is unusual, it is a good idea to check by reading the documentation that came with your video adapter.

 Note The default for this setting is based on the RMSIZE command in the CONFIG.SYS file.

DOS_SHELL (default
C:\OS2\MDOS\COMMAND.COM)

The DOS_SHELL setting allows you to specify the command processor to be used in the DOS session. If you are accustomed to using an add-on shell such as 4DOS, you can designate the path to the shell here.

 Caution   DOS shells that are not OS/2-aware may not work properly.

DOS_STARTUP_DRIVE
(default blank = OS/2 DOS emulation)

For those situations in which OS/2's DOS emulator doesn't run a program properly, you can boot a specific version of DOS or DR-DOS from within OS/2. Entering **A:** in this setting instructs OS/2 to load the boot disk in the diskette drive. Entering a path and filename tells OS/2 to load the disk image you defined, and boot as if the diskette had been loaded.

DOS_UMB (default ON)

Recent versions of DOS have been able to load some device drivers and utilities into memory above the 640K barrier. By managing the upper memory blocks (UMBs), DOS permits users to load device drivers with DEVICEHIGH statements rather than the earlier DEVICE statements, thus leaving more conventional memory free for the program.

Similarly, *terminate-and-stay-resident* (TSR) utility programs can be loaded into upper memory with the LOADHIGH statement. Some TSRs and device drivers, however, base their execution on management of those UMBs. To run them, change this setting to OFF.

DOS_VERSION (default 5.0)

Some DOS programs are version-sensitive. They check to see what version of DOS they are running on, and if they don't like the answer, they simply stop. OS/2 allows flexibility here as well, giving you the ability to specify, by program, which version of DOS you want OS/2 to pretend to be.

This is not the most user-friendly of OS/2 features, as specifying this information is a bit on the convoluted side. First, you must know the name of the executable program that requests the version information.

Programs are often loaded from menu systems or batch files, but those programs don't request the version number. It is the executable file, called by the batch file or menu program, that is looking for the DOS version.

If there is a batch file, either display it to the screen using the TYPE command or load it into your favorite editor. Look for the program name the batch file calls. It will not always be obvious. Batch files frequently set parameters with cryptic statements, change directories, and have one-word commands on some lines. Go to the directory indicated in the batch file and match filenames against the commands listed in the batch file. You will eventually find a file in the directory with an extension of .COM or .EXE that matches one of the lines of the batch file.

If there is a menu program, you may have to go into the directory where the program resides and find a file that lists the menu items and the commands called when you press that menu choice. There will be some sort of configuration file (look for an entry in the directory with an extension of .CFG or .MNU) that indicates which executable file is being called.

You can then enter the information into the **Value** field as follows:

program,major,minor,count

Program is the executable file that launches the application. *Major* and *minor* refer to the two parts of the version number. For DOS 3.31, for example, the major number is 3 and the minor is 31. Note that the minor is always a two-digit number, so for version 3.3, the minor should be entered as 30.

The *count* field specifies the number of times OS/2 should respond with the specified version number rather than the default. For example, entering **WP.EXE,3,30,3** causes OS/2 to tell WordPerfect that it is running under DOS version 3.3 the first three times WP asks, and respond with version 4 thereafter. (The authors have yet to come up with a good explanation for such a count!) If you specify the maximum, 255, OS/2 will always respond to that program with the specified version number.

DPMI_DOS_API (default AUTO)

The DOS Protected Mode Interface is an architected way for DOS programs to access memory above the normal DOS barrier. Programs written to take advantage of this function can either try to perform the DPMI services themselves or depend on the operating system to take care of it. In the AUTO setting, OS/2 monitors the program's requests and selects the appropriate mode. You can also select ENABLED to specifically instruct OS/2 to handle the memory translation, or DISABLED to force OS/2 not to do so.

Note   Windows programs expect the operating system to handle the DPMI requests.

DPMI_MEMORY_LIMIT (default 2)

The DPMI_MEMORY_LIMIT setting allows you to specify the number of megabytes of DPMI memory that should be available to the session. Note that OS/2 reserves this much memory for the session, so overstating the requirement can increase the amount of swapping in the system and the size of the swap file. The 2MB default is sufficient for most applications, though you may want to increase it for a Windows session.

DPMI_NETWORK_BUFF_SIZE (default 8)

Only useful in a network environment, this setting allows you to specify the number of kilobytes of memory to be reserved as a translation buffer for data transferred across a network by DPMI applications. If you are experiencing difficulty with a network-based DPMI program (such as a Windows program), try increasing this setting.

EMS_FRAME_LOCATION (default AUTO) and EMS_HIGH_OS_REGION (default 32)

Expanded memory specification (EMS) is a scheme whereby memory above the 1MB address, which can't be read directly by DOS, can be copied below that barrier in pieces. Those pieces are managed within a 64K area known as the *EMS frame*. OS/2 scans the device drivers in your system and allocates a frame area automatically. This setting applies to software that uses the Lotus/Intel/Microsoft Expanded Memory Specification (LIM EMS). You may notice problems when running programs that need LIM; there may be a conflict in which a DOS device driver or TSR tries to get to the same area of memory.

EMS_HIGH_OS_REGION provides a way to improve performance by allowing the frame to be larger than 64K. However, this may cause conflicts with some device drivers, so first try changing this setting to zero.

If you are still having problems, the next setting to adjust is the EMS_FRAME_LOCATION. If you scroll through the values in the pull-down list shown in Figure 11-5, you see that it is a series of memory addresses specified in hexadecimal. The trick is to find one that isn't being used by a hardware adapter, its device driver, or a TSR program. There is not much advice that can be given to assist you in locating such an address if OS/2 cannot do it for you in automatic mode. You are likely to have your best chance of success using addresses C000 and higher.

EMS_LOW_OS_REGION (default 384)

Some DOS programs have additional code to use conventional memory effectively as additional frame space, by remapping it. You might increase the performance of programs that do this mapping by raising this setting, which is a measure of kilobytes. Such programs are quite rare, however, and it is unusual for the user to modify this setting.

EMS_MEMORY_LIMIT (default 2048)

The EMS_MEMORY_LIMIT setting establishes the maximum amount of EMS memory (in kilobytes) that OS/2 should make available to the

Changing the EMS_FRAME value ✿

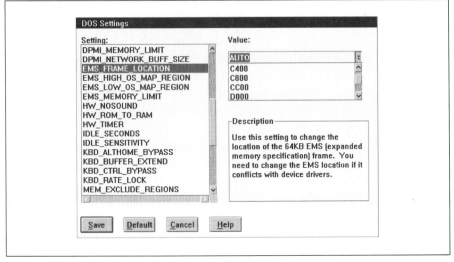

program. While some programs using EMS can benefit from raising this setting, the default of 2MB is sufficient for most applications. Remember that raising this much higher than needed uses system resources unnecessarily. This can be set to zero for programs that do not require expanded memory.

HW_NOSOUND (default OFF)

With a multitasking system, you probably will have more than one program running on OS/2 much of the time. If more than one of those programs makes heavy use of sound, it may be less confusing to simply turn the sound off for a session. If you're playing *Space Quest* in the office, you may also find it advantageous to turn the sound off. If you didn't do so before starting the session, you will be pleased to find that this setting can be changed at any time and will take effect immediately—quite handy when the boss walks in.

Don't let the double-negative confuse you; remember the setting contains the NOSOUND statement. The default setting of OFF means that sound is played. Changing the setting to ON silences the session.

HW_ROM_TO_RAM (default OFF)

The Basic Input Output System (BIOS) is the software that comes with your system and allows the operating system low-level access to the hardware. This software is provided on a Read-Only Memory (ROM) chip plugged into the motherboard of your system.

ROM has a great advantage over Random Access Memory (RAM) because ROM maintains its contents even when power is turned off. As with all things, there is a tradeoff here. Accessing information from ROM storage is slower than accessing RAM. Changing this setting to ON can improve the performance of the session by copying the contents of ROM into the faster RAM, and accessing the code from there.

IBM decided that OS/2 should not, by default, take advantage of this feature so they could provide the maximum amount of memory for programs. In most cases, however, the tradeoff is well worth it, and the user should change this setting to ON.

IDLE_SECONDS (default 0)

The vast majority of a computer's time is spent waiting for the user to take some action. Within a DOS program, this is typically handled via a technique known as *polling*. Polling simply means that the program repeatedly checks to see if the user has done something, such as enter a keystroke. Continuous polling can use up large amounts of the system's resources. While this may not have been a problem with DOS, in a multitasking system you don't want any single program to monopolize the system to the detriment of others.

For this reason, OS/2 monitors DOS programs closely. If OS/2 determines that DOS programs are in a polling loop, it lowers their priority to minimize the effect on other programs. These parameters allow you to manipulate how OS/2 does this to get the best system performance.

The IDLE_SECONDS statement establishes the delay, if any, before OS/2 begins monitoring the program for polling. In other words, if a program prompts you for input, OS/2 waits the number of seconds specified before beginning idle detection. The default of zero provides the best performance for most programs, meaning any program doing nothing while waiting for your input.

Some programs, such as games, may continue processing while waiting for your input. Having their priority lowered can cause performance problems with the ongoing action. To delay the idle detection, raise this setting for those programs.

IDLE_SENSITIVITY (default 75)

The IDLE_SENSITIVITY setting allows you to determine how OS/2 defines whether a program is polling frequently enough to be deemed idle. This setting represents a percentage of the total amount of time available to the program. If the program is polling at a rate higher than the specified percentage, OS/2 lowers its percentage.

Raising the IDLE_SENSITIVITY to 100 turns idle detection off, since a program can never poll more than 100 percent of the time. This can help performance in continuous-action programs such as games.

Lowering the sensitivity causes OS/2 to reduce the session's priority more quickly in a polling situation. This is more advantageous for programs that are inactive while awaiting user input, such as word processors.

Both of these settings can be changed while the session is active, so you can dynamically tune the performance of the system.

KBD_ALTHOME_BYPASS (default OFF)

When running DOS programs, OS/2 allows you to change your session from windowed to full-screen and vice versa by pressing ALT+HOME. However, some applications might require this keystroke for other tasks. Changing this setting to ON instructs OS/2 not to act on this key sequence, but to pass it through to your program.

KBD_BUFFER_EXTEND (default ON)

DOS can ordinarily store up to 16 keystrokes in a buffer, which is what permits typing ahead of the cursor. By default, OS/2 increases the buffer to 128 keystrokes. While not all programs can take advantage of this feature, the memory usage is slight, so there's little reason to change this setting.

KBD_CTRL_BYPASS (default NONE)

OS/2 uses CTRL key combinations as hotkeys. CTRL+ESC brings up the Task Manager, allowing you to bring any active session to the foreground. Pressing ALT+ESC switches to the next active session. Some DOS programs, however, need one of these keys for their own use. This setting allows you to select either CTRL+ESC or ALT+ESC, and instruct OS/2 to pass it through to the program rather than using it as a task switcher.

KBD_RATE_LOCK (default OFF)

The *typeamatic rate* is the speed at which keystrokes are repeated when you hold a key down. For example, when moving through the text in a document, the typeamatic rate determines how fast the cursor moves when you hold down an arrow key. Some programs change the typeamatic rate. Since OS/2 is a multitasking system, you might not want one program to change the cursor rate for others. Changing this setting to ON prevents this DOS session from changing the keystroke rate.

MEM_EXCLUDE_REGIONS (default none) and MEM_INCLUDE_REGIONS (default none)

These settings allow you to define specific areas of memory that should or should not be available for EMS or XMS usage. You can specify just the starting address, in which case a 4K section is reserved, or specify a starting and ending address.

MOUSE_EXCLUSIVE_ACCESS (default OFF)

OS/2 manages the mouse for both DOS and OS/2 sessions. Some DOS programs, however, try to manage the mouse directly. If, when running a DOS program, you see two mouse cursors, change this setting to ON. Then, when you click a mouse button in the DOS window, the PM pointer provided by OS/2 disappears, and you can use the pointer provided by the DOS program. Pressing the ALT key or either of the session switching hotkeys will restore the PM pointer.

PRINT_TIMEOUT (default 15)

The OS/2 spooler manages all print jobs in the system to avoid having two programs writing to the printer at the same time. DOS programs often do not close the printer, so the spooler isn't notified that printing is complete until the program ends. If you are printing from within a word processor, you might want to print a few pages and review them without leaving the program or you may want to go on to print other documents from the same word processor.

OS/2 handles this by monitoring the spool queue. If the DOS program hasn't added anything to the queue for the number of seconds specified in this setting, OS/2 closes the entry in the queue so printing can begin. If more than one program is printing simultaneously, output from the two programs could mingle. If you have a program that has long pauses between printing, you may need to raise this setting to prevent output mingling. Lowering this setting causes OS/2 to close the output more quickly, speeding the output to the printer.

VIDEO_FASTPASTE (default OFF)

Changing the VIDEO_FASTPASTE setting to ON can speed up the transfer of characters from the system clipboard when you're doing Cut and Paste to or from a DOS program. This can cause problems with some DOS programs that cannot handle quick delivery of the simulated keystrokes. If you find that characters are being lost in the transfer, make sure this setting is OFF.

VIDEO_MODE_RESTRICTION (default NONE)

OS/2 makes more conventional memory available to DOS programs than most versions of DOS. In fact, it is common for DOS sessions under 2.0 to have as much as 637K available. Still, OS/2 makes it possible for even more conventional memory to be available.

Contrary to popular belief, DOS can actually address more than 640K of memory. In fact, it can address 1024K, or 1MB. DOS reserves the space above 640K for device drivers and video memory. Depending on the video mode you plan to use, OS/2 can release some of that storage back to your program. If your program can restrict itself to the capabilities of a

CGA adapter (that is, 640 x 200 monocolor graphics, 320 x 200 4-color graphics, and 80 x 25 16-color text), select CGA from the pull-down list and your program will have an additional 64K of conventional memory. If your program doesn't require graphics at all and can use single-color text, select MONO and the program will gain 96K of conventional memory.

 Caution If after selecting one of these options your program tries to use a higher resolution capability, the program could write video information over your data. Check the program's documentation and specifications carefully before making any changes.

VIDEO_ONDEMAND_MEMORY (default ON)

In order to be able to restore it properly, OS/2 stores an image of the screen's contents when you switch out of a full-screen session. By default, the memory to do this isn't allocated until you actually switch out of the session. In extremely tight memory situations, it is possible that not enough memory (or swap space) would be available to save the screen—particularly if you are in a high-resolution graphics mode. This causes the program to terminate at that point. Changing this setting to OFF makes OS/2 reserve memory for the screen image when the program is started. If you are out of storage, OS/2 lets you know then, rather than risking terminating your program prematurely on a screen switch.

On the other hand, if you are that tightly constrained for resources, add memory. Leaving this setting in the default ON position allows programs to load more quickly, and keeps memory available for other programs until it is needed.

VIDEO_RETRACE_EMULATION (default ON)

Video retrace emulation is a fairly complicated term that describes a technique OS/2 uses to allow different sessions to be running in different modes and with different color palettes simultaneously. OS/2 keeps track of these differences when you switch between sessions.

This overhead does bring with it a slight performance penalty, and changing the setting to OFF can speed up some DOS programs. On the other hand, turning emulation off can cause the display of sessions to be restored improperly in some circumstances. The difference in performance is not dramatic, so it is usually best to leave this setting on.

VIDEO_ROM_EMULATION (default ON)

In most cases, the functions performed in the video ROM of your system can be performed more quickly in RAM; OS/2 has emulation software built in to take advantage of this fact. If your video ROM has added capabilities or speed improvements, change this setting to OFF to use those. In general, OS/2's RAM-based emulation is superior, and this setting shouldn't be changed, unless you spend most of your time at the computer playing games that manipulate the display directly. This setting can be changed at any time during a session.

VIDEO_SWITCH_NOTIFICATION (default OFF)

The VIDEO_SWITCH_NOTIFICATION setting determines whether OS/2 notifies the DOS program when it is switched from the foreground to the background. Most DOS programs, not having been written for a multitasking environment, have no way to detect this notification, and most standard video modes (CGA, EGA, VGA) have no way to use this notification. This setting should be changed to ON, however, if you are running a Windows application, since they are sensitive to switch notification.

VIDEO_WINDOW_REFRESH (default 1)

The VIDEO_WINDOW_REFRESH setting determines the length of time (in tenths of a second) between redrawings of this session's screen. The higher the value specified here, the smaller the impact of this session on the performance of other programs being run, particularly if the program uses video heavily. On the other hand, the program output may appear jerky or inconsistent if this is set to a high number. This setting can be changed at any time, so you can tune it for your program, observing the effect as you make changes.

XMS_HANDLES (default 32)

Extended memory is allocated in blocks, each of which is accessed via a handle. Each of these handles requires memory, so raising this beyond the amount needed abuses system resources. In most cases, the default value should be sufficient.

XMS_MEMORY_LIMIT (default 2048)

The XMS_MEMORY_LIMIT setting specifies the maximum number of kilobytes that this session can allocate for use as extended memory. The default of 2MB is sufficient for many programs, but the limit can be raised all the way to 16MB. Setting this limit too high can increase the amount of swapping required in the system, which slows performance. Your application's documentation should indicate the amount of extended memory required.

XMS_MINIMUM_HMA (default 0)

Nearly 64K of the High Memory Area (that is, the memory from 640K to 1MB) can be allocated to programs requesting it. There is no sub-allocation ability for that memory, however, meaning that only one program can access this memory within the session. Of course, unless this is a Windows session, you are likely only to be running one program in the window anyway. It is quite unusual for the user to ever need to adjust this setting.

Installing a Specific DOS Version

OS/2's compatibility with DOS and Windows is remarkable, and certainly one of version 2.0's strongest features. Still, there are some programs that have been written for explicit aspects of a specific version of DOS that cannot execute properly under OS/2's standard offerings.

In many cases there are ways to resolve the problem in order to allow the program to run within OS/2.

Sometimes a program absolutely depends on specific characteristics of a specific version of DOS. Or, you might prefer to use some of the characteristics of another environment, such as the two-column directory listing available in DR DOS. In fact, you already may have installed a specific DOS environment on your hard drive but let it run in its own partition and not within an OS/2 window. There are several steps involved, but taking advantage of the ability of OS/2 to boot another operating system within an OS/2 window can be accomplished in just a few minutes.

Creating a DOS Startup Diskette

To be able to boot another version of DOS, you must first have a copy of that operating system, and you will, of course, have to start it. To do that, bring OS/2 to an orderly shutdown, and boot the version of DOS for which you want to create a startup diskette, either from diskette or from the hard drive.

You must then create a bootable diskette with that operating system. In all known variations of DOS (including DR DOS), this can be accomplished by entering the command **FORMAT A: /S**

If you booted DOS from diskette, you will be prompted to remove your operating system diskette and insert an empty diskette to be formatted. The /S option indicates that after the diskette has been formatted, the system files will be written to the diskette's boot sector.

Creating the Startup Files

It takes more than the system files to run the operating system properly. You need a copy of CONFIG.SYS and AUTOEXEC.BAT on your startup diskette.

Copying from the Hard Drive

If you booted DOS from the hard drive you will be able to transfer the files you need to the startup diskette. With the new bootable diskette in drive A, enter this statement

COPY C:\CONFIG.SYS A:

followed by

COPY C:\AUTOEXEC.BAT A:

If you booted from a diskette, the files you need may or may not be available on the hard drive (they probably are if you are not booting into an OS/2 partition). If so, use the same technique to transfer the files.

Copying from Diskettes

If CONFIG.SYS and AUTOEXEC.BAT are on the boot diskette you used to start the system, you will need to copy them to your new OS/2 bootable DOS diskette. In that case, it is easier to create a temporary directory on the hard drive to store all the files you are going to need than to switch diskettes back and forth. Transfer the files in the temporary directory to the new startup diskette when you are finished. Creating a directory to hold these files also means that you won't accidently overwrite a file with the same name on the hard drive. Use a unique name for this directory, something like STARTDOS. To create the directory, issue the command **MD C:\STARTDOS** (or whatever name you have selected) from any prompt.

Put the boot diskette into drive A and use these commands:

COPY A:CONFIG.SYS C:\STARTDOS

COPY A:AUTOEXEC.BAT C:\STARTDOS

Then put the new startup diskette back into drive A and enter the following at the command line:

COPY C:\STARTDOS A:

 Note   If you booted from a diskette and do not have the CONFIG.SYS or AUTOEXEC.BAT files on that diskette, create what you need using your favorite editor, following the directions described in the next section. The individual lines contained in the files discussed are the only lines absolutely necessary for a DOS startup diskette.

Modifying the Startup Files

Once you have copied these two files to the new startup diskette, take it out of drive A and reboot the system. Be sure to boot into OS/2. Once the system has rebooted, put the startup DOS diskette back into drive A.

Modifying CONFIG.SYS

Some basic parameters guiding the configuration of the operating system are contained in CONFIG.SYS.

FSFILTER.SYS

There is one other file that must be copied onto the startup diskette. FSFILTER.SYS is a device driver that acts as a filter between the file system commands your DOS system will try to execute and the actual OS/2 file system. In other words, it lets your DOS get to OS/2 data. Copy this file to your startup diskette by entering this statement:

COPY C:\OS2\MDOS\FSFILTER.SYS A:

Now DOS needs to be told to load FSFILTER.SYS. Change the CONFIG.SYS file to do that. Using your favorite editor (see Chapter 7 for information on the editors included with OS/2), open A:\CONFIG.SYS. Insert the following line at the top of the file:

DEVICE=FSFILTER.SYS

This line must appear before any other device drivers (DEVICE=
statements) in the file.

Memory Managers

Review the other lines in CONFIG.SYS. If DOS is configured to use
extended or expanded memory, you may find HIMEM.SYS or
EMM386.SYS listed in device statements. These must be replaced with
the OS/2 version of these device drivers for correct memory management.
Either edit the original lines to match the example below or delete them
and add the following lines to the CONFIG.SYS file:

DEVICE=C:\OS2\MDOS\HIMEM.SYS

DEVICE=C:\OS2\MDOS\EMM386.SYS

Mouse Driver

DOS must be configured to use the OS/2 mouse routines. Browse
through the CONFIG.SYS file for a DEVICE= statement that loads a
mouse device driver (usually named MOUSE.SYS). If you find such a line,
remove it. The OS/2 mouse driver will be loaded through the AU-
TOEXEC.BAT file, explained in the following paragraphs.

At this point save CONFIG.SYS with your changes.

Modifying AUTOEXEC.BAT

DOS also allows you to specify instructions that are to be executed
whenever the operating system is booted by reading the instructions in
AUTOEXEC.BAT.

The OS/2 mouse driver must be added to the startup procedure on
the diskette. In your text editor, open the file A:AUTOEXEC.BAT and
insert this line:

C:\OS2\MDOS\MOUSE

Browse through the file looking for lines that don't have the complete path specified for programs to be loaded. You can either insert the complete path needed to load any command or program or, if there is room, copy any commands or programs listed in AUTOEXEC.BAT to the root directory of the startup diskette. Save your changes and exit the editor.

Testing the Startup Diskette

The startup diskette is now ready. To test it, open the OS/2 System folder, and from within it, open the Command Prompts to see the window shown in Figure 11-1.

With the startup diskette in drive A, double-click on **DOS from Drive A:**. Whatever DOS you've loaded onto the diskette should boot normally.

Configuring the DOS Session Defaults

The default is for DOS to load in a full-screen session, but you might prefer to run DOS in a window. To make this change, open the pop-up menu by clicking on DOS from drive A with mouse button #2. Open the Settings notebook and click on the **Session** tab to see the window shown in Figure 11-2. Click on the **DOS window** button to make the change.

Making an Image on the Hard Drive

If you are going to be running this version of DOS frequently, you may wish to be able to load it from the hard disk rather than the startup diskette. To do so, first create an image of the startup diskette. Put the startup diskette in the drive and type **VMDISK A:** *filename*, where *filename* represents the path, name, and extension you want to apply to the image file you're creating. Then return to the Session page of the **DOS from Drive A:** settings shown in Figure 11-2 and click on the **DOS settings** button to see the window shown in Figure 11-3.

Click on **DOS_STARTUP_DRIVE**. In the right side of the window, enter the complete path and filename to the image file in the **Value** field. Click on the **Save** button to store the information.

Click on the **General** tab and change the text associated with this icon to represent the version of DOS you're loading rather than DOS from drive A, for example DOS3.3.

From now on, double-clicking on the icon will cause your DOS version to be loaded from the image on the hard drive so you no longer need the startup diskette.

 Caution OS/2 opens the DOS session by loading the image file as if it were a diskette. As a result, the actual floppy disk drive cannot be used while this session is open. To use the diskette drive without closing the DOS session, enter the command **FSACCESS A:**, which releases the drive for general usage.

Running Windows Applications

While visually similar, there are many architectural differences between the DOS/Windows environment and WIN-OS/2, the Windows emulation software built into OS/2. A lot of the programming is the same, but WIN-OS/2 has had the original Windows programming modified to take advantage of some of the OS/2 features, such as the 32-bit file system and OS/2's preemptive multitasking scheduler.

WIN-OS/2, like Windows, is essentially a DOS application. Corresponding to other DOS applications running under OS/2, it has access to OS/2 virtual memory systems. In fact, most users find that they have fewer of the dreaded Windows UAEs (Unrecoverable Application Errors) when running Windows programs under WIN-OS/2 than they encounter when using native Windows.

Compatibility Issues

WIN-OS/2 is downwardly compatible for Windows; it runs applications that were written for versions of Windows before version 3.0. This is something Windows 3.0 itself cannot do. In addition, native Windows 3.1 actually has compatibility problems with some popular Windows 3.0 applications that perform well under WIN-OS/2.

At the time of this writing, OS/2 could only run applications written for Windows 3.0 and earlier. IBM is testing Windows 3.1 support and its release is imminent (it may even have been released by the time you read this). The Windows 3.1 in WIN-OS/2 will also be modified to take advantage of the OS/2 environment.

Incompatible Programs

Not all Windows applications will run in WIN-OS/2. Applications that must be run in Windows Enhanced mode will not run because WIN-OS/2 supports only Standard mode and Real mode.

There are also some Windows applications that are dependent on one or more of the mini-applications included with native Windows—the Calculator or Windows Write, for example—and these mini-applications are not included with WIN-OS/2. On the other hand, if you're using such an application, you probably have Windows installed on your system, so you can run them through WIN-OS/2.

Windows Multimedia Extensions

Another potential problem arises from programs that use Windows Multimedia Extensions. While these do work with OS/2, the migration routine that runs during OS/2's installation may not always set them up properly. Reinstalling these applications using WIN-OS/2 should clear up the problem.

Specific Compatibility Problems

As of this writing, there are a number of software applications that either cannot run under WIN-OS/2 or need special treatment in order to run. It's possible that by the time you read this, the compatibility issues will have been resolved for some or most of these packages. The following information is version-specific.

Action! Sampler 1.0 for Windows The DPMI_MEMORY_LIMIT WIN-OS/2 setting must be set to 5 or greater in order for this application to run.

After Dark for Windows To run After Dark in a WIN-OS/2 window, you need to change the object's settings to hide or minimize the icon on the desktop.

Aldus Pagemaker 4.0 for Windows The spelling checker cannot locate the dictionary, and you have to deselect the public setting in order to use the clipboard. In addition, if there is incorrect output when spooling Standard format files to the printer, set the printing to RAW mode using the following steps:

1. Go to the Printer icon on the desktop and click mouse button #2.

2. Select **Open**, and then **Settings**, and then **Queue Options.**

3. Make sure that **Printer Specific Format** is checked.

Aldus Persuasion 2.0 for Windows   You must use the parallel ports to print, and you have to deselect the public setting in order to use the clipboard.

Arts & Letters Graphics Editor 3.1 for Windows   The DECIPHS utility program requires that a DOS session be started from the Windows environment, and this is not possible. To run this program in a WIN-OS/2 window, change the object's settings so it is minimized to the desktop.

The directory created by Arts & Letters is named A&L, and the "&" character is a reserved character. To change to the A&L directory with the CD command, you must either prefix the "&" in A&L with a caret (CD A^&L) or surround the entire directory name with quotation marks (CD "A&L").

If you are running Arts & Letters and you get a system error you must restart the operating system before trying to run the program again; A&L will have left a portion of itself running when it stopped, and the program cannot start a new copy of itself while that portion is running. This also means that when you restart your system, Arts & Letters will start again. You should close that copy and start a new session by clicking on the icon.

Central Point PC Tools Deluxe 7.1 for Windows   Many of the utility programs require the start of a DOS session from Windows, and this is not possible. Start these programs from a separate DOS session.

The backup function of this application is similar to Central Point Backup for Windows, which is in the list of programs that perform restricted activities. If you have any difficulties backing up on a diskette, back up on an alternate device, such as a network drive or a tape drive.

CorelDRAW 2.0 for Windows   Install the program in a DOS session; run the program in a WIN-OS/2 full-screen session.

CorelDRAW 2.1 for Windows   To install this program, start a DOS session. Run FFIX /date ("date" must be lowercase). Run WIN-OS/2 from the command line and install the program. Exit WIN-OS/2. Then run FFIX /u. Run the program in a WIN-OS/2 full-screen session.

Drafix CAD Version 1.11 for Windows   This program must be run in a WIN-OS/2 full-screen session.

Drafix CAD Version 3.0 for Windows   This program must be run in a WIN-OS/2 full-screen session.

Form Publisher for Windows   Make sure the program's printer driver is installed before running the program.

FormBase 1.2 for Windows   The SHARE statement is automatically added to AUTOEXEC.BAT during this program's installation. Use an editor to remove the SHARE command from AUTOEXEC.BAT. When running this program and Lotus 1-2-3 in the same Windows session, this program must be started first.

FotoMan for Windows   This program must be run in a WIN-OS/2 full-screen session.

Harvard Draw for Windows   During installation under WIN-OS/2, you will see an error dialog box. Select OK in the dialog box and installation will finish successfully.

Harvard Graphics for Windows   During installation under WIN-OS/2, you will see an error dialog box. Select OK in the dialog box and the installation will finish successfully. When running in a window, the Color Selection windows do not show the Color Selection grid. This program must be run in a WIN-OS/2 full-screen session.

hDC FileApps 1.0 for Windows   This program uses the Windows Notepad for a README text file during installation. Indicate that you do not want to read the file, and the installation will continue.

HP New Wave 3.0 for Windows   Install this program under DOS. If you have problems with program or session termination, set UseOS2shield=0 in SYSTEM.INI (in the \OS2\MDOS\WINOS2 directory on your start-up drive). If that doesn't work, run the program in a full-screen WIN-OS/2 session.

Lotus 1-2-3 for Windows 1.0   You must set the DPMI_MEM-ORY_LIMIT DOS setting to a minimum of 3MB. After migrating the program to the Workplace Shell, copy the file 123W.INI to the \OS2\MDOS\WINOS2 directory.

MagiCorp for Windows   Running this program with other programs in the same WIN-OS/2 session could cause the system to halt, so run it by itself in a WIN-OS/2 full-screen session.

Mathcad 3.0 for Windows   To install this program, you must start a DOS session. Run FFIX /date ("date" must be lowercase), install the program (installation is a DOS program), and run FFIX /u.

Microsoft Codeview for Windows Version 3.0   This program must be run in a WIN-OS/2 full-screen session.

Microsoft Excel for Windows 3.0   You must deselect the public setting in order to use the clipboard. When using dynamic data exchange (DDE), run the program in the same WIN-OS/2 session as the Windows program it must communicate with.

Microsoft Money 1.0 for Windows   This program calls the Windows Calculator application. Use the OS/2 Calculator mini-application program in the Productivity folder.

Microsoft Project for Windows 1.0   The program must be installed in a DOS session.

Microsoft QuickC for Windows   This program must be run in a WIN-OS/2 full-screen session.

The Norton Desktop for Windows   This program makes the assumption that if it is not the first program loaded, another desktop is running, so include the UseOS2shield=0 statement in SYSTEM.INI (in the \OS2\MDOS\WINOS2 directory on your start-up drive). This program must be run in a WIN-OS/2 full-screen session.

Perform Pro 1.0 for Windows   This program must be run in a WIN-OS/2 full-screen session.

PFS: WindowWorks 1.75 for Windows   This program must be run in a WIN-OS/2 full-screen session.

Photostyler for Windows This program must be run in a WIN-OS/2 full-screen session.

Publisher's PowerPak 2.1 for Windows You must create the directory C:\OS2\MDOS\WINOS2\POWERPAK before running the installation program.

Quicken for Windows This program uses the Calculator program in the Productivity folder.

SQLWindows 3.0 for Windows This program occasionally accesses drive A. Keep an empty formatted diskette in drive A so you won't have "The A: device is not ready" error windows pop up.

The Way You Work (DOS/Windows) Run the installation for this program under DOS. After it is installed, it can be run either in a DOS or WIN-OS/2 session.

Turbo Debugger for Windows You must run this program in a WIN-OS/2 full-screen session. The screen is temporarily corrupted if you call the program from Turbo C++. To restore the screen, repaint by clicking the mouse on several different windows.

Windows Multimedia Extensions for Windows If you are using this program at the same time you are using another program that uses the audio adapter, there may be some erratic results. Using the OS/2 Multimedia Presentation Manager will prevent erratic results.

WINFAX PRO for Windows This program must run in a WIN-OS/2 full-screen session. If you are using DDE, don't switch from the WIN-OS/2 full-screen session or the DDE link might detach.

WordPerfect for Windows If you experience a problem with this program, change to the directory that contains WPWINFIL.EXE and enter **FIXWP WPWINFIL.EXE**. If you decide you want to run the program under DOS and native Windows 3.0 again, you must undo the fix by entering **UNFIXWP WPWINFILE.EXE**.

Migrating Windows Applications

When you installed OS/2, it tried to migrate your existing Windows applications so that they would appear on the desktop. This is one of those features that weren't quite right when 2.0 was first released, and some programs may not have migrated properly. If you have problems running a Windows application, try reinstalling it in a WIN-OS/2 full-screen session.

If you did migrate your Windows applications (at installation time or later, using MIGRATE), most Windows applications will execute in one WIN-OS/2 session. If you set up a Windows application and do not use MIGRATE, each program executes in its own WIN-OS/2 session.

Performance Differences

Since Windows is a DOS extender, the best way to start learning about performance issues is to look at the preceding chapter on running DOS applications. There are differences between Windows applications and plain DOS programs, as explained in the following sections.

Speed

Sometimes Windows applications run more slowly on OS/2. However, if you run Windows in a full-screen session (the same way you would run native Windows), the difference in performance is negligible.

In fact, some programs might even run more quickly because of OS/2's 32-bit file system. OS/2 also has the ability to run Windows applications on the OS/2 desktop in windows of their own. This technological achievement comes at a price. The performance slowdown when running Windows programs in this "seamless" mode is noticeable.

Still, it should be noted that most of the slowdown comes at program load time. The fact is, performance isn't affected as much as it appears. When you start native Windows, you don't really think much about the delay while Windows itself is loading, because you can see what is happening. The same is true when running Windows applications under WIN-OS/2 in full-screen mode; you can see the loading of Windows itself taking place.

When you start a seamless Windows session, the same Windows overhead must be loaded, but since you can't see what is happening, you may perceive that it is taking a long time to load the program. See Chapter 13 for tips on speeding up the program loading.

Memory

All Windows applications benefit from DPMI memory. Even if the program itself doesn't try to allocate extra memory, WIN-OS/2 uses it just as native Windows does.

Increase the DPMI memory limit (see Chapter 11) before starting the first application. The first application you run sets the DPMI memory available for all subsequent Windows applications that are run in the same session. Running multiple Windows applications in one WIN-OS/2 session reduces both memory and swapper-file needs.

System Startup File Considerations

It is fairly common to have a statement in the AUTOEXEC.BAT file prompt the user for input, such as a PAUSE statement. A quirk in the system OS/2 goes through to run Windows applications in WIN-OS/2 demands that there be no such statements in the AUTOEXEC.BAT.

Video

At this writing, seamless Windows applications running on the desktop are only possible in VGA mode. IBM is actively working on expanding this to SVGA modes.

The VIDEO_SWITCH NOTIFICATION parameter must not be changed while WIN-OS/2 sessions are open. If this setting is ON, make sure you wait until the Windows session is started before switching from the

Windows session to the WPS desktop. The setting should be ON if you are using an IBM 8514a or XGA adapter. You should also set VIDEO_8514A_XGA_IOTRAP to OFF if using an 8514a.

If you have difficulty seeing the icons in a WIN-OS/2 session running XGA, you may need to run the Control Panel to change the desktop color scheme.

If you are using Dynamic Data Exchange, be sure to leave it as an icon rather than opening it if you are running in 8514 or XGA mode.

Modes

The DOS settings discussion in the preceding chapter applies equally to Windows applications, and that chapter pointed out things that directly affect Windows applications.

There is one setting that applies only to Windows applications. Open the Settings menu for a Windows application; as you can see in Figure 12-1, the WIN-OS/2 settings are available.

WIN-OS/2 settings in the Settings dialog box ✿

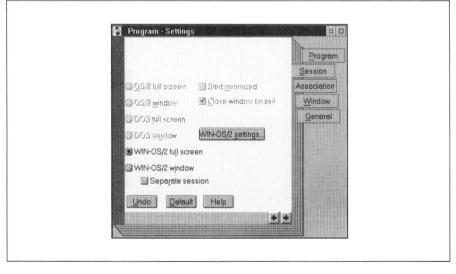

The button that had been labeled **DOS Settings** now reads **WIN-OS/2 settings**. Click on that button to see the dialog box shown in Figure 12-2. There is a new setting at the top of the list, **WIN_RUNMODE**, which lets you specify the mode in which the WIN-OS/2 session will operate.

Windows 3.0 applications should all run in Standard mode, while applications written for earlier versions of Windows should run in Real mode.

Note Real mode support is an advantage OS/2 has over Windows 3.1, which cannot run applications that require Real mode. The best solution is to select AUTO and let OS/2 determine which mode the application requires.

Changing Configurations

If Windows is on your system, do not run the Windows SETUP program. Instead, run the SETUP program in the \OS2\MDOS\WINOS2 subdirectory.

Setting the WIN-OS/2 running mode *

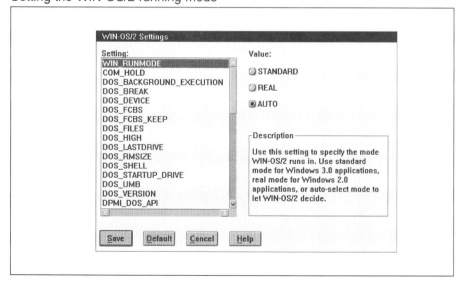

Device Drivers

The EXPAND.EXE utility program for WIN-OS/2 is located on OS/2 2.0 diskette 9. Use this program to expand Windows device drivers supplied by equipment manufacturers.

Printing

If your printer is connected to LPTx or LPTx.OS2, make sure that the OS/2 spooler is active and the Windows spooler is disabled. When the OS/2 spooler is active, Windows applications print jobs spool directly to the OS/2 spooler. Therefore, multiple print jobs can be spooled asynchronously from the same WIN-OS/2 session or multiple WIN-OS/2 sessions. This does not apply for printing to COMx devices, as there is no spooling for COM devices.

CHAPTER

Switching to High Octane

While you're probably impressed with OS/2's power, you may have noticed that you pay a price for it: the cost of the hardware required to use it. OS/2 2.0 cannot run on systems that don't have at least a 386SX processor and 4MB of memory. Functions such as preemptive multitasking and the Workplace Shell weren't possible on the desktop until such hardware became available and affordable.

Just as prices quoted in automobile commercials rarely include all the extras, the minimum hardware quoted by IBM doesn't represent a setup that most people would find acceptable. The difference in performance with even small increases in memory can be dramatic. Now that memory is more affordable, it doesn't pay to skimp on it. The difference in performance derived from an increase from 4MB to 6MB of memory is quite noticeable, and increasing from 6MB to 8MB brings even more improvement. However, with more than 8MB of memory, the law of diminishing returns begins to apply; although it is generally true that the more RAM you throw at software and operating systems the better, unless you have specific applications that take advantage of additional memory, 8MB is a realistic minimum for smooth performance.

When to Add Memory

While 8MB provides an acceptable amount of memory for productivity, many users strive for increasing performance beyond that needed for ordinary, day-to-day tasks. Some people turn into speed demons as they become more comfortable with computers; no matter how responsive their software, they continue their quest for speed, and add hardware and software solutions to reach a goal, which usually results in the setting of a new, higher goal. There is, however, a happy medium, which provides productivity and efficiency at a higher-than-average level without breaking the bank.

Checking the Swap File

The easiest way to determine whether you need to install more memory is to watch the size of the SWAPPER.DAT file. This file is used by OS/2 to store data segments that the system has temporarily removed from physical memory. Software consists of groups of pages of programming or data that are called into physical memory as they are needed. If an application calls for memory and there is not enough physical memory available to fulfill the request, OS/2 provides memory by taking the least frequently used data pages and moving them to the SWAPPER.DAT file on the hard disk. As applications continue to run and continue to ask for memory, the data is paged between physical memory and SWAPPER.DAT.

SWAPPER.DAT is in the subdirectory specified in the SWAPPATH statement in the CONFIG.SYS file. Unless you have changed the default established during the OS/2 installation, it is in the directory C:\OS2\SYSTEM. To ascertain its size, type **DIR C:\OS2\SYS-TEM\SWAPPER.DAT** at the command line.

SWAPPER.DAT changes its size continually as you work and your applications make memory requests. There is, however, an initial size allocated by OS/2 during installation. That size depends on the amount of physical memory your computer has. The more physical memory in your system, the smaller the swap file. The following table shows the initial size of the swap file for various available memory configurations:

Memory	Initial size
4MB	6144KB
5MB	5120KB
6MB	5120KB
7MB	4096KB
8MB	4096KB
9MB	3072KB
10MB	3072KB
11MB	2048KB
12MB	2048KB

Check the size of the swap file occasionally, while working in applications, to get an idea of the average size of the file. The size of the swap file changes quite a bit as your workload changes, so try to gauge an average size while keeping a close eye on the largest size and how frequently that size is reached. The swap file increases its size as needed, taking up valuable disk space, so if you can increase the amount of physical memory in your system you lessen the risk of running out of disk space.

A certain amount of swapping won't make an enormous difference in performance, and it shouldn't be your goal to make SWAPPER.DAT disappear. In fact, a SWAPPER.DAT file of 4MB or so is quite a comfortable area. If the swap file starts getting a lot larger than that, it is a clear indication that adding memory will improve your system's performance.

 Tip To determine the amount of memory you need to add to your system, a good rule of thumb is to subtract four million from the size of SWAPPER.DAT during a normal workload.

Application Memory Use

Different types of applications use varying amounts of memory. And, depending on how good the programmers are, the memory an application uses may or may not be manipulated efficiently. Table 13-1 shows an approximation of memory usage by various application types. However, remember to take into account the various combinations of application types that are running at the same time and impacting memory usage.

For instance, if you are working in a spreadsheet program, a great deal of memory is used while you are actively keying in information. If you

TABLE 13-1 Application Memory Use

Element	Memory (MB)
OS/2 Operating System	3.0
HPFS	.3
DOS Sessions	
DOS full screen	.3
Each additional DOS full screen session	.2
DOS Windows session	.3

TABLE 13-1	Application Memory Use (continued)

Element	Memory (MB)
Each additional DOS Windows session	.3
WIN-OS/2 session	2.0
Each additional WIN-OS/2 session	1.0
Spooling (when active)	.5
DDE	.4
Clipboard	.2
Application Types	
Communications	.5
Database	1.0
Engineering	3.0
Game	.6
Graphics	1.5
Spreadsheet	1.5
Word Processor	1.0

put the spreadsheet into the background and work on another chore, most of the time the spreadsheet won't be taking up memory because there is little for it to do when it is not in an interactive mode. But, if you use macros or other automated features that permit the program to read in data from a disk file and then perform computations, the spreadsheet program will continue to use memory; in this case, consider adding physical memory if these processes seem slow.

If you have a robust accounting package and it is time to close the fiscal period for a series of accounting modules (Accounts Receivable, Accounts Payable, General Ledger, and so on), you can start these tasks and then move them to the background while you open and work on another application. Again, having plenty of physical memory is likely to be very important with this scenario.

A communications program using your modem needs to have everything in memory for as long as the connection is open, so that anything that needs to be sent or received can be given the operating system's full attention, even if other applications are being used at the same time. Again, if this applies to your normal working pattern, consider adding more RAM to your system.

Disk Caching

You can also improve performance by using a *disk cache*, a storage buffer that contains frequently used instructions and data. Accessing data from memory rather than the disk is significantly faster since your computer does not have to access the hard disk, search it for information, and then bring that information into memory. Through the use of sophisticated prediction techniques, the cache software anticipates what you're likely to want to read from the disk next and copies it into memory in advance. When your program asks for the information, it will be loaded from high-speed memory rather than disk. A multitasking platform like OS/2 can get even more advantage from a cache by doing disk reads and writes when nothing else is going on, without affecting the rest of the system.

Lazy-Writes

While the key performance gains from caching are on long reads of sequential information because the caching software reads ahead in anticipation of the next data required, there is another useful performance technique available with a disk cache. When information needs to be written to the disk, OS/2 2.0 makes available a technique called *lazy-writing*, which takes data bound for the disk and stores it in the disk cache. The software that caused the disk write is informed that the write is complete as soon as the information gets into the cache—which happens much more quickly than if it had to wait for the information to reach the disk. The cache software then writes the data in a separate process, waiting for a time when the disk is idle. This not only provides faster throughput for the particular software program, it means that all incoming requests from all open software applications are freed from the need to wait for disk-write operations, either their own or any others. The entire response time for your system is optimized.

As wonderful as this additional productivity can be, there are some tradeoffs. First of all, if you do not have a lot of physical memory, using storage space for data waiting to be written to disk may cause so much swapping that you lose the benefits. In addition, lazy-writing increases slightly the risk of data loss in the event of a power failure or a faulty shutdown during the brief time between the program sending the data (it believes it sent the data to the disk, but it is not there yet) and the actual process of writing to the disk. Still, if you are concerned about data integrity and aren't concerned about a decrease in performance, you might want to turn lazy-write off.

The DISKCACHE Statement

For FAT file systems, the statement controlling the disk cache in CONFIG.SYS is

DISKCACHE=*n*, LW, T, AC:x.

n=the size   The *n* parameter is a number from 64 to 14400 indicating the number of blocks of storage that is used for control information and programs in the disk cache (remember that only data is swapped to the hard disk, program code is discarded). Each block of storage is 1024 bytes, which is one kilobyte. The default value is 64KB.

LW=Lazy Write   The appearance of the LW parameter indicates that Lazy Write is in use. To turn off Lazy Write, remove the parameter; there is no ON or OFF indication in the statement. The default is to have the LW parameter in the statement.

T=threshold size   This is a number between 4 and 128 that signifies the threshold for the number of sectors that can be placed into the cache. The default value is 4.

AC:x=autocheck   This parameter indicates that the operating system will perform an autocheck for the drive indicated by "x"; the autocheck determines if the file system on that drive is in an inconsistent state. This can happen if files were left open when the computer was turned off, usually caused by a failure to run the **Shutdown** choice from the desktop menu or a loss of electrical power during operations. When this parameter is in the statement, the operating system runs CHKDSK with the /F option to correct any problems. Every time you format a drive for a FAT file system, OS/2 updates the DISKCACHE statement to add that drive.

Sizing the Disk Cache

OS/2 assigns a default size for a cache during installation, based on the amount of physical memory installed in your system. If there is 5MB or less in the system, the default disk cache size is 64KB. With 6MB or more, the disk cache size defaults to 256KB. The size of the disk cache is specified in the first parameter of the DISKCACHE statement in your CONFIG.SYS file. Unlike the swap file, the size of the disk cache is not dynamic—it will not automatically grow larger when you are loading more data into memory.

The more memory you have available to allocate for the disk cache, the more likely it is that the information needed will be in memory, and the faster your system will perform. However, there are some tradeoffs to consider. Allocating too much memory to the disk cache may cause your system to swap more frequently, nullifying the gains from caching.

It is sometimes advantageous to elevate the size of the disk cache to a value above the OS/2 default. However, increasing the size decreases the size of available storage that applications can use. You may want to experiment with various sizes of disk cache until you feel you have increased performance.

The CACHE Command

For installable file systems such as HPFS, caching is controlled by the CACHE command. During installation, if you select the HPFS file system, caching is set up for the primary partition. To change the parameters of the cache, do so as part of a RUN statement in CONFIG.SYS or by entering CACHE with the appropriate parameters at the command line. Entering the command without a parameter causes the operating system to display the current values for CACHE.

The syntax for the CACHE command is given here:

CACHE /LAZY:state /MAXAGE: time /DISKIDLE: Time /BUFFERIDLE: time

LAZY   This parameter is ON or OFF. The default is ON.

MAXAGE   This parameter is a statement of time, in milliseconds, before data is written to the disk, regardless of whether or not there has been idle time for the disk. The default value is 5000.

DISKIDLE   The DISKIDLE parameter sets the time, in milliseconds, that a disk must be idle before data from cache memory can be written to it. The default value is 1000.

BUFFERIDLE   The BUFFERIDLE parameter is the amount of time, in milliseconds, that the cache buffer can be idle before the data within it must be written to disk. The default is 500.

 Note   The minimum amount of DISKIDLE time must be larger than the value for BUFFERIDLE.

The HPFS manages the cache, which is divided into blocks of 2KB, by transferring data that is read from and written to disk into the cache. When an application requests data, if it is not present in the cache, the HPFS looks for the least recently used block and, if necessary, writes that block's data to disk, and then uses the block for the newly requested data. This creates a high probability that often-used data will be found in the cache and therefore reduces the number of disk-reads.

To enhance productivity further, within the HPFS cache is information about directories that enables almost instantaneous access to the appropriate directory whenever data needs to be obtained or written.

CONFIG.SYS Settings

There are several statements in CONFIG.SYS that can increase productivity, but generally there is a tradeoff to consider. Changing any of the parameters of CONFIG.SYS statements should be done one at a time, so you can judge the effects before making other changes. If you change too many things at once, and productivity doesn't improve (or worsens), it will be hard to figure out which alteration was the culprit.

PRIORITY_DISK_IO=   This YES/NO choice indicates the input/output priority for applications running in the foreground. When YES is specified, any application running in the foreground will have priority for disk I/O over any application running in the background. Depending on your application types and the way you work with them, there are as many (or more) reasons not to say YES as there are to do so. For example, if you frequently update databases (perhaps your accounting program's posting routines) in the background and move to a word processor in the foreground in the meantime, giving disk priority to the foreground task doesn't make much sense.

SET DELDIR=   Naming a directory to hold deleted files so that you can undelete them if you choose to sounds like a handy feature. However, for a high-octane system, this may be a counterproductive tool. Tracking and saving every deleted file to disk may slow system performance. In fact, by default, this setting is commented out in CONFIG.SYS but many users, anxious to have the facility undo a mistake, make the line "live". Software companies such as Norton and Central Point provide undelete facilities for FAT systems, and Gamma Tech has a similar package for HPFS files.

VIDEO_WINDOW_REFRESH   This value sets the time that elapses before a window is redrawn. The range can be from .1 second to 60 seconds. If you increase the value, you increase the delay between redraws for graphics applications that frequently write to video memory. While this sounds, at first blush, as if it would be terribly annoying, consider what it does for you—the processor is free to work with other applications, updating them, during the elapsed time. Again, changing this value may be useful if how you work justifies the delay. If your work in a graphics package doesn't consist of rapid and frequent changes to the screen image, and you don't need instantaneous response, and you have a database or spreadsheet running in the background, the longer interval between updates may be just what you need for additional productivity.

PRINTMONBUFSIZE= This sets the buffer size, in bytes, of the parallel port device driver and is used with the print monitor programs. You can increase the size of the buffer and improve the speed of data transfer to the printer(s) connected to the parallel port.

DOS_BREAK When BREAK is on, the system checks continuously for a CTRL+BREAK or CTRL+C key combination so you can stop an application from running. While this is frequently a handy device, the process of constantly polling for the key combinations slows down your system. The default for this setting is OFF.

VIDEO_FASTPASTE This ON/OFF setting increases the speed of Cut and Paste transfers between the clipboard and a DOS session. It only affects characters, not graphics. If you use Cut and Paste a great deal and need speed while working, turn this setting to ON. Otherwise, it is not particularly productive to ask for all this attention from the system over this action; leave the OFF default.

AUTOEXEC.BAT Settings

Your AUTOEXEC.BAT file, read during bootup, affects only DOS sessions and has no effect on OS/2 software or OS/2 sessions. Because it affects DOS, it also affects all WIN-OS/2 sessions. The file should contain only those commands needed when a DOS session is started and the AUTOEXEC.BAT file that was created for you during OS/2 installation should rarely be modified. There is no reason to have the commands found in this file on a DOS system. Path statements and prompts are not needed because they are handled by OS/2.

 Caution Do not permit any software program to alter AUTOEXEC.BAT during installation. As a safeguard, make a copy of the file under a different filename. If you install software that changes it but doesn't warn you, you can copy back the original.

If there is some DOS command necessary for a particular application, write a batch file to call that command and run that batch file after you open the DOS session. Or, because it is usually preferable to avoid the command line and stay in the graphical interface, use a program template to create an entry for this application, and have that template point to the batch file.

Program Settings

In Chapter 11, which covered the running of DOS applications, we discussed using the IDLE_SENSITIVITY and IDLE_SECONDS settings to tune performance for programs that use polling techniques. That chapter also made the point that having memory settings higher than necessary wasted resources and could increase swapping. In addition to that problem, the system overhead to manage that memory additionally impacts performance.

If your DOS or Windows program doesn't use EMS or XMS memory, you can improve performance by setting both of these to zero allocation.

The improved performance gained when Windows programs are run in a full screen session (discussed in Chapter 12) is also possible when DOS programs are run in a full screen session. Still, many people prefer to run Windows programs on the same desktop as OS/2 programs. The performance of Windows applications run seamlessly can also be improved by running them all in the same session.

That sounds like a conflict—Windows applications running separately on the OS/2 desktop, but all running in the same session. As mentioned in Chapter 12, a lot of the performance difference is due to the time spent loading the WIN-OS/2 overhead. Look at the Settings notebook of a Windows application, as shown in Figure 13-1. The button labeled **Separate session** is blank, indicating that the default is for all Windows applications that are running seamlessly to execute in the same virtual Windows sessions. This means that after the first Windows application is loaded, subsequent programs won't have to reload the WIN-OS/2 overhead.

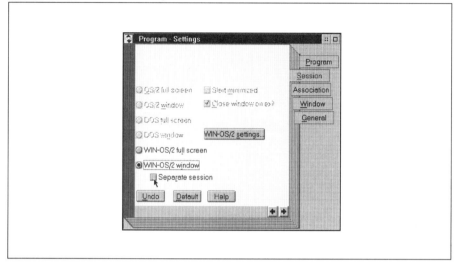

FIGURE
13-1

Windows application settings ✿

This is a substantial performance improvement, but it comes at a price. Since these programs all run in the same session, a UAE in one can bring down all other Windows applications, just as it does with native Windows. Of course, all of your OS/2 programs, and even DOS programs in other sessions, will continue to run.

Remember also that the memory allocations specified for the first Windows application will be shared by all other Windows applications in the same session. Thus, that first application should have substantially more memory allocated than it requires for its own needs.

Tip Set up the Windows calculator to start at boot time and allocate it much more memory than it needs. The calculator does not use CPU cycles when it sits idle, but it will ensure that WIN-OS/2 is preloaded, with plenty of memory, when you want to run a Windows application.

Another advantage of running your Windows applications in a shared session is that you can change the Windows clipboard from **Public** to **Private**. They can still share information since they're in the same session, and you get another performance boost.

Switching Between Windows Applications

OS/2 sessions are set up by default so that if you double-click on the icon of an object that is already open, the system simply switches you to that already open session. WIN-OS/2 sessions, however, don't have that ability. Each time you double-click on the icon of a Windows application you start a new session, using more system resources and increasing the performance delay of swapping. Use the Task Manager menu to move to the already-opened session.

When you exit a WIN-OS/2 session, the Dynamic Data Exchange facility (called Data Update in the OS/2 Task Manager menu) and the Windows clipboard both remain open. This saves time loading subsequent WIN-OS/2 sessions. On the other hand, if you know that you aren't going to be loading another WIN-OS/2 session (or at least not for a while), speed up the rest of the system by going to the Task Manager and closing these processes.

Hardware Considerations

The physical components of the computer system you are using are a considerable determinant for performance. For example, many current video adapters have extra processing power to speed up your system, particularly when you are operating in graphical environments such as the Workplace Shell. Moving up to one of these adapters can noticeably improve your system.

The speed of your disk drive is important as well. The days when 28-millisecond access time was considered high performance are long gone, and you should be looking for access times in the teens.

And, there is no substitute for raw horsepower. While OS/2 2.0 can indeed run on a 16MHz 386SX processor, you will not get the best performance. Using a 25MHz 386 system will noticeably impact performance and higher MHz rates will provide even more power.

Increasing Productivity

Some of the little niceties that increase your day-to-day productivity will occur to you as you run your favorite applications under OS/2, and many of them are application specific. However, there are some common sense approaches that you should bear in mind.

Loading and Closing Applications

If you use an application every day, try putting it in the Startup folder so it loads when the system starts. Or, move the application's icon out of the folder it is in, and bring it directly onto the desktop. Any keystrokes (or mouse strokes) you can eliminate increase productivity. Another productive maneuver is to create a separate folder for several of the applications you use regularly and have that folder open at bootup.

If you find you are closing and reloading the same applications frequently, remember that you can minimize an application instead of closing it and then retrieve it, either by selecting it from the Window List or opening the Minimized Window Viewer.

Hard Disk Space

The more hard disk space you have available, the better. With plenty of available storage, you can install new software or additional functions for existing software without worrying about whether or not you are going to have a problem with your swap file. If your accounting software has the capacity to save financial history details for many years, that's a convenience that frequently is unavailable because of storage space.

The best way to clean house on your hard disk is to take a hard look at the functions you really need and use. There are, for example, a great many functions and utilities that are part of OS/2 that may no longer be useful to you. If you no longer use the tutorial, save disk space by deleting the tutorial file, which is \OS2\HELP\TUTORIAL\TUTORIAL.HLP. If you installed all or most of the productivity aids and games and find you are not using some of them, clean house there too.

To best clean house, do not attempt to find the particular files that run the utilities you need—it is easier and safer to delete all the files in \OS2\APPS and OS2\APPS\DLL. Then, use the INSTALL program to install those items you know you will use. If you aren't sure about a particular utility, don't install it; you will gain more productivity by keeping the disk space instead of installing the utility. You can always install it later if you find you really miss it.

CHAPTER

Productivity Applications

ith OS/2 2.0, IBM has included a wide variety of programs that let you become productive immediately after installing the operating system. Indeed, a great deal of your software needs may be taken care of without you ever having to buy a software package. To examine these applications, open the OS/2 System folder, then open the Productivity folder within it for a view similar to that in Figure 14-1.

Note The applications you see in your Productivity folder reflect the selections you made when installing OS/2. These are optional parts of the operating system. If you decide to add any that were not installed originally, it's easy to do so via the Selective Install icon in the OS/2 System window.

The Calculator

Double-click on the Calculator icon to open the following window: *

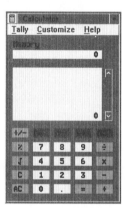

This is a great example of using a graphical interface to show how to use an application.

The menu item **Tally** refers to the "paper tape" record of your entries. The pull-down menu under **Tally** allows you to clear or print this tape. Click on the **Customize** entry in the menu bar to see the configuration

The Productivity folder

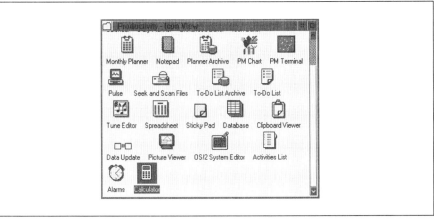

options. The first two entries in the pull-down menu allow you to switch the Calculator between two-decimal mode, such as you would find in an adding machine, and floating point mode, where more or fewer decimal places will be shown, depending upon what is needed.

The Calculator automatically switches Num Lock on, so you can use the numeric keypad for entry. When you make another window active, OS/2 switches Num Lock back off. OS/2 keeps track of the Num Lock state for each window, and restores it when that window becomes active. If for some reason you don't want Num Lock on for the Calculator, click on it in the **Customize** pull-down menu.

Note Those devoted to alternate input techniques can use the mouse to move the pointer to the desired number and click to enter it.

Clicking on **Colors** in the Customize window brings up the dialog box shown in Figure 14-2. This allows you to change the appearance of the Calculator to your personal preferences. You can also modify the appearance of the paper tape to your preference by clicking on the **Font size** entry.

FIGURE
14-2

Customizing the Calculator ✿

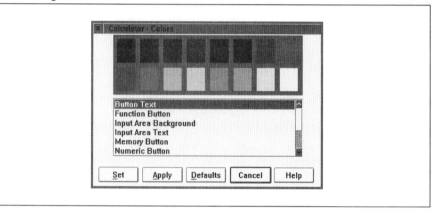

The Clipboard Viewer

The Clipboard Viewer provides a way to view the contents of the system clipboard, the storage area used when you utilize cut and paste functions. When you cut or copy, the information is stored in the clipboard. When you paste, the information is retrieved from the clipboard. The Clipboard Viewer is a way for you to monitor the information as it passes through the system.

Double-clicking on the Clipboard Viewer icon opens the viewer in its minimized state. To use it, you first must restore it. There are three different ways to do that:

☐   Press CTRL+ESC to bring up the Window List and double-click on **Clipboard Viewer**.

☐   Open the Minimized Window Viewer from the desktop and double-click on the Clipboard Viewer icon.

☐   Press both mouse buttons simultaneously to bring up the Window List.

Viewing the Contents

To see the contents of the clipboard, select **Display**, then select **Render**. The last data you sent to the clipboard will be displayed.

Option

The Options menu provides a choice between designating the clipboard as **Private** or **Public**.

When you select **Private**, information that is cut or copied to the clipboard is only available to Presentation Manager programs. If you are also running WIN-OS/2 sessions, they will have a separate clipboard.

If you select **Public**, WIN-OS/2 sessions can share information with OS/2 sessions. The clipboard for both sessions must be defined as **Public**.

Moving Data

To copy or move data from one OS/2 program to another, select the data you want to use and use the Cut or Copy command. That puts the information into the OS/2 clipboard. Make the receiving program the active window and move the mouse pointer to where the information is to be inserted. Use the Paste command in the Edit menu of your program to insert the data. (The documentation for the specific software may present slightly different instructions for these techniques.)

Importing Data

If you placed data into the WIN-OS/2 clipboard (which was a private clipboard, as is the OS/2 clipboard in this example), bring it into the OS/2 clipboard by selecting **File**, then choosing **Import**. Any information in the WIN-OS/2 clipboard is available, and you can use the Paste command to insert the data in the window you make active.

Exporting Data

If the clipboards are private and you need to copy or move information from the OS/2 clipboard into a WIN-OS/2 clipboard, first use **Cut** or **Copy** to move the data to the OS/2 clipboard. Select the Clipboard Viewer, then select **File** and **Export**. The data is now available for any WIN-OS/2 session.

The Database

One of the primary uses of a computer is the storage of data. Database applications have become one of the most popular kinds of computer programs because they frequently provide the best vehicle for both organizing and retrieving stored information. A database can be structured in a number of ways, such as relational, object-oriented, or flat file, depending on your needs and your experience with database designing.

Many database programs sell for three times the price of OS/2 and occupy the same amount of disk space. While the database included with OS/2 isn't as functional as most of these products, it is still extremely useful for managing small amounts of data, such as a phone list. In fact, it even includes a dialing function, so if your computer is connected to a modem, OS/2 can automatically dial a number for you.

Building a Database

Open the database to see the following window: *

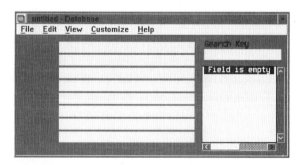

Each record in the database is composed of up to eight lines of information. It might be useful to think of the database as a collection of 3×5 cards, with each card having eight lines and each line capable of holding up to 30 characters. Each database can hold up to 5000 such cards or records.

The first step in creating a database is to assign headings for each of these lines. Click on **Edit** to view the following pull-down menu: ✱

Edit	
<u>R</u>estore record	Ctrl+R
<u>C</u>opy	Ctrl+Insert
<u>P</u>aste	Shift+Insert
Clear <u>l</u>ine	Ctrl+L
Clear <u>a</u>ll lines	Ctrl+C
<u>D</u>elete current record	
Ca<u>n</u>cel edit	Ctrl+Q
<u>G</u>raphics...	
Edit line <u>h</u>eadings	
<u>A</u>dd a new record	Ctrl+A

Click on **Edit line headings** to assign a name to each line.

The left side of the window changes color and the cursor moves to that section. Enter the headings you want to use for the database, pressing ENTER after each line to move to the next line. Each heading is limited to eight characters.

When you have completed entering your headings, click on **File**, then **Save** from the pull-down menu to see the following dialog box: ✱

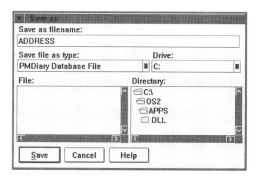

The file type has already been specified as a Database File. Enter a descriptive filename for your database, and click on **Save** to return to your database.

Tip   You don't need to specify a file extension when naming your database. The database will automatically add the extension .$$F to identify it as a database file.

Entering Information

Now you can enter records into your database. Press ENTER when you finish each line to move to the next line. When you have completed the record, click on **File** and **Save** to store that card. To add another card, click on **Edit** again, and this time select **Add a new record** from the pull-down menu. As you add records, you will see the first few characters of the first line of each card appear in the list box on the right side of the window. When you are through (and have saved the last record), simply close the window to exit the database.

 Tip   Use the **Graphics** entry in the Edit pull-down menu to dress up your information with pictures that help convey information.

Accessing Your Database

To retrieve the information in a database, click on **File**, then click on **Open** from the pull-down menu to see the following dialog box: *

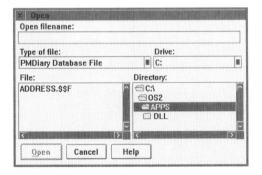

If the file you want is listed, click on it, then click on **Open**, or simply double-click on the filename. If the file you want is not shown, move through the directory to find the appropriate directory just as you have done in many other similar dialog boxes—the continuity of the Workplace Shell again makes things familiar.

The **Search Key** field helps you locate a specific record in your database. As you enter characters into the **Search Key** field, the database changes the card displayed to try to match the key you enter. When you enter a character, the database brings the first card that starts with that character to the forefront. If no card starts with that character, the database will display the card that comes closest to matching. As you continue typing characters, the database continues to change cards to try to match your key.

Of course, you may not always want to use the first line of the record for searching. Click on **View** to see the following pull-down menu: ✳

The heading for each line is displayed. Click on the line that you would like to use as your search key, and the list box on the right side of the screen changes to reflect those values. Entering information into the **Search Key** field causes the database to match cards having that information in the selected line of the record.

Printing Your Database

You can print a single card or the entire database at any time. First tell the database how you would like the output to appear. Click on **File**, then click on **Print list format** from the pull-down menu to see the dialog box shown in Figure 14-3.

The database predefines output as consisting of four columns across the page. By default, only one four-column line per record is printed, and that line consists of the first four fields in the record. Use the arrows beside each column to change the sequence in which the information is

FIGURE
14-3

Printing the database ✿

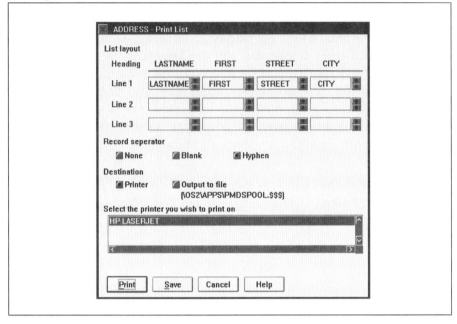

printed and instruct the database to print more than one line per record, as shown in Figure 14-4.

The **Record separator** buttons (the word "separator" is incorrectly spelled on your screen—IBM isn't perfect) allow you to determine what method, if any, should be used to separate the records being printed. If printing address labels, you would probably want a blank line between records. You can also choose to have a line drawn across the page by selecting **Hyphen**, or instruct the database to list one record after another with no separator.

The **Destination** buttons allow you to specify whether you actually want to print this report or simply send it to your fixed disk in report format. The addresses being printed here could, for example, be used by your word processor for merging addresses into a form letter by reading the report file generated.

If you have more than one printer installed, select which you would like to receive the report. Clicking on the **Print** button at the bottom causes this report to begin printing. Clicking on **Save** causes this format to be

Configuring the printing *

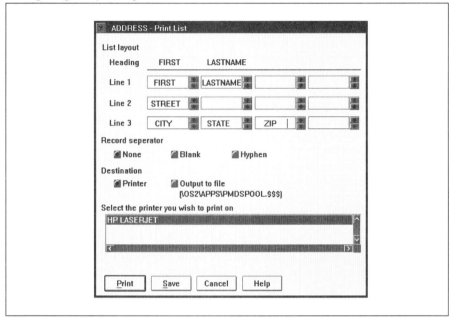

saved as the default format for reports from this database. To re-create this report in the future, you need only click on **File**, then click on **Print** from the pull-down menu, and this report format will be used automatically.

Direct Telephone Dialing

You can instruct the database to use the modem attached to your computer to dial the phone number stored in any record in your database. First, however, the database needs to know a few things about your setup. Click on **Customize** to see the following pull-down menu: *

Click on **Dial setup** to see the following dialog box: *

The first section of this box allows you to specify the serial port to which your modem is attached. The **Dialing control text** field is for specification of any control characters that must be sent to your modem in order for it to dial. The most common command set for modems is the Hayes commands. For Hayes-compatible modems, enter **ATDT** in the **Dialing control text** field. If your modem is not Hayes compatible, check your modem's documentation for instructions on the codes required to tell your modem to take the phone off the hook and wait for a dial tone.

Similarly, the **HangUp control text** field is for the commands to be sent to the modem to instruct it to hang up the line. For Hayes-compatible modems, this command is ATH.

Next, bring up the record containing the phone number that you wish to dial. Then click on **File** and click on **Dialing function** to bring up the following dialog box: ✿

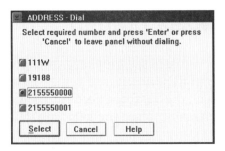

OS/2 is an international product, so it is impossible for the database to be able to determine what is a valid phone number by studying your data. Instead, it shows the value of each line that starts with a number.

Simply click on the button beside the correct phone number, then click on **Select** to dial the number.

You should be able to monitor the call's progress from your modem's speaker. If the person you are calling answers, you can pick up the handset and converse normally. When you want to hang up, either because the line is busy or you have finished your conversation, click on the **Enter** button in the dialog box to instruct the modem to close the connection.

Viewing Field Totals

The database automatically keeps a running total of the numeric fields in your records. Look again at the View pull-down menu. At the bottom are entries to display or print the statistics report. Click on **Display statistics report** to see a Totals window similar to the following: *

Field	Non-Blank	Numeric	Total
number	3	3	1.0087e+005
card	3	0	0
limit	2	2	4500
lastbill	3	3	424
	0	0	0
	0	0	0
	0	0	0
	0	0	0

Like the dialing function, these statistics look at the first character in each line. If it is a number, the field is considered numeric, and the database reads the field to the first nonnumeric character and uses that value to calculate the total. Thus, in the example, the street addresses were totaled, as well as zip codes and phone numbers. If, for example, you had a record for each of your credit cards, you could look at the total of each of the balance lines to see your total debt.

The Notepad

The Notepad, as its name implies, is designed to make it easy for you to jot quick notes to yourself. Opening the Notepad reveals the window shown in Figure 14-5. Each notepad is composed of five pages. Each page can hold up to 25 lines of text, with up to 180 characters per line.

Entering Data

As you enter information, the window automatically scrolls to show the current cursor location. Use the ENTER key to move from one line to the next. The TAB key moves from one page to the next, and SHIFT+TAB moves to the previous page.

Note   The TAB key functions can sometimes take effect slowly, so don't be alarmed if at first they appear not to work.

As you move through the pages, the first line on each page will always be visible, helping you navigate through your notes.

FIGURE 14-5

The Notepad ✿

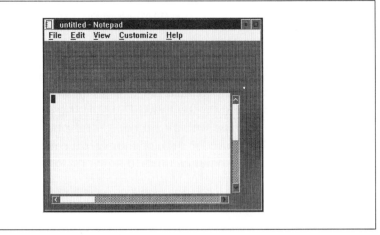

Tip You can see the complete text of any line without scrolling the window by double-clicking on the line. A message box will pop up showing the full line.

As with many of the productivity applications, you can choose **Graphics** from the Edit pull-down menu to make your notes more interesting.

Printing Data

You can open and save your notes from the File pull-down menu and you can also print your notes. Click on **Print** from the File menu to see the dialog box shown in Figure 14-6.

This dialog box allows you to tailor the appearance of the printed output with any of the following alterations:

☐   Print only the page you have brought to the front or all pages.

☐   Specify whether blank lines are to be printed or ignored.

☐   Adjust the number of lines to print per page (the maximum is 25, since you cannot have more than 25 lines on a Notepad page).

☐   Adjust printer line length. Most standard narrow carriage printers are limited to 80 characters per line using the standard monospaced font, while wide carriage printers can accommodate 132 characters on a line.

☐   Specify whether to print the output or send it to a file on the fixed disk. If you are printing and have more than one printer attached to your system, select the printer to which output is sent.

The To-Do List

The To-Do List provides an opportunity to list your chores, assign priorities to the tasks, and then sort the list according to priority, assuming you want to accomplish your chores in priority order.

FIGURE
14-6
Printing notes ✿

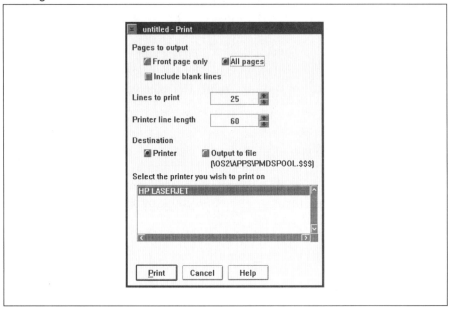

Making a List

To begin a new To-Do List, open the program by double-clicking on its icon in the Productivity folder. Select **File**, then **New** to produce the To-Do List window shown in Figure 14-7.

FIGURE
14-7
The To-Do List window ✿

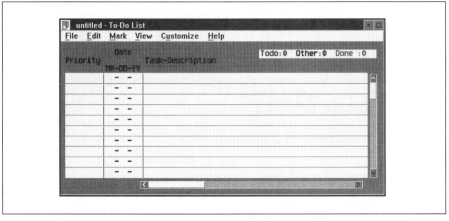

Go to the first line and enter a priority for the task, using one or two characters. The program will sort in alphanumeric order, meaning that it will read numbers from 1 to 9 and letters from A to Z. It is probably best to stick to an uncomplicated system for priorities, perhaps using the numbers 1 through 5.

Use the RIGHT ARROW key to move to the **Date** field and fill in the date. (You can set an automatic date for the current date by choosing **Autodate** from the Edit menu.)

Use the RIGHT ARROW key to move to the **Task-Description** field to enter a description of the task. If you wish, you can enter a graphical picture to enhance the description by clicking on **Edit**, then **Graphics** to produce a variety of pictures, as shown in the following: ✿

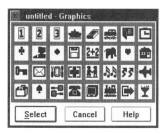

Saving a List

Once you have an entry or two in your To-Do List, save the file by clicking on **File**, then on **Save**. Name the file; the system will add the extension .T to indicate this is a To-Do List file.

Modifying the Entries

Open the To-Do List program and click on **File**, then click on **Open**. Select the file you want to work on. You can add, modify, and delete items.

As you complete the tasks, mark them as completed. Choose **Mark** to bring up a list of the choices you have for completed items, as shown in the following: ✿

Mark	
Mark current item as completed	Ctrl+M
Mark item and date stamp	
Mark item & add line to archive	
Add line to archive then delete	
Unmark Line	
Archive all completed lines	
Archive all completed lines then delete	

Archiving Entries

You can archive entries for future reference, either in addition to deleting the entries or without deleting the entries from the current To-Do List.

Archived entries are stored in a separate file and are retrieved via a separate application: the To-Do List Archive, also found in the Productivity folder. Opening that application produces the window shown in Figure 14-8.

You can sort, view, and print the entries in the To-Do List Archive file, once you have opened the appropriate file. To sort the entries, click on

The To-Do List archive ✿

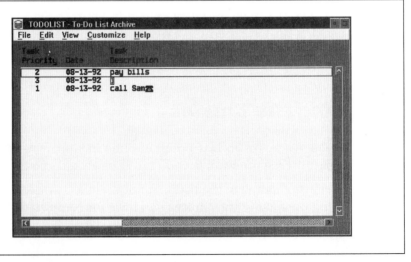

View, then on **Sort**. To view a specific entry, click on **Edit**, then click on **Find**.

The Sticky Pad

The Sticky Pad is similar to the Notepad in that it allows you to jot down quick reminders to yourself. Rather than having the information stored in a Notepad file to be retrieved, however, the Sticky Pad allows you to post these reminders on the desktop, where they stand out. Open the Sticky Pad program to see the following window:

The black area at the top of the note will be filled in by the program with the current date and time as soon as you begin writing the note. When you complete the note, tear it from the pad by moving the window for that note out of the main Sticky Pad window. You can now minimize the note and an icon will appear in the lower-left corner of the desktop as a reminder of the sticky note and number that is stored there. Double-clicking on that number will reopen the note. You can have up to ten sticky notes at any one time.

 Tip Selecting **Icon** from the Customize pull-down menu allows you to change where the sticky icons are stored on the desktop.

The PM Terminal

Accessing computer bulletin boards and information services is often done by use of a "dumb" terminal—that is, a machine with no inherent intelligence other than the ability to send, receive, and display data. Computer users can access these same services using a *terminal emulator*. Terminal emulation software allows your computer to appear to be any one of a variety of different terminal types to the host computer. Opening the PM Terminal displays the window shown in Figure 14-9.

There are a variety of entries predefined in the phone book. Access any of these services by double-clicking on the desired entry, or by selecting the entry and clicking on **Start** from the Session pull-down menu shown in the following: ❉

Session	
Start	Enter
Stop...	F4
Add...	Alt+Insert
Change...	Ctrl+C
Delete...	Delete
Setup profiles...	Ctrl+P

Since IBM couldn't know the local access numbers by which you can connect with these services, the first time you start a service you see the dialog box shown in Figure 14-10. This allows you to specify the phone number as well as any special prefixes or suffixes required by your telephone network to reach that service.

FIGURE 14-9

The PM Terminal ❉

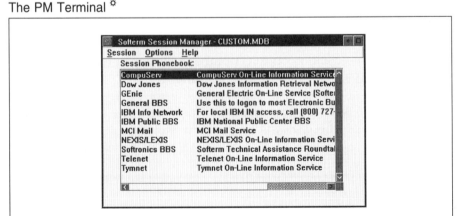

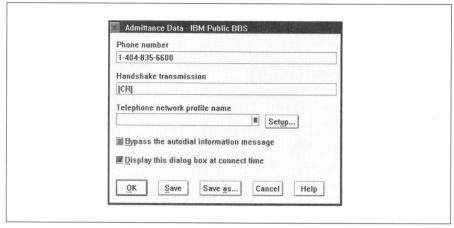

FIGURE 14-10 Entering Data in the PM Terminal ✿

Terminate the connection by selecting **Stop** from the Session menu. That menu also allows you to add, change, or delete entries in the phone book.

The **Setup profiles** option allows you to tailor the emulation used by the program to match the characteristics expected by the host. These will vary based on the service being accessed. Contact the administrator of that service for the settings required.

The Spreadsheet

Many numeric processes can be handled using a spreadsheet model, shown in Figure 14-11. Like a bookkeeper's journal, each spreadsheet is divided into rows and columns. Each block within the spreadsheet is referred to as a *cell.* Specific cells are addressed by their column and row. The cell in the upper-left corner is in column A, row 1, and so is referred to as cell A1. This program limits each spreadsheet to 26 columns (A-Z) of 40 rows each.

Each cell can contain a number, text, or a formula. It is good practice to use text across row 1 and down column A to label the fields in use so that all of the items in your spreadsheet will be easy to identify.

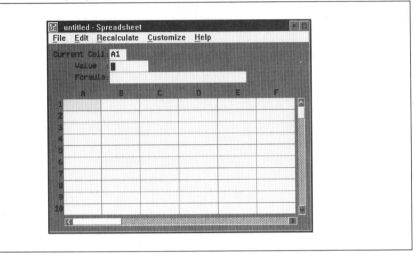

| FIGURE |
| 14-11 |

The spreadsheet program ✻

Formulas

You use formulas to indicate that the content of a cell is not a specific number, but rather the result of a calculation of the values in other cells. For example, if the contents of cell C4 should be the sum of cells B3 and D8, you enter the formula **B3+D8** in C4. Changing the value of either B3 or D8 and recalculating the spreadsheet causes cell C4 to change automatically. The spreadsheet supports addition (+), subtraction (-), multiplication (*), and division (/).

Users often total entire rows or columns, and there is a summation operator (@) for that purpose. If cell B40 is to contain the sum of all entries in the B column, you can enter the formula **B1@B39** in B40. Likewise, you could put the total of row 5 in the far-right column by entering **A5@Y5** in column Z5.

Tip You can also total a rectangular region. For example, entering **B3@C4** totals the four cells within that area.

Manipulating the Data

You can open, edit, save, and print your spreadsheets through the File menu in the same manner as the other productivity applications described.

The Icon Editor

The Icon Editor allows you to create new icons and modify existing ones. In addition, you can use this program to create and edit bitmap graphics and pointers (the icon that moves across the screen as you move the mouse).

Creating a New Icon

From the Productivity folder, open the Icon Editor to see the window shown in Figure 14-12.

FIGURE
14-12
The Icon Editor ✿

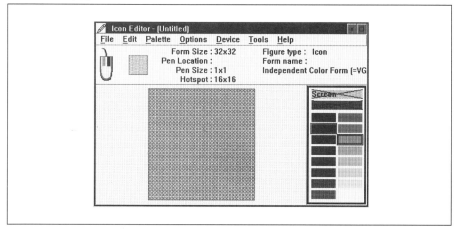

Click on **File** to pull down its menu. Click on **New** to see the following dialog box: ✿

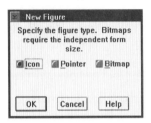

Select the **Icon** button, and click on **OK**. The empty square in the middle of the window is the canvas on which you create your icon. The color of this window is not important; it represents an invisible area and any part of your icon that contains this color will be transparent, letting the desktop background show through.

Move the pointer into the drawing area, and watch the pointer turn into a square. This square represents the tip of a pen, with which you can draw the icon. The default size is a single-pixel square, which permits extremely fine control over your drawing. On the other hand, it can take longer to fill in large areas with this size pen point. Click on **Options** and then click on **Pen size** to see the following cascaded menu, from which you can change the size of the pen point: ✿

Options		
Test	Ctrl+T	
Grid	Ctrl+G	
✓X background	Ctrl+X	
Draw straight	Ctrl+-	
Pen size	→	✓1 x 1 Ctrl+1
Preferences	→	2 x 2 Ctrl+2
		3 x 3 Ctrl+3
Set pen shape	Alt+J	4 x 4 Ctrl+4
Hotspot	Alt+K	5 x 5 Ctrl+5
		6 x 6 Ctrl+6
		7 x 7 Ctrl+7
		8 x 8 Ctrl+8
		9 x 9 Ctrl+9

The Icon Editor performs like a limited-function paint program. Select a color to use by clicking on that color from the palette presented on the right side of the window. Moving the pointer over the drawing area reveals a square the size of the current pen point. Pressing button #1 changes the area within that square to the new color. You can drag the pointer with button #1 to paint in a free-form fashion, coloring as you move the pointer. The resulting icon's appearance can be monitored in the small square beside the mouse graphic at the top of the window.

Changing the Color Palette

To change a color in the palette, first select that color by clicking on it, then click on **Palette** and **Edit color** to see the following dialog box: ✲

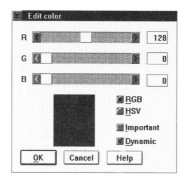

By moving the slider on the appropriate color bar, you can adjust the red, green, and blue components of the color individually and get the precise shade desired. Alternatively, you can click on the **HSV** button, and the sliders will change to indicate the Hue, Saturation, and Value components of a color.

The actual resulting color will depend upon the display adapter in your computer. Colors that cannot be displayed directly by your adapter are simulated by a process called *dithering*, the insertion of small dots of black or white to darken or lighten the base color. Icons, because of their size, can change significantly by the color of a single dot. Consequently, avoid dithered colors and paint your icons only with colors your display adapter can show directly.

The **Important** check box indicates that no matter what the display adapter, this color must be displayed. Program developers activate this for applications that are used on different display types.

The **Dynamic** check box indicates that the color in the sample box will continue to change to reflect the current value as you move the slider, rather than waiting for you to click on the arrows to select a specific value.

Once you have the color you want, click on **OK** and the new shade will replace the original in the palette. If you expect to use your new colors frequently, store the new palette using the **Save** or **Save as** choice.

When you start a new Icon Editor session, use the **Load** entry from the menu to restore your changed palette. You can, in fact, have several different palettes to reflect specific needs. If you have made changes, and know that you will be using this palette most of the time, choose **Select the default palette** to make this the color set presented every time you start the Icon Editor.

Drawing Tools

The Icon Editor has a few tools commonly found in paint programs to help your creative efforts. Click on **Edit** to see the following pull-down menu: *

Edit	
Undo	Alt+Backspace
Cut	Shift+Delete
Copy	Ctrl+Insert
Paste	Shift+Insert
Clear	Delete
Select	Ctrl+A
Select all	Alt+A
Stretch Paste	Alt+I
Fill	Ctrl+Delete
Flip horizontal	Ctrl+H
Flip vertical	Ctrl+V
Circle	Ctrl+C

There are several entries here to simplify icon development. To create a solid rectangle, for example, click on **Select** and the pointer changes to cross hairs. Move the pointer to one corner of the rectangle and drag the cross hairs with mouse button #1 to the opposite corner. The rectangle will be outlined. Select the color for the rectangle from the palette and click on **Fill** from the Edit menu to paint the rectangle.

Circles and ellipses can be drawn in much the same way. First, select the outline of the area in which the circle or ellipse should be drawn, just as you did for the rectangle. Select the color from the palette, and click on **Circle** from the Edit menu.

The same technique is used to reverse sections of the drawing, using the **Flip horizontal** and **Flip vertical** entries in the menu.

Other Options

Click on **Options** to see the pull-down menu. The **Test** entry is used for creating new pointers, and allows you to see your drawing as a pointer when the arrow is moved into the drawing area. The **Grid** entry changes the paint area into a series of squares. This can be very helpful when you are trying to align elements of your icon.

The **X background** can also be helpful in aligning elements, as well as serving as a test for the visibility of the icon when its transparent areas are over a visually busy portion of the desktop.

When using a mouse or a trackball, many people find it difficult to draw a straight line. The **Draw straight** choice is extremely helpful when you need horizontal or vertical lines; when this mode is activated, drawing lines becomes very straightforward. Move the pointer to one end of the line and hold down mouse button #1. Drag the pointer in the desired direction (up/down, or left/right), and a straight line will be drawn, no matter how much your hand zigzags.

Caution The Draw Straight mode determines the type of line being drawn from the very first movement of the mouse. It is important that your first move be in the desired direction or the Icon Editor could incorrectly conclude that you are drawing horizontally rather than vertically.

You can use **Set pen shape** to get a nonsquare drawing area. Use **Select** to define the shape desired, then click on **Set pen shape** to modify the pen point.

The **Device** entry on the menu bar provides a mechanism for developers to define different versions of an icon for different display types. Leave this in the Independent Color Form mode for your icons.

Copying Graphics

With a highly graphical application, such as a game, it can be fun to create a new icon for that game out of one of its characters or screens. This is especially useful for DOS programs, which don't come with OS/2 icons.

Open the program and when the desired image is on the screen, click on the window's system menu, and select **Mark**. Use the mouse to mark the area that you want to turn into an icon. Click on the system icon again to get the system menu, and click on **Copy**.

Now open the Icon Editor. Click on **File** and **New** to create a new icon. Then click on **Edit** and **Paste**. The image you copied into the clipboard will be rendered into icon format. You can then save the new icon, and attach it to your program.

Tip   When you save a new icon, use the extension .ICO for the filename. That is the default extension for the Icon Editor, and most other programs looking for icons know to look for it.

Personal Planning Aids

A number of applications available in the Productivity folder can help you plan your time, meet your schedules, and make your deadlines. The applications listed here and described in the following paragraphs, are all related:

- Alarms
- Tune Editor
- Daily Planner
- Monthly Planner
- Calendar
- Activities List

When a modification or addition is made in one of these applications, it is reflected in the others.

Alarms

You can set alarms to go off during the day, either directly through the Alarms program or by invoking the Alarms program through other productivity applications (details on those are in the following sections).

Setting Alarms

Opening the Alarms program in the Productivity folder brings up the Alarm Setup panel shown in Figure 14-13.

To set an alarm, click on **Alarms**, then click on **Set alarm** to bring up the window shown in Figure 14-14. Fill in the appropriate fields to set your alarms. When all the information is entered, click on **Set** to set the alarm (or click on **Cancel** if you change your mind). The fields and options are discussed in the following sections.

Setting the Alarm Number   Use the arrows to select the alarm number you want to set in the **Number** box. You can have ten individual alarms stored.

FIGURE
14-13

The Alarms Setup panel *

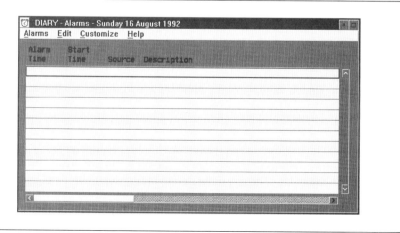

FIGURE
14-14

Setting the alarm ✿

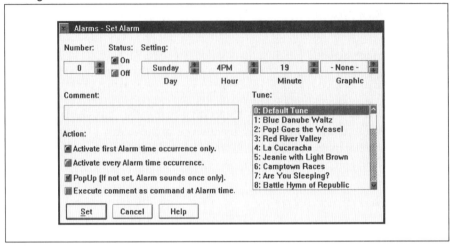

Alarm Status   The status of an alarm is either On or Off. Set the status with the **On** and **Off Status** buttons. If the alarm is set for On, all the input fields will appear and each of them can be modified.

Setting the Day   In the **Day** box, set the day(s) of the week the alarm is to sound. You can choose every day, weekdays, or Saturday through Friday.

Setting the Hour   In the **Hour** box, choose the hour the alarm is to sound. You can set any specific hour from 12 midnight through 11 P.M., or you can choose every hour.

Setting the Minute   In the **Minute** box, select the minute portion of the alarm time.

Choosing the Graphic   In the **Graphic** box, select a picture that will appear when this alarm goes off. Use the arrow to view the names of the pictures.

Alarm Reason Comment   Type a description of the reason for the alarm in the **Comment** field. If you opt to have PopUp messages with your alarm (information on PopUp follows) the description will appear on the screen when the alarm sounds.

Choosing an Alarm Tune   In the **Tune** list box, use the slider arm to view the titles and select a melody to play when the alarm goes off.

Activating Occurrences   To have the alarm sound once, when the setting first occurs, select **Activate first Alarm time occurrence only**. After the first alarm, the alarm will be turned off.

To have the alarm sound every time this alarm setting arises, select **Activate every Alarm time occurrence.**

PopUp Alarm Message Display   Choose **PopUp** to display a window with information about the alarm when the alarm occurs. Without PopUp, a tune plays at the time the alarm is to sound, but there is no accompanying explanation of the reason for the alarm.

Execute Comment   To execute a command or program when the alarm is set to go off, choose **Execute comment as command at alarm time** You must type the name of the executable file, including the path and the filename extension, in the **Comment** field.

Customizing Alarms

Click on **Customize** on the Alarms menu bar to see the choices shown in the following: ✿

The menu selections are described in the following paragraphs.

Alarm Sound Limit   Use the **Sound limit** selection to choose the number of times an alarm tune plays. Use the arrows to change the count, then click on **Set**.

Alarm Snooze Period   Like many alarm clocks that are found on bedside tables, the Alarms program provides a snooze feature. Choose the **Snooze period** selection. Use the arrows to change the value of the number of minutes before the alarm repeats, then click on **Set**.

Colors and Font Size   Use the **Colors** and **Font size** selections to customize the appearance of the Alarms program.

Set Master Planner File   You can open a Daily Planner file to tell the Alarms program to set alarms indicated in the Daily Planner. More information on the Daily Planner program follows.

The Tune Editor

You can create and edit the tunes that are used with alarms and save those tunes in files. Each file can hold up to 36 tunes. The tune file that exists in the Tune Editor is PMDIARY.$$A and it contains a number of familiar strains.

Playing Tunes

To hear any of the songs in the existing tune file, open the Tune Editor by double-clicking on its icon in the Productivity folder. Click on **File**, then on **Open** and open PMDIARY.$$A to see the window shown in Figure 14-15. The tune presented is Tune 0, the default tune for Alarms. To hear it, click on **Play**, then click on **Play current tune**.

FIGURE 14-15

The Tune file ✿

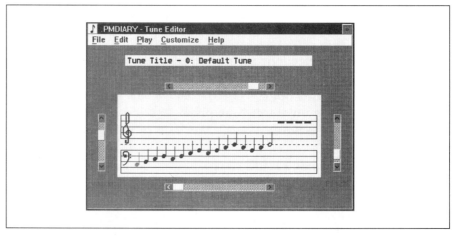

To change the tune, click on **File**, then on **Open tune** to bring up the list of tunes in the current file.

Creating Tunes

If you can read music you will find it fairly easy to compose a tune in the Tune Editor. If you can't read music, you can still have fun experimenting with sounds (and eventually you may even teach yourself how to read music).

To create a tune, open the Tune Editor by double-clicking on its icon in the Productivity folder, which produces the window shown in Figure 14-16.

To place a note on the staff, either move the slider located at the bottom of the window or move the mouse pointer to the appropriate location and click with mouse button #1.

Select the **Value** of the note by moving the slider on the left side of the window.

Select the **Pitch** using the slider on the right side of the window or by moving the mouse pointer to the correct location and clicking button #1.

The **Tempo** is controlled by the slider on the top of the window.

FIGURE
14-16

Creating a tune ✿

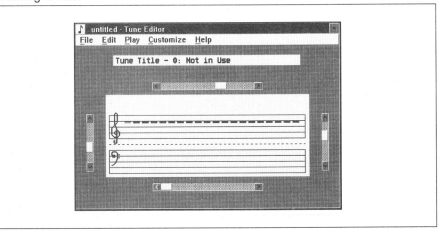

Fine-tune your tune by selecting from the choices in the **Edit** menu, as shown in the following: ✿

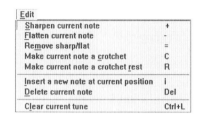

Edit	
Sharpen current note	+
Flatten current note	-
Remove sharp/flat	=
Make current note a crotchet	C
Make current note a crotchet rest	R
Insert a new note at current position	i
Delete current note	Del
Clear current tune	Ctrl+L

When you have finished, play your tune to see if you need to make more changes. Then, name that tune. Create a new file to hold that composition and add new compositions to it as the creative spirit moves you.

The Daily Planner

The Daily Planner enables you to keep a record of your activities. You can plan future activities, log those tasks you have completed, set alarms to remind you of appointments, and store your records in case you have to refer to them in the future.

Entering Activities

When you open the Daily Planner, a blank planner page is presented with the current date as the default. As shown in Figure 14-17, the following fields need to be filled in: **Start, End**, alarm time (indicated by the ringing alarm clock), alarm tune (the stacked "A" and "T"), activity type (the check mark), and **Description of Activity**. Each is described next.

Start   Enter the time the task or activity is to begin. Give the hour and minute followed by an A or P (for A.M. or P.M.).

End   Enter the ending time for the activity.

FIGURE
14-17

The Daily Planner ✿

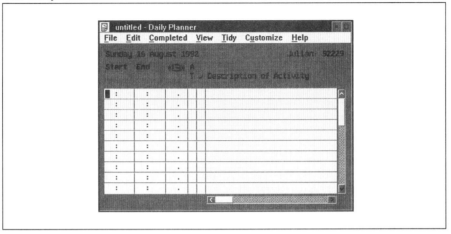

Alarm Time   Enter the number of minutes before the start time that you want the alarm to sound. Enter a number between 0 and 59. This is not a required entry.

Alarm Tune   Choose the tune that you want to hear when the alarm goes off. To select a tune, click on **Edit** on the menu bar, then click on **Select alarm tune** to see the list of available tunes, as shown in the following: ✿

Use the scroll bar to see the entire list of tunes available, click on the desired ditty, and click on **Select**. The number or letter attached to the tune will appear in the alarm tune column of your Planner page.

Activity Type   The Planner offers a chance to indicate the type of activity this item represents. Click on **Edit**, then on **Activity type** to see the list of types. Choose one, if it fits the activity, and the line will change colors. This is not a required field.

Description   Fill in the **Description of Activity** field, using up to 180 characters. You can add a graphical reminder of the activity by choosing **Graphics** from the Edit menu and picking a picture from the choices displayed.

Changing Dates

You can move to other dates and enter or view activities by selecting **View** from the menu bar and clicking on **Next day** or **Previous day**, as shown in the following: ✿

View	
V̲iew complete entry	Ctrl+V
Ne̲xt day	Ctrl++
P̲revious day	Ctrl+-
Return to t̲oday	Ctrl+T

A shortcut for moving from day to day is to use CTRL++ (hold down the CTRL key and press the plus sign) to move forward and CTRL+- (the CTRL key and the minus sign) to move backward.

Saving the File

Click on **File**, then on **Save** to save the entries. Enter a filename and the system will add the extension .D, which indicates that this is a Daily Planner file.

The most productive way to save your Daily Planner is to keep only one file; the easiest filename to use is your own name. The file will not get overly large because you are able to delete and archive the entries at will. However, some people like separate files for different types of activities or different date periods.

Modifying the Entries

Once saved, retrieve your Daily Planner file by clicking on **File**, then clicking on **Open**. When the list of Daily Planner files is presented, click on the appropriate one and then click on **Open**.

Mark as Completed   When an activity has been completed, you can indicate that fact by clicking on the activity and selecting **Completed** from the menu, which brings up the following window: ✿

```
Completed
  Mark line as completed                    Ctrl+M
  Mark line and add to archive
  Add line to archive then delete
  Unmark line as completed

  Mark all lines as completed
  Mark all lines and archive
  Mark all lines, archive then delete
  Unmark all lines as completed

  Archive all completed lines
  Archive all completed lines then delete
```

The choices regarding lines should be considered if you are only interested in the selected activity. Marking a line as completed does not remove the line from the Daily Planner for that date. You can, however, delete the line or archive it and delete it.

You can also mark all the activities for the date with the choices offered.

Archiving   To keep a history of your activities, you have the option of Archiving entries. As you archive entries, they are placed in a separate file that has the same name as your Daily Planner file but has the extension .D$A. To view, modify, or delete entries in the Archive file, use the Planner Archive folder in the Productivity folder.

Deleting an Entry   To remove an entry, click on the appropriate line, choose **Edit**, and then click on **Remove line**.

Tidying Up   If you don't want to bother going in and out of your Daily Planner file to delete and archive activities, you can periodically tidy up the file.

Selecting **Tidy** from the menu presents a range of choices that are self-explanatory, as the following shows: ✿

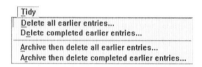

Customizing the Daily Planner

Choose **Customize** from the menu to change the color scheme and fonts that are presented when you open the Daily Planner.

Printing

Choosing **Print** from the File menu sends a list of activities to the printer. You can choose the number of days you wish to include in the printed list, starting from the current date. Use the up and down arrows to change the number of days you wish to print information about.

The Monthly Planner

To see an overview of your Daily Planner for any month, open the Monthly Planner by double-clicking on its icon in the Productivity folder.

Click on **File**, then on **Open** to see a list of your Daily Planner files. Open one of them and the Monthly Planner will present your schedule as illustrated in Figure 14-18. Activity times are shaded and at the beginning of the shaded portion is an indication of the activity. If you had selected a graphic for the activity, that graphic is on the screen. If no graphic was selected, the first two letters of the activity description are presented.

FIGURE 14-18

Getting a Daily Planner file *

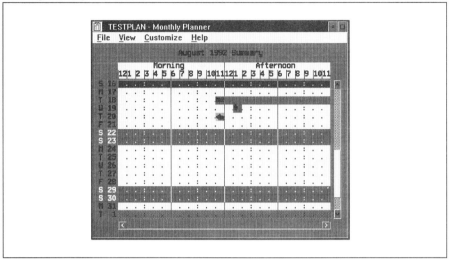

Viewing an Entry

With the mouse pointer on the appropriate date line, double-click to bring up the associated Daily Planner day.

While the Daily Planner is open, you can add, delete, change, or complete any entry just as if you had opened the Daily Planner from the Productivity folder.

The Calendar

The Calendar presents a more abbreviated view of your Daily Planner activities than does the Monthly Planner. Open the Calendar by double-clicking on its icon from the Productivity folder. Click on **File**, then on **Open** to see a list of your Daily Planner files. Select the appropriate file and the Calendar will use colors and shading to indicate the dates in which activities are scheduled, as shown in the following: *

Viewing the Entries

Double-clicking on a date will bring up the appropriate Daily Planner day. You can modify any entries for any dates in the Daily Planner and when you close the Daily Planner and return to the Calendar, any new dates with activities will be indicated.

The Activities List

The Activities List is a quick way to view the entries in the Daily Planner. Open the program by double-clicking on its icon in the Productivity folder. Click on **File**, then on **Open** to select the Daily Planner file you want to use. As shown in Figure 14-19, the Activities List for the entire file is presented in date order. You can find any particular item by clicking on **Edit**, then on **Find**.

To change the order of the list, click on **View**, then on **Sort** to bring up the following dialog box and descriptions of available choices for arranging the list: ✿

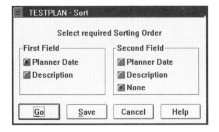

The Activities List *

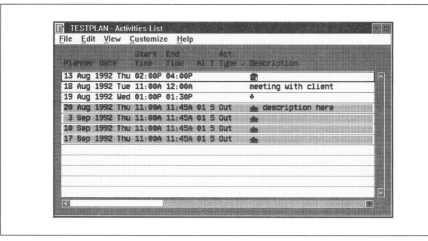

When you have the list arranged in a way that suits you, print it so you have a constant copy of your work handy, even when you are not in front of your computer.

Seek and Scan

The icon marked Seek and Scan invokes PMSEEK, a utility that enables you to search your hard disks for files or for text. Double-clicking on the icon produces the window shown in Figure 14-20.

Finding a File

To locate a file, type the name of the file in the **File name to search for** field. To direct the search, click on the **Drives to search** buttons for the disk drives you want searched. You can select more than one button. (If you specify a drive as part of the path of the filename you are searching for, the drive button will be ignored.)

During the search, matching filenames will be presented in the **Files found** list box. If you want to stop the search, click on **Stop**. Select the file you need by clicking on the filename.

FIGURE
14-20
The Seek and Scan Files dialog box *

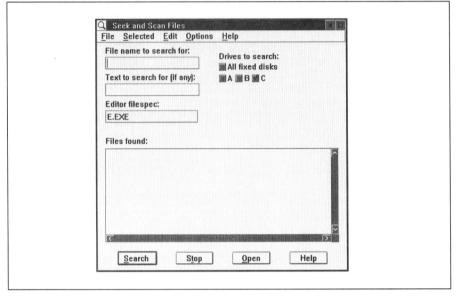

Opening a File

If the file you select is a text file, you can open it in order to view or edit it, using an editor. You must have the name of an editor program in the **Editor filespec** field. To open the file, click on **Selected**, then on **Open**.

Speed up the process of editing files found by using Drag and Drop. Make sure you can see the minimized editor icon while you are using PMSEEK.

Select the file by pressing mouse button #1, then press and hold mouse button #2 and drag the pointer (which will have changed its shape) over to the Editor icon. When you release the mouse button, the Editor will open with the selected file in the window.

Running a File

If the file that is selected is a program file, run it by clicking on **Selected**, then on **Process**.

Processing a File

To process a command such as ERASE or COPY on the selected file, click on **Selected**, then on **Command**. Selecting **Command** opens a window in which you type the command.

Finding Text

Type a string of text in the **Text to search for** field to find files in which that text appears. The filename(s) will be displayed in the **Files found** list box.

To configure how text is hunted, click on **Options** to display the choices available. If you select **Display found text**, the text itself, along with surrounding text, will be displayed, as shown in Figure 14-21.

Caution Selecting **Display found text** will slow the search considerably. If you do not want to display the text, as soon as PMSEEK finds a file with the text it will display the filename and move on. If you want the

The results of clicking on **Display found text** in the Options menu of the Seek and Scan Files dialog box ✿

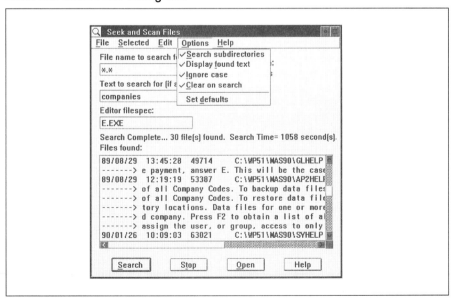

text displayed it will continue to search each file for every occurrence of that text before moving on.

Saving the Results

Once the list of files and/or the displayed text have been presented, you can choose to save the display as a file. Select **File**, then **Save**. A window will open for you to insert the name of the file, and a total of the entries saved in that file will be displayed, as shown in the following: ✿

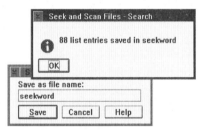

CHAPTER

Games and Fun

When the thrill of entering data into the accounting software has paled, when facing the blank screen of your word processor produces the tremors that accompany writer's block, when the boss is out to lunch, it's time for some fun. OS/2 provides plenty of opportunity to relax and enjoy yourself.

OS/2 Games

The Games folder is in the OS/2 System folder. When it is opened the following choices are available: ✱

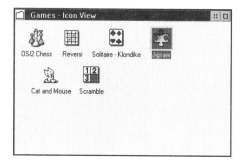

Double-click on the icon of the game you want to play.

Cat and Mouse

Not really a game, Cat and Mouse is an exercise that helps you learn how to use a mouse. Even if you are comfortable using a mouse, you'll find it a pleasant diversion.

The exercise is based on your moving the mouse. When you move the mouse, the cat chases it. When you stop the mouse, the cat nods off until the mouse moves again. As long as Cat and Mouse is open, the mouse will lurk around your screen. If you open other applications, you'll see it occasionally peek out at you from behind a window. When the cat dozes off in the absence of mouse movement, you'll see it curl up, close its eyes, and snore (several Z's will be shown over the sleeping form). If you are using software that doesn't require a mouse, such as a database or a text-based word processor, click on the mouse once in a while to wake the cat.

Cat and Mouse Controls

Opening the Cat and Mouse program produces the following window, which gives the current settings for the **Cat Set-up Control Panel**: ✿

The control panel regulates the play time, speed, and length of the steps the cat uses. Slide the control bar for each to change the settings and click on **Register** to apply the new settings. Restore the original settings by clicking on **Default**.

Play Time   In the **Play Time** field, you adjust the amount of time the cat plays with the mouse before deciding to rest.

Speed   The cat can move faster or slower as it chases the mouse, depending upon the setting of the **Speed** field.

Step   The **Step** field setting adjusts the length of the strides the cat uses when chasing the mouse.

Playing Cat and Mouse

Click on **Hide** to empty your screen of everything except the cat. Then watch the cat run all over the screen and try to catch it with your mouse. Once the mouse is on the cat, click on it to "tag" the cat. Any windows that were open on the screen will return.

If your coordination is off a bit, or the boss walks into your office, hitting the ALT key has the same effect as catching the cat.

 Note   The settings on the control panel govern the movements of the cat no matter which animal is the pursuer.

Scramble

This is a computer version of an old game that children (and many adults) play by moving tiles around inside a plastic casing. As with the hand-held game, the object of this computer version is to get the tiles into a logical order. There are several different games to choose from. Double-clicking on the Scramble icon produces the Scramble window shown in the following: ✿

After you learn how to move the tiles, you'll learn how to play the various Scramble games.

Moving Tiles

Putting the mouse pointer on a tile produces an arrow that shows the direction in which the tile can move. A tile can only be moved if it is adjacent to the blank space; the arrow will point to the blank. If there is no blank space next to the tile, no arrow will appear and the tile cannot be moved. Clicking on the tile moves that tile in the direction of the arrow (if there is no arrow the system will beep to indicate an error).

You can also use the arrow keys on the keyboard to move tiles. If a tile is poised to move in a specific direction, pressing the appropriate arrow key moves that tile. If you press the LEFT ARROW, the tile that has the blank spot to its left will move left into the blank spot. If there is no tile with a blank spot to its left, the system will beep at you.

Numbers Scramble

When you first open Scramble, the tiles show the numbers 1 to 15, arranged in ascending order, with the last square a blank. If you want to play the Numbers version of Scramble, click on Game and then click on Scramble to rearrange the numbers so they are out of order. The object is to reorder the tiles. Most people play the game to produce ascending numbers but it is just as much fun to start with the number 15 and work backward.

Frisky Cats!

Frisky Cats! is another Scramble game choice. Click on **Game** and then on **Open** to produce the following choices: ✿

To select **Frisky Cats!**, either click on the name and then click the **OK** button, or double-click on the name.

The window that opens brings up a picture showing several poses of the cute feline creature you met in Cat and Mouse. Click on **Game** and then on **Scramble** to jumble the order of the tiles. This game is more difficult than Numbers since you have to remember what the original picture looked like.

OS/2 Logo

Selecting this game produces a scrambled picture of six OS/2 logos, each in a different color. Your job is to unscramble the picture. Unfortunately, the color scheme does not match that of the OS/2 logo decals that were packed in the box that you received when you bought OS/2. So even if you proudly placed a decal on your computer or monitor, it won't help you with this game.

Autosolve

If your frustration level is easily reached, click on **Game** and then on **Reset** to have OS/2 put the tiles in the correct order.

Reversi

Another computer game based on a product sold in a box (under the name Othello), Reversi requires some thinking and planning in both offensive and defensive tactics. Double-clicking on the Reversi icon produces the following game board: ✿

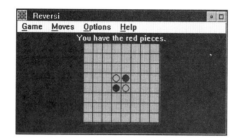

The computer manipulates the blue circles and you control the red ones. The object of the game is to have more red circles on the board than blue ones when the game ends. You turn your opponent's blue circles red by strategically surrounding blue circles with red circles. When all the squares are filled or neither player has a legal move available, the game ends and the score is displayed.

Moving the Circles

A move is the placement of a circle into a blank square so that a circle (or a line of circles) of one color is flanked on both sides by the other color. Once a color is flanked by the other color, the outflanked circle changes to the color of the circles that lie on either side of that circle or row. Flanking can be horizontal, vertical, or diagonal. Clicking on a blank square that fulfills this requirement puts a red circle there. As you move the mouse around the board, if a square will complete the flanking maneuver the pointer changes from an arrow to a crosshatch mark. If you click on a square that is not showing a crosshatch mark, the system will beep at you.

 Note   One move often will produce a flanking in more than one direction.

Playing Reversi

The game opens ready to play. Red (you) must make the first move, unless you pass and force the computer to go first. To pass, click on **Moves**, then on **Pass**. You may decide, after you have played a number of games, that there is an advantage to giving the computer the first move. There is no built-in advantage to you either way; if an advantage is present it is because of your own particular playing style.

 Note   Except for this discretionary pass to begin the game, you can only pass when you have no legal move open to you.

When it is the computer's turn, it flashes a message informing you that it is thinking. The time involved in thinking will change as the skill level changes (see the discussion of levels in the upcoming "Selecting the Skill Level" section).

Hints

Remember to plan a defensive as well as an offensive strategy each time you move. That means that choosing a move that merely turns a great many blue circles to red circles is not necessarily the best strategy.

There is an advantage to getting your red circles into the boxes along the edge of the game board. If you can get a red circle into one of the squares along the edge, that circle has less chance of being outflanked. In fact, once you've played enough, you'll learn how to make sure circles on the edge don't get outflanked. At the same time, it is possible to "tempt" the computer to permit its circles to be outflanked in the edge squares.

The four corner squares are the most desirable. A circle placed there cannot be outflanked by the opposition. However, the squares next to these corners can be the most dangerous, since you may be giving the computer an opportunity to outflank that circle and, in doing so, land in the corner. Particularly dangerous are the squares in front of the corners, on a diagonal. Avoid placing a red circle there.

Try to keep the pattern of circles compact; don't go far out on a diagonal or into the next-to-last rows early on in the game.

You can ask the computer for a hint by clicking on **Moves**, then clicking on **Hint**. The computer will place a crosshatch mark in the most advantageous square (don't worry, the computer really tries to help you, it doesn't set you up for its own victory).

Selecting the Skill Level

Clicking on **Options** presents this choice of skill levels: ✿

The level that is grayed out is the current one; the default is **Beginner**. Choosing a higher level, of course, affects only the skill level of the computer. You will have to depend on your brain and experience to raise your own skill level. The computer thinks for a longer period of time when the playing level is raised, which does slow down the game slightly. However, offsetting that is the added challenge you face playing an adept opponent.

Solitaire

The OS/2 version of solitaire is Klondike Solitaire. For the uninitiated, that means it is the basic solitaire game where the object is to find the aces and build on them, suit by suit. You do this by stacking cards in descending order along seven columns. These columns are not stacked by suit, but must be laid upon each other in alternating colors in descending order of the value of the cards.

The game ends when the stacks of similar suits are complete through to the king, or when no further plays are possible.

Playing Solitaire

Double clicking on the icon brings up the window shown in Figure 15-1.

Tip Click on the Maximize button in the upper-right corner of the window to make the playing area full-screen.

Transferring Cards to Columns

Begin moving to other columns any face-up cards that are capable of being moved. A card can be moved if it will complete these requirements: it must be the opposite color of a card in another column and the next card in descending numerical order. For instance, you can move a black 4 onto a red 5. Drag the card by the drag-and-drop technique using either mouse button. You don't need to place the moving card directly on the receiving card; if you release the button when the card you're moving is anywhere on the correct column, the card will drop into place automatically.

FIGURE
15-1

Klondike Solitaire ✿

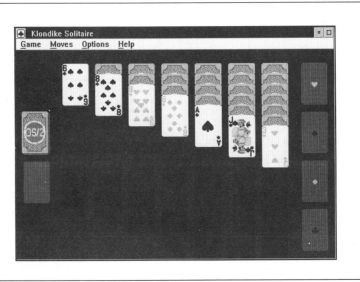

If a move results in an empty column, you may move only a king (and any cards on top of that king) onto the empty column.

Continue to move any *exposed cards* until you have no more legal moves available (sometimes the opening deal exposes cards that provide no legal moves at all, a bad sign but not necessarily fatal).

Exposing Cards from the Deck

Whenever you run out of legal moves using the exposed cards, you can begin to expose the cards in the deck. Click on the deck to turn over a card or several cards; the variation of the game determines the number of cards turned over from the deck. The default game variation is to draw three cards at a time from the deck and *flip* (turn over and start again) the deck as many times as you care to continue to play. More discussion of the possible variations follow later in this chapter.

When you draw three cards you can see all of them but you only have access to the card on the top, as shown here:

If you can move that card onto a column or a stack (the stack is discussed in the following section), the card below it is available for movement.

Starting the Stack

If an ace appears, either drag it over to the appropriate stack on the right of the playing area or double-click to have the system place it on the stack. If a 2 of the same suit as an ace in the stack becomes available, move it to the stack.

Tip Don't be too hasty to move a 3 on top of a 2 if all the stacks haven't been started. You may need the 3 to remain in the column in order to provide a place to park a 2 of a suit that has not yet had an ace placed on the stack.

The Options Menu

Klondike Solitaire gives you a number of options to choose from; you see the list of alternatives by clicking on **Options** to produce the following window: ✿

Colors

Clicking on **Colors** produces the following choices: ✿

The seasons refer to the color of the background. If you want to change the colors of the elements on the playing area, select **Edit** and change the red, green, and blue values of the colors using the slider bar.

Sound

You can choose to have the system beep at you when you attempt an illegal move. Toggle the beep ON or OFF by clicking on **Sound**. Incidentally, the illegal move will be refused whether you wish to be beeped at or not.

Score

Scoring can be turned OFF or ON. The choices offered also include an option to reset the score and start again instead of letting the score accumulate as you play.

Scoring for solitaire is as follows:

☐ You begin the game with 500 points.

☐ To play a game, you must ante up 52 points.

☐ Each card moved to the stack is worth 5 points.

☐ Each flip of the deck deducts 25 points.

☐ You lose 5 points if you take a card from the stack and put in back on a column.

Time

Clicking on **Time** activates a readout of elapsed time on the playing area. Clicking on **Time** again toggles off the readout.

Drag Cards

Another ON/OFF toggle, when **Drag cards** is turned OFF, the card you are manipulating is miniaturized as you drag it and pops back to full size when you place it on the column or stack.

Variations

This choice determines the method by which you get cards from the deck. The choices are shown in the following, with the current variation grayed out: ✿

Draw 3, Flip none
Draw 3, Flip 3
Draw 3, Flip unlimited
Draw 1, Flip unlimited

Animation

This is the speed at which cards are dealt, with choices varying from slow to very fast. When the system deals the cards you see the movement from the deck to the columns. Choosing **None** means that cards will pop into the proper place automatically. While this speeds up the game, it does detract from the illusion of real play.

Card Back

This option lets you choose which design you want on the back of the deck of cards. There are nine choices; the current choice has a check mark next to it, as shown in the following: ✿

Special Moves

You have several options for special moves while playing, as shown in the following: ✿

Moves
Take back	Ctrl+T
Replay	Ctrl+R
Cheat	Ctrl+C
Auto finish	Ctrl+F

Take Back and Replay

To undo your last move, click on **Take back**. To reverse your undo, click on **Replay**.

Cheat

This is one of those little things that distinguishes OS/2 from other graphical operating systems. The **Cheat** option permits you to make one move regardless of whether or not the move is legal. You could put a red 5 under a red 3 if you wished. While you are cheating the pointer changes color. Each click of the **Cheat** option permits one move, but you can click **Cheat** as often as you feel you need to.

 Caution If you cheat and win, OS/2 will stage a victory celebration for you—complete with fireworks—and announce not only your glorious victory, but also the number of times you cheated during the game.

Auto Finish

When it is clear that you will win and you don't want to go through the effort of dragging or clicking the remaining cards from the columns to the stacks, click on **Auto finish** to let the system move the cards for you, after which the victory celebration will display.

The Game Menu

The two choices in this pull-down menu are shown in the following:*

If you think the game you are playing cannot be won and you don't want to keep trying, click on **New (Deal)** to initiate a fresh deal.

Auto play is not terribly exciting, but if you need a demonstration of the game it is useful. Some people use it to show the fun of running a multitasking system, letting Solitaire autoplay in one window while running other applications in other windows. To stop it, click on **Auto play** again.

Hints

Always remember that it is more useful to take cards from a column than from the deck. If you have a black 9 on a column and a red 8 available on another column and the other red 8 is on the top of the deck, choose the red 8 from the column. Exposing the face-down cards on the columns is a consistently more productive practice.

Try to use cards from the most full column first. For example, if one column has a red 6 at the bottom and there are two black 5's available, pull the 5 from the column with the largest number of face-down cards.

Don't rush to move cards over to the stack—you may need them on the column in order to move a lower card of a different color that is on a column you want to start exposing.

You can move laterally, taking part of one column to another column. Sometimes this is useful to exchange cards of the same number and color in order to move one of them to the stack.

Chess

Opening the chess game produces the following window that asks you to set up the players for the game: ✿

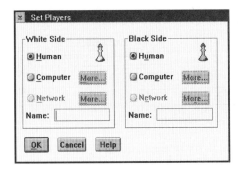

You can play the computer, another person at your computer, or even someone who is playing from a different workstation if you are on a network.

Choosing Players and Colors

You must tell the computer what type of players are playing and select a color for each player. Select **Human** or **Computer** or give a network ID if it is a human at another workstation. Incidentally, while the traditional colors for chess are black and white, and OS/2 Chess uses that terminology, you'll probably find that the black pieces are red. There is no explanation for this anywhere in the OS/2 Chess online documentation. It does, however, make the board more colorful.

If you are not on a network, the network option will not be available. If you are on a network, click on the **More** button to see a list of known network IDs.

If you select the computer for either player, click on the **More** button to determine the level of expertise at which you want the computer to operate.

The human player may be identified by name, but it is not necessary. When you have finished filling out any fields that you wish to, click on **OK** to display the chess board shown in Figure 15-2.

Moving the Chess Pieces

Chess is a fairly complicated game and it would be impossible to attempt to teach it here. If you have any experience at all with chess, or at least understand the way each piece moves, you can have a lot of fun with OS/2 Chess.

You move the pieces with the drag-and-drop method—either mouse button will work.

The menu items available in Chess are varied and plentiful.

Chess ☼

Game Choices

Clicking on **Game** produces the pull-down menu shown here: ☼

New

New starts a new game at any time. When you click on **New** you are asked if you would like to save the current game. Answering yes stores the game in its present condition, along with the names of the players and the date. You are not asked to name the file; OS/2 gives it a unique filename and stores it as OS2\APPS*nnnn*.PMC where *nnnn* is a numerical arrangement that seems not to be sequential.

Load

Clicking on **Load** produces a list of saved games so you can choose the one you want to resume.

Save

Click on **Save** at any point to store the game at the current point. Even if you continue to play, you are able to reload the game at any time and pick up play from the point at which you saved it. This is a clever way to see what would have happened had you made a different move just after saving the game.

Delete

Clicking on **Delete** brings up a list of all saved games. Highlight the game you want to delete and click on the **Delete** button.

Print

If you want to study or even preserve for eternity the condition of the board at any point in the game, clicking on **Print** produces a graphic printout of the gameboard.

The Options Menu

Clicking on **Options** produces this pull-down menu: ✿

Set Players

Clicking on **Set Players** produces the same window seen when you first open the Chess game. Use it to change the name of the human players and the level of the computer's skill.

Set Position

Use this option to move all the pieces except the kings off the board so you can place them wherever you wish to start a game. This gives you an opportunity to reenact a game you may have read about or played at some other time in noncomputer form.

Set Colors

This option produces the following window, in which the board and background colors can be changed to any combination of hues that pleases you: ✿

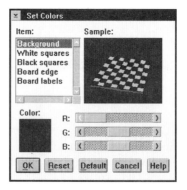

Select the item you want to re-color and move the **R**, **G**, and **B** (red, green, blue) sliders to produce the colors you want.

Sound

Toggle the error beep OFF and ON by clicking on this choice.

Warning Messages

If you make an illegal move you may opt to have the system tell you why it is illegal by choosing to have warning messages ON. If you toggle this choice OFF, the system refuses to place an illegally moved piece but provides no explanation.

Label Board

Toggling this option to ON results in the board being labeled with alphabetic characters in the horizontal positions and numeric characters in the vertical positions. This is useful in Algebraic Chess Notation, the notation method used by OS/2 Chess.

There are a number of different ways to annotate a chess game and the use of Algebraic Chess Notation is a common one. Every move can be recorded by the starting and ending squares involved in the move, using the row and column labels on the board. (A brief explanation of Algebraic Chess Notation is given later in the chapter.)

Keyboard Entry

Those comfortable with the Algebraic Chess Notation system can enter moves via the keyboard. When you choose this option, you are presented with the following window: *

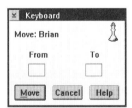

The player whose turn it is to move is noted by the system, and the cursor waits for the notation labels to be entered. If you plan to play most of the game through the keyboard, drag the Keyboard window so that it is no longer in the game window. As you type you can see the pieces move on the board.

Time

Just as in a match, the elapsed time for each move is kept by the system. As soon as a move is completed, the other player's clock starts. When that move is made, the first player's clock begins again. To see this, click on **Time** to bring up the following Time Elapsed window: ✺

Take Back Move

You can undo the last move you made by clicking on this option.

The View Menu

The View menu gives you an opportunity to see information about the game in progress as well as make some changes in the setup.

Move Status

Clicking on **Move status** produces the following window: ✺

Game Record and Algebraic Chess Notation

A history of the game's progress (in Algebraic Chess Notation) is presented in the Game Record window, shown in the following: ✿

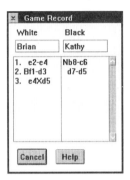

Understanding the notation is not difficult if you understand the codes. A letter indicates each piece except pawns, which have no letter marking in the notation. The pieces are represented with these letters:

Knight N
Bishop B
Rook   R
Queen   Q
King   K

A move is indicated by a hyphen between the starting and ending square. If the move results in the capture of a piece, an X is placed between the starting and ending square. If the move puts the opponent's king in check, a plus sign is used; if checkmate then two plus signs.

For example, Nb6Xd8 indicates that a knight, starting on b6, captured a piece by moving to d8.

Valid Moves

All of the available valid moves for the current player are listed in the Valid Moves window, shown here: ✿

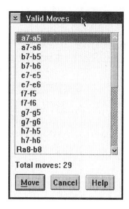

If you are the current player, click on the move you want to make. Use the slider bar to move through the list if it is longer than the window. As the game goes on, of course, this list gets shorter.

Analysis

This is the computer's suggestion for the best line of play.

Captured Pieces

A graphic representation of the pieces that have been captured is presented in the Captured Pieces window, shown in the following: *

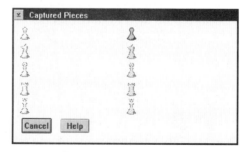

Rotate Board

You can rotate the board as though it's on a lazy Susan by using the slider, as shown in the following: ✿

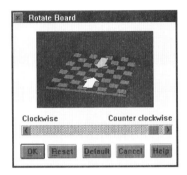

Flip Board

This choice turns the board 180 degrees.

The Network Menu

The Network menu options permit you to send a message to another player, list the network users, and disconnect yourself from the network.

Hints

Chess pieces are not equal; some are more powerful than others and therefore considered more valuable. Chess players never tire of the debate about assigning values to pieces but it is not easy to arrive at an evaluation system. Too much depends on the position of a piece on the board or whether or not it is vulnerable. However, it is generally agreed that a bishop is more valuable than a pawn and a queen more valuable than any other piece.

During the beginning phases of a game, the center of the board is more important and you can use your less valuable pieces to try to control those squares. The opponent still has plenty of less valuable pieces to use for a counterattack and you don't want to lose a rook, for instance, to a pawn.

Don't spend time moving the same piece several times; this makes it difficult to gain momentum for an attack.

Decisions on tradeoffs change depending on the progress of the game. At the beginning, it may be worthwhile to trade a bishop for a good capture while protecting a knight. While there are still a lot of squares filled, the bishop is often less mobile. Towards the end of the game, with a better chance of having a clear diagonal path, the bishop should be protected and the knight sacrificed.

It is always a good idea to set up for the capture of a valuable piece just before making an aggressive move to put the opponent in check. While the king is being protected, you take the other piece.

It is a rule of thumb in chess that if you castle early you protect your king better.

Jigsaw

After opening this object by double-clicking on the Jigsaw icon, click on **File,** then on **Open** to select which puzzle to play. As you see in the following window, you have access to all the drives and directories to find puzzles: ✿

By default, you are pointed to the directory where OS/2 has placed the puzzles provided with the system.

The **Open filename** field displays a mask for files with an extension of .BMP. A puzzle with the filename of OS2LOGO.BMP is listed in the **File** field. Double-click on that to open the puzzle. As Figure 15-3 shows, the puzzle is assembled so you can see what it looks like.

Jumbling the Puzzle Pieces

The first step is to break up the picture into its jigsaw pieces. Click on **Options**, then on **Jumble** to produce a pile of puzzle pieces as shown in Figure 15-4.

Arranging the Pieces

The first thing you notice is the lack of workspace—you don't have the space available that you do when solving a physical jigsaw puzzle. Most people use the edges of the table or puzzle board to hold pieces until they figure out where to put them.

A picture of the completed puzzle ✿

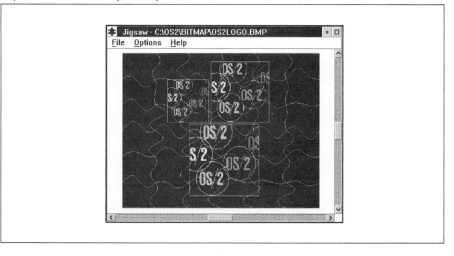

FIGURE 15-4 Jumbled puzzle pieces ✿

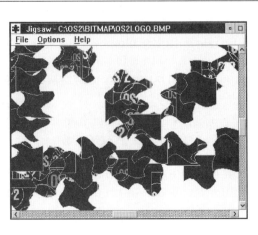

You can create some workspace by making the puzzle pieces smaller. Click on **Options**, then on **Size** to change the size between small, medium, or large.

Tip The smaller the piece, the more room there is to work. However, at the small setting, the details of any printed characters on each piece disappear and you will have to rely on shape to assemble the puzzle. Most of the time choosing medium works best.

Assembling the Puzzle

The drag-and-drop technique, using mouse button #2, moves the pieces.

Begin moving pieces around the game area with an approach much the same as that used when assembling a physical jigsaw puzzle. Generally, people fill in the edges first. It is easy to see which pieces are edge pieces, so move those toward the appropriate sides of the game area.

Note It is never necessary to rotate a piece.

As you place the pieces along the proper edges it is useful to pile the other pieces up in the middle of the board to create working room for yourself. This procedure, as shown in Figure 15-5, gives you a clearer view for assembling the edges.

Now begin to move the edge pieces, starting with placement of the corners. Then, matching shape and contents, put the individual pieces together. Of course, many of the shapes are similar (OS/2 didn't want to make this too easy) but you will hear a two-tone beep when you have made the right connection.

Note Once connected, pieces will stay together when you move them.

After the sides are assembled, begin on the pile of pieces you left in the center of the game area. Using shape and contents, finish putting the puzzle together.

Selecting a New Puzzle

Click on **File,** then on **Open** to bring up the Open window. Again, the field marked **Open filename** is filled in with *.BMP. But, it is highlighted,

 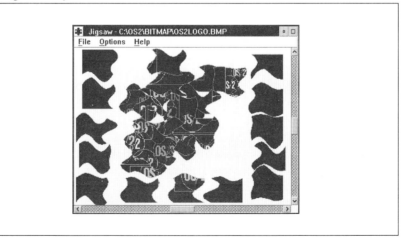

Stacking center pieces in the center ✿

which means that as soon as you press any key the current entry is replaced by the keystrokes you make. Type *.* and press ENTER to see the other puzzles available. If you chose to install additional bitmaps during the OS/2 installation process you will see an entry named LIGHTHOU.VGA in the list of files. Double-click on that to bring up a new puzzle.

Adding Games

There are plenty of sources for games and fun for OS/2. Your local user group, electronic bulletin boards, and the OS/2 forum on CompuServe are all likely sources.

CHAPTER

Selecting Software

*T*he ability of OS/2 2.0 to run DOS, Windows, OS/2 16-bit, and OS/2 32-bit applications means that it can run more software than any other desktop operating system. This gives users of OS/2 an edge in software purchasing, since almost any application written for a PC can be purchased with confidence.

This wide range can also bring confusion. Which packages will run best? Which will integrate well with other programs in the system? Which will slow down other programs running simultaneously? Which will require additional hardware?

DOS Programs

The ability to run multiple DOS programs from the Workplace Shell Desktop is an attractive feature of OS/2 2.0. It helps you move to OS/2 without having to replace your software. You can continue to operate all of your DOS programs and benefit from OS/2's faster file system, Workplace Shell, and preemptive multitasking.

Usually, DOS applications are more economical to purchase, but that should not be a significant yardstick now that you have moved to OS/2. DOS applications aren't written to run in a window, nor are they written to share information dynamically with other applications. OS/2, of course, assists in bringing DOS programs closer to the state of the art that OS/2 represents by furnishing DOS windows and by providing a cut-and-paste mechanism to and from those windows.

DOS applications, however, cannot fully exploit the capabilities of OS/2. They don't detect and adjust to changes in window size and they don't support Workplace Shell functions such as drag-and-drop. They don't have access to the Adobe Type Manager (ATM) fonts. Most importantly, they aren't programmed to use multiple threads that provide efficiency for overlapping functions. Remember, a multitasking operating system affords more than the ability to run multiple applications at the same time—that same multitasking environment empowers individual software programs to do more than one thing at a time, providing that power is programmed in.

Also, most software companies currently put new features, new capabilities, and new innovations only into their Windows and OS/2 versions.

The main exception to this is in the world of games, which continue to be developed predominantly for DOS.

All in all, while DOS compatibility is great for allowing you to continue to run existing programs, you should probably not consider buying much new DOS software in the future.

Windows Programs

Windows programs bring much of the visual interface that OS/2 users expect, and some do use some degree of multithreading to improve performance. Many Windows programs support integration features such as Dynamic Data Exchange (DDE). For the most part, running multiple Windows programs in OS/2 provides a very stable environment; many users prefer OS/2 to native Windows because of the preemptive multitasking environment. If you need to, review Chapter 12 closely to determine compatibility problems before purchasing any Windows applications.

OS/2 Programs

While many OS/2 programs fully exploit the capabilities of the operating system, some do not do justice to OS/2. One way to determine how fully software uses the power of OS/2 is by noting how the software "got" to OS/2. Almost all OS/2 software can be traced to one of three roots:

☐ It was ported from DOS (or Windows) to OS/2.

☐ It was converted from DOS (or Windows) to OS/2

☐ It was written for OS/2

At this point in the history of OS/2, the majority of OS/2 software falls into the first two categories. As explained in the following paragraphs, there is a difference between a ported program and a converted program, with the latter more desirable. Of course, you probably can't tell by looking at the software package in a retail store whether the software was ported or converted, so a key phrase to look for is "exploits OS/2." Also, make it a habit to read reviews and comments in publications you believe to be accurate and trustworthy. In the following discussions, all references to DOS include Windows.

Ported DOS Software

When a software company opts to take a DOS program and port it to OS/2, it provides a quick way to supply software to OS/2 users. *Porting* means that any parts of the original DOS program that would cause problems in OS/2 are changed. Depending upon the language in which the software was written, this can be onerous or quite simple. Developers have to be aware of the restrictions imposed by the protected hardware mode that OS/2 operates in; they have to be aware of the memory management issues. Some things that the software may have done in DOS are unacceptable in OS/2. Even if you are not a programmer, if you think about the things you've learned about OS/2 you can see why certain programming procedures may cause problems.

For instance, remember the section titled "Checking the Swap File." in Chapter 13. One of the things you learned was that the operating system swaps data out of memory and then brings it back when your applications need it. Only the data is saved for your use. However, also in memory are the program files that run the applications. When OS/2 needs the memory for other things, those program files aren't swapped to disk and retrieved when you want to move on in your work. OS/2 discards program code because it knows where it is on the disk and can retrieve it as needed.

That sounds very efficient, unless you write a program that alters the original programming code during use, depending on changes the user makes. In DOS, those changed programming instructions remain in memory; when you exit the software, the code is saved back to disk in a changed condition. In OS/2, that changed code can be (and probably will be) discarded and the original version of the program brought into memory when needed. DOS programmers who wrote self-modifying code had to restructure their approach in order to port their programs to OS/2. However, since that style of programming is not the standard, most DOS developers were able to port their software to OS/2 with minimal effort.

The bottom line is that ported programs are merely DOS programs with anything that interferes with OS/2 taken out. That's not quite the same thing as exploiting the power of OS/2.

Converted DOS Software

DOS applications *converted*, or rewritten, to take advantage of the power of OS/2 are more productive than ported programs. Converted programs go through all the alterations that ported programs do, and are then reexamined and rewritten to add additional strength and fully utilize OS/2's power. For example, not only are the protected mode hardware issues considered and any problems avoided, in many cases programmers take the opportunity to look carefully at those portions of code that interact with hardware and rewrite them.

Consider the interaction with the parallel printer port. A program must be redesigned so it no longer grabs the port (as it can in DOS) since that port is shared by all applications running at the same time. A proper conversion means the programmers may have rewritten the portions of code that control the printing and implemented separate threads, multitasking within the software. If the code is rewritten, printing is a separate task and your work in the application is more productive. Other functions within the software may also have been examined for the possibility of creating separate programming threads to take advantage of the multitasking abilities of the operating system.

While this conversion takes more time than a simple port, the result is software that operates more robustly under OS/2 and, given the choice, you should opt for it.

If the program is a Presentation Manager application (more on this later in the chapter), a real conversion was probably effected.

Software Written for OS/2

Applications written for OS/2 are designed from the ground up to exploit the multitasking capabilities of the operating system. The individual tasks performed by the software are programmed as separate threads to maximize productivity. This empowers sharp response while performing background operations.

There are few things more frustrating than the prolonged appearance of an hourglass or clock on the screen. It is a clear indication that the program has decided you cannot do anything else on the system until it finishes some task. Certainly there are times when this can't be helped, but a surprising amount of individual tasks within a single software application can be multitasked. By and large, a program should always let you perform more than one task at a time.

Even if the program must prevent you from doing any other tasks, it should release the keyboard and mouse so you can interface with other programs.

 Note   OS/2's preemptive multitasking makes sure that other programs continue to run in the background. The application doesn't have to allow that explicitly. On the other hand, you don't want a program that allows periods of time during which you can't bring other windows to the foreground and use the mouse or keyboard.

OS/2 2.0 also enables 32-bit programs. These are programs that exploit OS/2's ability to work on larger amounts of data, providing greater capacity and speed. They will almost certainly be faster than their non-32-bit equivalents. If the program is a spreadsheet, it will likely handle more rows and columns. If it is a communications program, it will probably handle faster connection speeds. If a word processor, the program will keep up with your keystrokes even while programs such as spell checking or grammar checking run in the background. In other words, 32-bit programs are likely to be the best purchase for optimizing productivity.

User Interface Issues

The look and feel of the software you purchase should match the OS/2 interface, creating a consistent workplace that makes moving between software applications less burdensome.

Common User Access Programs

Software programs that use the standards of IBM's CUA (Common User Access) specifications offer a menu bar containing File and Help in addition to software-specific menus, provide contextual help whenever you press F1, and present dialog boxes that have a consistent look and feel, including OK and Cancel buttons.

Additionally, applications that conform to CUA ensure that you will know, automatically, quite a bit about running the program. Details such as the layout of the menu bar, accelerator keys, and so forth are common across all CUA applications, greatly simplifying the learning process.

Presentation Manager Programs

Software properly written for OS/2 interacts with the Presentation Manager. PM programs can access any device attached to your system for which OS/2 has installed a driver.

PM programs also can access the ATM fonts in your system, improving the look of your screens and reports. Properly written programs will utilize not only the fonts you installed with OS/2, but also any additional ATM fonts you acquire and install later.

Workplace Shell Programs

Workplace Shell programs have been written specifically for OS/2 2.0, and will be 32-bit programs. Workplace Shell functions, such as drag-and-drop, provide many new features to simplify using your system. Programs should be written to exploit this interface, including such features as accepting files dropped upon them.

 Note The Workplace Shell is new for version 2.0 of OS/2. The number of applications exploiting it is not large just yet, but the number is growing rapidly.

Hardware Issues

The protected mode character of OS/2 makes hardware compatibility a significant issue.

Memory

OS/2 shields the user from most concerns regarding the amount of memory a program requires. Its virtual memory function allows the program to see as much memory as it needs. Still, an exceedingly large program can increase the amount of paging taking place, which may adversely affect performance. This may not necessarily pose a problem, but you may need to do some tweaking in order to prevent problems. (For details, see Chapter 13.)

Displays

These days most programs are written to support all standard video adapters and resolutions. OS/2 makes that easier, in fact, by providing a generic interface that can be resized automatically. Still, not all programs support all adapters. Make sure that your configuration is supported.

Special Adapters

If the software requires a specialized adapter card, make sure that there is an OS/2 device driver for that card.

Getting Advice

When making a major software purchase, it pays to spend some time reviewing the choices before making a decision. There are several resources available to help you do that.

Dealer Assistance

At one time, when people returned to the same dealer for all computer needs, the dealer was a great place to get good advice and assistance in understanding hardware and software issues. However, the proliferation of discount superstores and the mail order channel means that well-informed dealers are not as easy to find as they used to be. There are exceptions, and it is worth your time to seek them out, but if you typically shop for price instead of maintaining a relationship with a dealer you trust, you are well advised to check other resources as well.

Publications

There are dozens of computer-related magazines, most of which are carried in bookstores. A quick review of many of them shows detailed side-by-side comparisons of related products. This should make it easy for you to find the product that best suits your needs.

Online Services

Another good resource is electronic access to local bulletin boards and online services like CompuServe. Most major software vendors have a presence somewhere on CompuServe, PRODIGY, GEnie, or BIX. This gives you an opportunity to talk directly with the vendor and with the users of the vendor's products.

User Groups

Computer user groups, established under the philosophy of "user helping user," exist all over the country. Within each of these organizations are usually special interest groups (or SIGs) that meet to share information. SIGs are formed around specific software packages or software types. Most user groups have an OS/2 SIG, and any retail computer store or local electronic bulletin board system can point you to the user group meetings. The feedback you get from people actually using the software you are considering is better than any marketing hype found in advertisements. Talking to users means you can learn how the product really works for those who depend upon it.

Other Issues

As you look at reviews, ask questions, and even call the vendor (a good idea that is surprisingly easy to accomplish with many software companies), consider several issues that extend beyond the straightforward functionality of the software's day-to-day ability to complete tasks.

Installation

Because the installation procedure is frequently an omen of things to come, a program that takes frustrating hours to install is unlikely to make you happy over time. The installation program should detect your hardware, configure itself automatically, and give you the flexibility of deciding which subdirectory to place it in. And it should *never* automatically update your CONFIG.SYS or AUTOEXEC.BAT files without giving you the opportunity to see the changes suggested and permitting you to make them manually if you wish to.

Online Assistance

Opening a manual each time you want to try something can be exceedingly frustrating. Applications should have full reference information online, including contextual help, which is the capability of the program to detect what task you are involved in and bring up help panels that are directly related to that task.

A tutorial is also a great help. It is often beneficial to walk through sample tasks using demonstration data before trying them with your data.

Configurability

You should be able to tailor the application to your specific needs and wishes. Application designers must try to set up a reasonable set of defaults for a program. Things such as report layout, window size and location, colors, fonts, accelerator keys, and usage of other features may all be established in advance by the vendor.

It is presumptuous of the vendor, however, to assume that their configuration is the best one for you. Programs should provide an easy technique with which to alter these settings to mold the environment precisely to your needs.

Once you have changed what you want to change, you should be able to make your preferences the default setup. You don't want to go through a customization process each time you run the program.

There may be situations in which you would like to save multiple configurations; the software should provide this facility. The Workplace Shell, for example, allows you to set up several different entries in the Scheme Palette for the desktop layout. You can change your current setting at any time by simply dragging the appropriate scheme to the desktop.

The Warranty

In the past, the only warranty on most software was on the distribution diskettes themselves. They could be returned for a replacement set (often with the user paying shipping and handling to replace the vendor's manufacturing error). Now, you frequently get 30 to 90 days to evaluate the package. If you find it unsuitable, you can return it for a complete refund. That policy is true of OS/2 itself. The dealer or other company from which you purchased the product may offer such an evaluation period, even if the software vendor does not.

For OS/2, one of the issues to consider is the one of hardware compatibility. If the product is apparently not "talking" to OS/2 drivers, that is ample reason to return it.

 Note   No product will be warranted to be an answer to a specific computing need. That is highly subjective; it is up to you to determine whether the software works in your environment before purchasing it.

Support

There should be a period (often the first 30 to 90 days) during which telephone support is free. Following that period, many software vendors have established schemes for supporting your day-to-day use of the product. It is important that the support organization includes technical personnel who understand OS/2 and the attendant issues.

 Caution   Some vendors provide telephone support via 1-900 telephone numbers, which have an automatic fee added to your phone bill.

Sometimes support via bulletin boards and online services has advantages over telephone support. On the phone, you are only going to ask about your specific problem. While browsing online discussions, however, you are likely to find a number of valuable tips and techniques to enhance your use of the product. You might find additional files for downloading, with enhancements such as additional macros or bug fixes. Look for other OS/2 users for specific hints and procedures about maximizing your use of the product.

Update Policies

All software is updated, enhanced, fixed, and otherwise altered on a regular basis. The vendor should have some way of notifying you of changes and new versions as soon as they are available. Additionally, software vendors writing applications for OS/2 should be aware of updates and enhancements to the operating system and adjust their programming accordingly.

CHAPTER

Insiders' Tips

*T*hroughout the development and beta testing of OS/2 version 2.0, quite a number of people had the opportunity to play with the operating system. Since the release of the final product, the same people have continued to test and stretch the powers of OS/2. Corporate computer supervisors and users have experimented and learned a great deal, and consultants have seen user problems and innovations at client sites. From all of these people, most of whom have helped other users just beginning their adventures with a powerful multitasking operating system, we have collected tidbits, shortcuts, undocumented errors, and undocumented tricks. Some of the more interesting and useful items are presented in this chapter.

To start off, if you have installed the optional bitmaps, click on the Workplace Shell desktop background once with mouse button #1 and press CTRL+ALT+SHIFT+O (that's the letter *O*, not a zero).

Installation Tips

During the installation process there may be some problems, caused either by your hardware/software configuration, general system problems, or even a disaster like a power outage. All of those things have happened to users, who have offered the following solutions.

Grabbing the README File

A README file is contained on the OS/2 diskette set, and there is a lot of good information in that file about installation. However, you can't get to the file until you have installed OS/2. After reading the file, if you discover you have some of the hardware and/or software that may cause problems, you may have to go through some of the installation procedures again.

There is a way to see the README file before beginning the OS/2 installation. The README file is on diskette #6, and you can manually unpack the file and read it before installation.

1. Boot the Install disk and, when prompted, insert disk #1.

2. When there is a prompt telling you that you can press ESC to cancel installation, do so. You will get a command prompt for drive A. Copy the file UNPACK.EXE from disk #2 onto your hard disk. Insert disk #6 into drive A. Make your hard disk the current drive and type **UNPACK A:\REQUIRED . /N:README**.

The README file will be on the hard disk. You can reboot your computer normally, load the file into a word processor, send it directly to the printer or view it with the TYPE command.

Recovering from an Aborted Installation

You may on occasion have your installation aborted, for example, if there is a power loss. If you have passed the first reboot and are into the main graphical installation, you can pick up the installation procedure at the point of stoppage without going through all of the preliminary steps.

1. You must know which disk was being unpacked when the procedure stopped.

2. Subtract that disk's number from 16 and add 1. For example, if you were on disk #9, then your magic number would be 8.

3. Boot from the Install disk, and insert disk #1 when prompted to do so.

4. When you are told you can press ESC to cancel, do so. This results in a command prompt.

5. Use a text editor to edit the CONFIG.SYS file on the hard disk. There is a line starting with FIRSTDISK and you need to edit that to be FIRSTDISK= (*the disk that was being unpacked at the time of failure*). (See step 1.)

6. In the line starting with NUMDISKS, edit that so it reads NUMDISKS= (*the number from step 2*).

7. Remove the diskettes and reboot from the hard disk. You will see the install panel. Select OK, Install, and all defaults. You will be

prompted for the disk from step 1, and all of your previous installation choices will have been saved.

 Tip As mentioned in the chapter on installation, after installation and
before you run any DOS or Windows programs, shut down your system.
This only needs to be done once, immediately after you are finished
installing OS/2 2.0.

Fixing Hardware Problems with Install

There have been reports of installation problems or failures due to
hardware issues, sometimes because of incompatible hardware and other
times because of incompatible system setups.

Hard Disk Controllers

Some customers with AT-bus(ISA) systems have had disk controllers
that are not recognized or supported by 2.0. OEM drivers for their disk
controller may not yet be available. Some of the symptoms include an
extremely slow installation procedure, a lot of noise (like a grinding
sound) from the hard disk during the installation, errors in FDISK during
installation, and error messages about unrecognized disks.

1. Use DOS to edit the CONFIG.SYS on diskette #1, which is the first
   diskette after the Install diskette. Change the line
   BASEDEV=IBM1S506.ADD to REM BASEDEV=IBM1S506.ADD.

2. Boot the Install diskette and go through the installation procedure
   up through the first five diskettes.

3. You are told to reinsert the Install diskette. After you do that and some
   files are copied, you are told to remove the Install diskette and press
   ENTER to reboot. Do not remove the diskette; leave it in drive A.

4. Press ENTER with the Install diskette in the drive and the system will
   reboot. However, it is booting into the Install diskette. You will be

told to insert diskette #1. Do so. Watch the screens carefully and look for the screen that tells you to press ESC to exit. When you see that message, press ESC.

5. This brings up a command prompt. Enter the following commands:

   RENAME C:\OS2\IBM1S506.ADD IBM1S506.XXX
   COPY C:\OS2\IBMINT13.I13 C:\OS2\IBM1S506.ADD

6. Remove the diskette from the drive and reboot your system. When you are booted up, the installation program will begin again at the point where it left off.

General Hard Disk Problems

Sometimes there is a general failure during installation and it is clear from the error messages that the problem is with the hard drive. Look for one of the following problems:

☐ The hard disk may be corrupted and near failure.

☐ OS/2 is unable to identify the adapter. Do you have some type of no-name, incompatible system?

☐ The drive is compressed using a stacker utility (although an OS/2 version of Stacker is in development, at the time of this writing it had not been released).

☐ There is a Beta version of OS/2 2.0 on the hard disk (you can install OS/2 2.0 over a copy of OS/2 1.3). If you have Beta 2.0, you must reformat the drive.

☐ There is a problem with the hard disk controller.

Supported Drives

OS/2 specifically supports hard drive adapters that conform to the Western Digital chipset interface standard, which includes almost all of the MFM, RLL, IDE, and ESDI adapters and Adaptec, Future Domain, and IBM SCSI adapters. This is true for ISA and EISA bus machines.

In addition, there is generic INT13 support for all other hard disk adapters, including devices like Iomega's Bernoulli and SyQuest's removable media products.

CD-ROM support is included, but as of this writing the OS/2 CD-ROM driver does not work with every available CD-ROM device. However, the DOS device drivers can be configured and installed to provide CD-ROM support for DOS and Windows programs.

BIOS Problems

There are many manufacturers of PC equipment and many versions of each of their products. OS/2, more sensitive to hardware issues than DOS, may need a more recent BIOS than that installed in your system. If you suspect BIOS problems, check with the manufacturer regarding compatibility with OS/2. There has been a rumor floating around since the release of OS/2 2.0 that AMI BIOS chips that are not very recent will not support the new version of the operating system. We have not found that to be true; in fact, a large portion of this book was written using a machine with an older AMI BIOS, booting into OS/2. It is a fact, though, that there have been problems with older AMI Keyboard BIOS. This problem extends to software beyond OS/2; WordPerfect support personnel have dealt with this problem many times, for instance.

Specific Hardware Compatibility Problems

There are some potential compatibility problems with the following adapters and devices.

All Adaptec Adapters   SCSI hard disks must be configured as SCSI target ID 0 or 1 to be able to start up from that hard disk.

Adaptec AHA-154x   With an IBM 0661-320MB SCSI drive, the adapter BIOS will not recognize the drive as target 0 or 1 (drives 80, 81). For OS/2 2.0, the drive can be used as a non-startup drive.

Adaptec AHA-174x   For the IBM WDS-3180-80MB SCSI and IBM WDS-3160-160MB SCSI drives, the adapter will not recognize these drives when configured in Standard Mode (AHA-154x emulation). The

AHA-174x adapter should be configured in Enhanced Mode, which is supported by the OS/2 2.0 drivers.

Future Domain TMC-850/860/875/885 w/BIOS revision level 7.0 and Future Domain TMC-1660/1670/1680 w/BIOS revision level 2.0 In IBM Models 35 and 40, when the Future Domain adapter is controlling the startup diskette, you may get the message "Disk read error has occurred" when you start the Installation diskette. Contact Future Domain for a free BIOS upgrade.

SCSI Adapters The AMI "Fast Disk" and AMI "Fast Disk II" SCSI adapters are incorrectly identified as Adaptec adapters. Before the first reboot and after you have completed installation, delete from CONFIG.SYS any line with the following:

BASEDEV=AHA1xxx.ADD (where x can be any character)

Make sure the line BASEDEV=IBMINT13.I13 appears in CONFIG.SYS.

Bernoulli Boxes 44 and 89MB drives will work if connected to any SCSI card other than Bernoulli's own card. The drive will work as a large diskette and will be non-bootable.

PROCOMM+ The SCSI MCA adapters do not work and you should contact PROCOMM for information about OS/2 support.

IBM 16-bit SCSI Cards (early versions) Early versions of the IBM 16-bit SCSI adapters may experience problems and erroneously report that the device is not functioning. You can get an upgrade from IBM.

Display Hardware Problems

If the installation procedure stops after diskette #6, your VGA adapter might be causing a problem. You need to get your hands on the documentation that came with the adapter. If the adapter has auto-sense capability, find out how to turn it off. If the adapter has various resolutions available, make sure the adapter is set to 640x480 mode.

Miscellaneous Installation Tips

Be sure your CMOS setup parameters are set properly. There have been a number of problems reported that turned out to be connected to CMOS inaccuracies, particularly regarding floppy disk drives.

Shadow RAM should be disabled. RAM should have sufficient wait states and precharge cycles.

The AT bus should run at 8 MHz if there is an indication that it will not be reliable at a higher speed (check the documentation or ask the manufacturer).

If you are using the IBMINT13.I13 driver to access an MFM, RLL, or ESDI hard drive, and the hard drive has more than 1024 cylinders, make sure the sector translation mode is enabled.

Certain Quantum IDE hard disks will need a ROM update, which is available at no charge from Quantum.

Like DOS, OS/2 2.0 "out of the box" can only be installed from drive A (unless your BIOS supports booting from drive B) or across a network. If you have the wrong disk size, go back to your dealer and exchange the disks. Another alternative is to swap floppy drive cable connectors and change the CMOS parameters, and then install from the new drive A. If the floppy drive cable connectors are not the same, use an adapter.

 Tip   There is software on Compuserve (GO IBMOS2) that allows you to install OS/2 from drive B.

Mouse Tips

There have been some occasional problems reported with 50 MHz systems (AT-style bus) with a mouse, where the mouse gets out of sync. Input will function through the keyboard, but it is recommended that you shut down the system and restart to get the mouse back in sync.

The mouse selection menu provided when installing is a bit confusing to Logitech Mouse owners. The Logitech Mouse selection should be chosen only if you have a Mouse Systems PC Mouse or a Logitech C7 or

C9 serial mouse. All other Logitech pointing devices are Microsoft-compatible, and you should select the appropriate Microsoft driver.

Other Pointing Devices

There is an undocumented function you can use with the mouse device driver. If you have another pointing device such as a tablet or touch screen, it can be used in addition to the mouse.

Install the device driver for the device with a DEVICE= statement in CONFIG.SYS (the device must have an OS/2 device driver). Then, add the following to the end of the DEVICE=C:\OS2\MOUSE.SYS line:

STYPE=xxxxxx$

where the xxxxx$ is the name of the device (from the device driver manual).

When you reboot, both pointing devices will be available to you.

COM Ports

OS/2 COM ports do not have to be defined in sequence, and you could have a COM4 without having a COM3. DOS, however, will probably have some problems if there is a gap in the port definitions. To avoid any problems in DOS, you can define COM ports that do not have any physical adapters attached in the COM.SYS statement. These substitute definitions will serve as placeholders.

COM1 and COM2 are assumed to have standard values and do not need to be set up unless you have non-standard values to tell the operating system about.

To enable COM3 or COM4 on an ISA system, place the following line in CONFIG.SYS:

DEVICE=*X*:\OS2\COM.SYS (*n,a,i*) (*n,a,i*)

where

□   *X* is the drive where OS/2 is installed

    ☐ n is the COM port that you are attempting to access

    ☐ a is the communications port I/O address (03E8, 02E8, for example)

    ☐ i is the IRQ level, which is usually a jumper setting on the I/O adapter

For example, to put COM3 at address 03E8 on IRQ5 and COM4 at address 02E8 on IRQ10, use the following statement:

DEVICE=C:\OS2\COM.SYS (3,03E8,5) (4,02E8,10)

The I/O address and IRQ level are usually found in the manual that came with your adapter. Sometimes these are fixed, but usually they can be reset via jumpers or switches. If the values are fixed or the available settings are not broad enough to avoid a conflict, you are going to have to buy a more versatile adapter or simply never use both adapters at the same time.

Setting the IRQ on an ISA System

Table 17-1 shows the 15 standard Interrupt Request Level assignments on ISA systems, which will give you guidelines for changing the COM3 or COM4 port adapters.

The IRQ levels shown as Open have no standardized assignment. When you set IRQ values for COM3 or COM4 ports, you will probably find these IRQ levels available without conflicting with another adapter.

If you don't have two parallel ports installed, IRQ5 may be used for COM3 or COM4. Be judicious about this, however, because it will cause problems if you install a second parallel port later. Also, make sure no other non-standard device is using IRQ5.

When trying to avoid conflicts, you could discover that 8-bit adapters cause problems. Except for IRQ9, only 16-bit adapters can use IRQ levels higher than 7. Table 17-1 shows that the low-numbered IRQ levels

TABLE
17-1

Standard IRQ Assignments

IRQ	Device
0	System timer
1	Keyboard
2	Secondary interrupt controller (cascade)
3	COM2 (serial communications port 2)
4	COM1 (serial communications port 1)
5	LPT2 (parallel port 2)
6	Diskette
7	LPT1 (parallel port 1)
8	Realtime clock
9	Open
10	Open
11	Open
12	Open
13	Math coprocessor
14	Hard disk
15	Open

already have some function assigned. It may be that the only way to avoid some IRQ conflicts is to buy a 16-bit adapter.

Interrupt conflicts are particularly common for non-standard 8-bit adapters. For example, the SoundBlaster adapter is configured at the factory to use IRQ7, which is the ordinary assignment for LPT1. You may never notice this while running under DOS because DOS printing usually does not use the interrupt. OS/2 2.0 does use it, though, and the conflict can cause printing problems.

Some people have found that, after years of running their systems under DOS, the interrupt on their parallel port card doesn't even work or perhaps doesn't exist. Under DOS, this usually has no effect, but with OS/2, the problem becomes apparent as printing either becomes erratic or just doesn't occur.

Displays

To have a colorful, interesting command line prompt in OS/2 sessions, edit CONFIG.SYS. Try setting the SET PROMPT= statement to

$e[32;40m$e[1m[$P]$e[0m

Using that string in the Prompt statement in AUTOEXEC.BAT will accomplish the same thing in DOS, as long as you have loaded ANSI.SYS.

Display Problems

There are some known problems with display adapters that pop up occasionally due to incompatibilities with settings of software or hardware.

SVGA Display

The following Super VGA boards have been tested and found to work with OS/2 2.0 for DOS applications that make use of SVGA modes. It is important to note that there were a limited number of boards tested, and it is quite probable that there are many more adapters that are supported.

☐ Orchid ProDesigner IIs by Orchid Technology (ISA and MCA versions)

☐ Trident TVGA by Trident Microsystems, Inc. (8900b and c levels)

☐ STB PowerGraph VGA by STB Systems, Inc.

☐ Video Seven VRAM II by Video Seven

☐ Boca Super VGA by Boca Research Inc.

☐ VGA Wonder XL Series by ATI Technologies, Inc.

☐ Paradise VGA Professional by Western Digital Imaging

☐ ATI 8514 Ultra

Note The 8514 Ultra by ATI must be installed as an 8514. It will default to high-resolution mode. You must update CONFIG.SYS so that the statement DEVICE=\OS2\MDOS\VVGA.SYS is changed to DE-VICE=\OS2\MDOS\VSVGA.SYS.

If you are going to run Windows or OS/2 applications in SVGA modes, you need to contact the manufacturer of your computer or SVGA video adapter in order to get device drivers and installation instructions.

SVGA ON Program

If you have one of the video adapters listed above or another video adapter that you are sure is supported by OS/2 2.0, and you want to run DOS or Windows applications that will use SVGA, you have to turn on OS/2 2.0 SVGA support.

The OS/2 Installation program detects the video chip in the system, not the type of adapter the video chip is on. As long as you are sure you have a configuration that is supported by OS/2, you can enable SVGA.

To do so, use the SVGA.EXE program that resides in the \OS2 directory. The syntax is SVGA [ON] [OFF] [STATUS]. To turn on SVGA, type **SGVA ON**, which generates a file named SVGADATA.PMI in the \OS2 directory. The command must be entered at a DOS full-screen command prompt; do not enter it from a DOS window session. Reboot your computer after turning on SVGA.

Note Typing **SVGA OFF** at a full-screen DOS prompt deletes the .PMI file (you must reboot after entering the command), and entering **SVGA STATUS** returns the chipset type that the operating system believes your adapter contains.

When you have SVGA ON, you can use 132 column modes in an OS/2 full-screen session and you can paste an SVGA image to the clipboard.

Many different SVGA boards have unique characteristics, and you may find that some boards work better with SVGA OFF.

SVGA Redraw Problems

With some SVGA displays, if you switch to the PM desktop while the screen is still redrawing, you may find problems with the display on the desktop. Switch back to the SVGA screen until the redraw finishes.

DOS Display Errors

If you receive the error message SYS3176 whenever you attempt to open a DOS session or DOS application, you may be able to solve the problem, which is related to SVGA support in OS/2, using the following steps:

1. In CONFIG.SYS, set RMSIZE to 624 instead of 640.

2. Change the DOS setting in the object for HW_ROM_TO_RAM to ON.

Using ANSI.SYS

If you want to use ANSI colors and characters in your DOS sessions, you must add the statement DEVICE=C:\OS2\MDOS\ANSI.SYS to CONFIG.SYS. Remember, you must reboot to have changes made in CONFIG.SYS take effect.

8514 Display

If you have an 8514, in order to run a WIN-OS/2 full-screen session you need to change the DOS Settings so that VIDEO_8514A_XGA_IOTRAP is set to OFF and VIDEO_SWITCH_NOTIFICATION is set to ON.

When running a WIN-OS/2 full-screen session with an 8514 adapter in high-resolution mode, be careful not to switch to another session while an application is updating the screen or while the hourglass is on the screen.

Network Issues

To view the contents of a network printer object, some users have found it productive to use a long refresh interval or to set the interval to 0 (no refresh interval). Experiment with your system to see which works best.

If you move the network object into a folder from the desktop, the network printer-object template will not be there the next time you boot up. Move it back to the desktop and restart the system.

Printers

There have been some reports of "workaround" solutions for certain printers that were troublesome when used with OS/2 2.0. As problems and solutions are reported for other printers, the information will become available on CompuServe (GO IBMOS2) and BBSs.

Cannon Bubblejet   Use one of the following drivers:

☐   For the BJ10E, the IBM42xx driver will emulate an IBM Proprinter X24E.

☐   For the BJC800, the OS/2 Epson driver will emulate an Epson LQ2550.

☐   For the LBP8 III+, use either of the above, depending on the emulation you want.

HP DeskJet, DeskJet+, DeskJet 500, DeskJet 500C   Install   the OS/2 Epson driver and select HP DESKJET 500. The HP DeskJet 500C will not produce color output even using the HP DeskJet 500 device support in the Epson printer driver.

HP LaserJet   If there is an existing driver when you install the OS/2 HP LaserJet printer driver, delete all the old *.FNT files first. Delete the printer driver from the OS/2 Workplace Shell printer object, and answer Yes when asked if the driver files should be deleted from the hard disk.

HP PaintJet and PaintJet XL   Use the Micrografx PaintJet printer driver (SMGXPJET.DRV), which you will find on Printer Diskette 3.

IBM 3812, 3852, 5152, 5182, 5201-1, 5216   Printer drivers were not shipped with OS/2 2.0 for these printers because they have been out of service for a number of years. However, you can use the printer drivers shipped with OS/2 Version 1.3, which can be downloaded from Com-puServe (GO IBMOS2) or ordered via the order card in your OS/2 package.

NEC P3200   Use the OS/2 Epson driver and choose EPSON LQ-850.

NEC P6200   Use the OS/2 Epson driver and choose EPSON LQ-2550.

STAR NX-1000   Use the OS/2 Epson driver and choose EPSON LX-800.

Non-Supported Printers

If your printer is not supported by an OS/2 2.0 printer driver, check the printer documentation to see which emulations are available and then select the appropriate driver to match the emulation. Also, call the manufacturer to see if an OS/2 driver is available.

Printing Problems

During investigation of problem reports, a number of printing prob-lems have been addressed and solved.

Nothing is Printing

If nothing prints to a parallel port, make sure you have installed the correct printer driver for your printer. If the printer driver is right, check the following things:

☐   Make sure your parallel ports are configured properly. See the IRQ section above.

☐   Make sure your cable meets the correct specifications. Some cables do not and therefore cause printing problems. Cables that are too long are frequently a problem. A 6-foot maximum has been found to be important on some high-speed microprocessor systems, and a 10-foot maximum should generally be applied.

☐ Some cable does not have all the interface signals wired. This did not cause a problem with DOS, because DOS does not use all the signals in the parallel-port interface. But additional interface signals are used to send data under OS/2 2.0. Purchase a cable that has all the signals wired.

If you still cannot print, and you are convinced it is not caused by any of the above problems, there might be a problem with your I/O adapter. Some older parallel-port adapters do not generate hardware interrupts. These adapters usually work correctly under DOS, since DOS does not use hardware interrupts to print. The OS/2 2.0 operating system waits for the printer to send an interrupt to indicate that the printer is ready for more data. If your adapter does not provide this signal, you need to buy one that does.

Another indication of an interrupt problem is erratic printing, such as the printing of one character followed by an error message on the printer or the constant illumination of one of the lights on the front of the printer.

Printing Stops

Printing stops usually occur in a DOS application that is printing PostScript. Here is a possible solution:

1. Cancel the print job that caused the printer to stop printing.

2. Open the printer-object settings notebook to the Queue page.

3. Turn off the PRINT WHILE SPOOLING checkbox.

4. Resend the print job.

Printer is Offline

If you send a print job to an offline printer, and then put the printer online and say Yes to the Retry query on the screen, the job may not print correctly. Instead, cancel the job and send it again (after making sure the printer is online).

Printing in DOS, Not in OS/2

If your printer worked well under DOS, but does not work under OS/2 2.0, that is the symptom of a problem with your IRQ or printer cable. See the previous sections for solutions.

Print Job Spools but Does Not Print

The spooler will not print a job until the sending application closes the print-data stream. There are some DOS applications that do not close the print-data stream right away.

If you can see your print job as an icon with an arrow pointing to the document in the Job Icon View window, the job will not print. The arrow must point from the document to the printer. Until the application closes the data stream, this will not happen.

Use the DOS_DEVICE DOS setting to load the C:\OS2\MDOS\LPTDD.SYS device driver. Then the PRINT_TIMEOUT DOS setting can be used to close the print job without your having to close the offending application.

Print Job Goes to Multiple Spool Files

Some DOS applications open and close the printer data stream for every character, line, or page, creating separate spool files. If the software company does not have a fix for the problem, you will have to disable the spooler, using the Spooler object in the System Setup folder.

If this problem only occurs with complex printouts and does not seem to be a problem with the entire application, you can increase the DOS setting PRINT_TIMEOUT value.

Printing from a WIN-OS/2 Session

If your printer is connected to LPTx or LPTx.OS2, check that the OS/2 spooler is active. Also, make sure the WIN-OS/2 printer does not use the Print Manager by disabling the Printer icon in the WIN-OS/2 Control Panel.

When the OS/2 spooler is active, WIN-OS/2 software prints directly to it, so print jobs can be spooled from one WIN-OS/2 session or multiple WIN-OS/2 sessions.

If you are using LPTx but are unable to print from any other session, you must use LPTx.OS2 for WIN-OS/2 printing. If you are printing to a redirected port, you must use LPTx.OS2.

Fax Support

If your fax adapter operates well as an ordinary modem, but does not work correctly as a fax device when you are in a DOS session, it is probably a problem with the VCOM.SYS device driver. VCOM.SYS sometimes introduces timing distortions into the commands that are used to control the fax device but are not a part of the asynchronous communications used for normal modem communications.

There are no standards established for fax controls, so if this is happening, it may mean that the only solution is to purchase an OS/2-based fax device driver and application software. Check with the fax adapter manufacturer for information on availability of OS/2-based software.

You can also try removing the VCOM.SYS statement from CONFIG.SYS. While this may make your fax adapter work well, it might have other disagreeable side effects.

One of the things VCOM.SYS does is to provide a performance-expediting function. Without VCOM.SYS, you may have to lower the baud rate of your modem transmissions. In addition, some applications, such as Prodigy, require VCOM.SYS. You need to weight the alternatives before making a decision about these solutions.

If you have an ISA bus system, you can change the fax adapter so that only part of your system detects it. Then do all operations in a single DOS session. You can accomplish this by setting up your fax adapter as COM3 or COM4. Since there are no standards for COM3 or COM4 on an ISA system, OS/2 2.0 will not recognize the adapter unless it is defined for the system in the CONFIG.SYS file. (See the section on COM3 or COM4 setup earlier in this chapter.)

To create this configuration, set the hardware switches on the fax adapter to indicate either COM3 or COM4. Use a setting that is available and that does not conflict with any other adapters in your system. You can keep VCOM.SYS in CONFIG.SYS, but do not define the fax adapter settings to the COM.SYS device driver. When OS/2 2.0 starts up, it will not recognize the fax adapter, but the normal communications ports will still get the gains of having VCOM.SYS working for you.

Then set up a DOS session that loads the DOS software you use for faxing and also loads the DOS device driver used to manage the fax adapter (if it came with a driver). This single DOS session should now be able to access your fax adapter without problems.

If this doesn't work, it is probably because the DOS software treats the adapter as a COM port instead of directly accessing the adapter as hardware. This means, of course, that DOS will not see the adapter either. The big problem is that this single DOS session controls the adapter. Other DOS or OS/2 sessions will not be able to access it at all.

IBM is working on a fix for this problem, but in the meantime, the solution to fax problems is the use of OS/2-specific device drivers and software.

HPFS in a Nutshell

While there are lengthy technical explanations about the advantages of HPFS, there are some easily understood issues surrounding this file system. As consultants and technicians listened to questions and offered responses, there emerged a pattern of explanations that users of every level could understand.

Advantages

The following list contains the most frequently mentioned benefits of using HPFS.

- Long file names—up to 254 characters including the path.

- Contiguous storage of extended attributes—the files and the attributes stay together.

- An amazing immunity level against any file fragmentation.

- Better media error handling.

- Support for larger file storage devices (up to 64 GB).

- Faster disk operations, especially on large hard disks, on systems with more than 6 MB of RAM.

Disadvantages

Users who choose not to install HPFS or who find obstacles to its use and change back to a FAT system frequently base their decision on factors related to their own particular hardware configurations or software use.

- Not currently supported on removable media, so that, for instance, diskette backup software will lose the name and extended attributes of files.

- Native-mode DOS cannot access an HPFS partition. However, DOS and Windows sessions running under OS/2 will be able to use any files that are named with the standard 8.3 convention, even if those files are stored on HPFS volumes.

Virus Issues

At present there are no known OS/2-specific viruses. However, DOS or Windows viruses could possibly infect an OS/2 2.0 system, so the antivirus software you use for DOS or Windows is still useful. IBM has an antivirus package that runs under OS/2 directly, and others are being developed.

OS/2 2.0 is likely to be extremely resistant to viruses. Viruses running in one virtual DOS/Windows session would probably be confined to that session. Since most virus infection is implemented through low-level disk access, the fact that OS/2 curtails such access makes infection much less likely. Even if a virus does enter via DOS or Windows, it is unlikely to disrupt your entire system.

Folder Problems

All OS/2 consultants, support personnel, and technicians have handled many telephone calls from panic-stricken users who have found that folders suddenly disappeared from the desktop.

Restoring Lost Folders

One user dragged the OS/2 System object into a drive folder. After completing the tasks being accessed from the drives folder, the user closed it, along with all the drive objects. After that, he could not get to the OS/2 System object. What had happened was that the drives objects were in the System object, but the system object was in the drives object.

For a solution, you must remember that all folders are represented in the OS/2 file system. Once you realize that, you see that you can use the OS/2 command line to fix things.

The folder is a subdirectory in the file system. The OS/2 Desktop is represented by the directory OS!2_2.0_D for FAT systems and OS!2 2.0 Desktop for HPFS systems. If you list the directory, you see something like this (depending upon what you chose to install):

```
TEMPLATE <DIR>
MIMIZE <DIR>
INFORMAT <DIR>
NETWORK <DIR>
```

```
OS!2_SYS <DIR>
DOS_PROG <DIR>
```

You will notice that the names of the subdirectories match the names of some of the icons on your desktop. Move down one level into OS!2_SYS (the System folder), where you find a directory structure akin to this (you should recognize the names of icons found in the System folder):

```
DRIVES <DIR>
STARTUP <DIR>
SYSTEM_S <DIR>
COMMAND_ <DIR>
GAMES <DIR>
PRODUCTI <DIR>
```

The MOVE command moves the folder (which is a subdirectory within the file system) to the proper place. To move the OS/2 System folder to the Desktop, go to the subdirectory where OS!2_SYS is now located and enter **MOVE OS!2_SYS C:\OS!2_2.0_D** to move the folder back to the Desktop.

 Caution Under normal circumstances, you should not play around at the command line, moving folders. Do this only if a folder becomes inaccessible from the Workplace Shell.

Deleting Stubborn Icons

There have also been situations in which a user moved an icon onto the Desktop and then could not get rid of it. One clever workaround has been suggested.

Create a new folder on the Desktop (call it GARBAGE or something else that you won't forget). Move the icon you want to get rid of into this folder. Then go to an OS/2 command line and, as above, go to the directory where the Desktop subdirectories are located. Empty and remove the Garbage subdirectory.

Corrupted INI Files

Sometimes the Desktop gets corrupted, which can mean anything from missing icons to unreadable icons to the dreaded "white screen"—a solid white display. This occurs because something untoward has happened to your INI files.

There is an undocumented feature in OS/2 2.0 that will back up your INI files and CONFIG.SYS and reset the ones that were established during installation. However, any modifications (such as shadows and associations) since installation will be gone, and you will have to create them again.

Reboot your system. As soon as you hear a beep from the system speaker after the Power on Self Test, press ALT+F1. Hold these keys down until you hear continuous beeping from the system because your keyboard buffer is full.

This will back up your old INI files and CONFIG.SYS. You will see a message during the boot process confirming the backup. If you do not see the message, it did not work and you should try again. This will not erase any files from your disk; it will only restore your Desktop to a "newly installed" state. The INI files in \OS2\INSTALL will be copied and will become the active INI files.

If you have corrupted INI files or lose objects such as the "wait" clock or your fonts, and the above procedure does not help, you can retrieve them by remaking your INI file. To do this, boot from the Install disk. Press ESC after following the prompt to insert disk #1, which will bring up a command prompt. Go to the hard drive that has the \OS2 directory and go into that directory. Type **MAKEINI OS2.INI INI.RC.** Then reboot. This command looks at the installation INI file and your current INI file, merging objects from the latter into the former. This usually restores any lost objects.

If your Desktop objects are so far gone that you cannot use the Desktop, there is still the extreme, last resort, procedure. Boot from the Install disk and escape to a command prompt as described above. Delete the \OS!2_2.0_ D directory and everything underneath it. Then try the remedy described first in this section.

An Ounce of Prevention

Since INI file corruption can occur from an improper shutdown or an electrical failure, it's a good idea to prepare ahead so you don't have to use the procedures discussed above.

Back up your INI files regularly. One way to do this is by adding this line to CONFIG.SYS:

```
CALL C:\OS2\XCOPY.EXE C:\OS2\*.INI C:\OS2\*.INX
```

which creates a copy of the INI file as an INX file. If you really want to be safe, and to make sure that any changes you make along the way are also backed up (so if you change your mind you can go back one previous configuration), add two lines to CONFIG.SYS:

```
CALL C:\OS2\XCOPY.EXE C:\OS2\*.INX C:\OS2\*.INY
CALL C:\OS2\XCOPY.EXE C:\OS2\*.INI C:\OS2\*.INX
```

which copies your last backup of the INI files to yet another backup and then copies the current INI files to the backup version. Two generations of INI changes are saved.

Also, there is an excellent shareware program on CompuServe (GO IBMOS2) that backs up your desktop configuration and can restore it.

Bug Fixes

As wonderful and powerful as OS/2 is, and even with all the beta testing and field testing that was conducted before its release, the operating system has a few bugs. (There have been few software packages released in perfect working order.)

IBM offers Service Paks to fix bugs, and a number of bug fix files have been uploaded by IBM to section 17 of IBMOS2 on CompuServe.

Service Paks can be ordered by anyone with an IBM customer number directly from IBM. (Most IBM customer numbers are held by large corporate sites.)

OS/2 users without customer numbers can get Service Paks from authorized IBM dealers. Some dealers do not know this program exists, so be patient while you explain it to them and insist that they make the necessary telephone calls to get you what you need.

Shutdown Problems

In some situations (a low-resource problem, for example), the final shutdown message may fail to appear after a shutdown is performed. To make sure that shutdown is complete, wait until you are sure that all disk activity has stopped before turning off or restarting your computer.

If you restart your system by pressing CTRL+ALT+DEL instead of turning off the machine, there are some differences. For instance, if you had used the ARRANGE choice on the Desktop folder pop-up menu, the icons you had placed in specific places on your Desktop were rearranged, possibly in a way that you do not like. Restarting your system this way recovers your icon positions.

If you opened several folders, shutdown may take longer because the system is saving the positions of the icons. You can restart your system without doing a shutdown, but do this only if you are sure you will not lose anything else that is important.

If you shut down your system but do not receive the message "Shutdown has completed. It is now safe to turn off your computer...", wait for all disk activity to stop, and then press CTRL+ALT+DEL.

Mouseless Shutdown

If you lose your mouse functions and want to shut down the system to fix things (or, if you are working in OS/2 without a mouse and the shutdown is one of the things you can't find an accelerator key for), follow these steps:

1. At the Desktop, press CTRL+ESC.

2. Cursor up to the OS/2 Desktop entry and press ENTER.

3. Press SPACEBAR to deselect all of the currently selected icons.

4. Press SHIFT+F10 to bring up the Desktop menu.

5. Cursor down to the Shutdown option and press ENTER.

Forced Shutdown

Once in a while there are reports of software that hangs the computer so badly that there is no way to get to the Shutdown command and you must reboot.

Before assuming that you have lost the keyboard, press CTRL+ESC and have patience. Many times, after a long wait (30 seconds is not unheard of) the Window List will appear, permitting you to close applications.

If this doesn't work and you find that you have to reboot, a frozen keyboard makes the CTRL+ALT+DEL sequence unavailable. If you have a reset button, that is an alternative. For users without a reset button, there is an option besides a total power-down and the resulting slower restart. Some users have reported that holding down CTRL+ALT and pressing NUM LOCK twice starts the OS/2 system memory dump routine. The system will ask for a diskette to be placed in drive A for the purpose of generating a CREATEDD disk. While you don't really care about the creation of a CREATEDD disk in this situation, one of the advantages of the CREATEDD function is that it frees your keyboard for a CTRL+ALT+DEL reboot.

Automatic Startup

Any programs running when your system is shut off will start up automatically when you next reboot. Any programs located in the startup folder will also load when you boot. In addition, any programs invoked in your STARTUP.CMD file will load when you boot. There are things to be aware of if you want programs to load automatically at startup and ways to prevent the action if the automatic startup is unintentional.

Note If you turn off your computer with a program running that you started from the command line, OS/2 will see the command session and open that upon reboot, not the application that the command session had loaded.

Loading from STARTUP.CMD

This file is read and the commands in it are executed before the Workplace Shell is started up. Be very careful not to issue an executable command that requires the Workplace Shell.

Arresting Automatic Startup

If you have to reboot because a program hung the system, or if you turned off the machine accidentally without closing down all applications, you may want to prevent those open applications from starting up when you restart the computer.

Reboot the computer and as soon as the mouse pointer appears, press CTRL+SHIFT+F1. Hold those keys down for about 15 seconds until the Desktop icons appear. If nothing happens and the light indicating hard disk action goes off, you may have hung up. Let go of the keys for a second or two and then hold them down again until you see the Desktop icons. Once the Desktop has initialized, check to see if any programs are open with CTRL+ESC. If so, double-click on the appropriate ones and close them normally.

Laptops

First of all, if you travel with a laptop or notebook computer, you know that you have to show airport security personnel that it is a working computer. If you have to wait for OS/2 to boot, you may miss your plane. Keep a DOS boot diskette in drive A for this situation.

Adjusting LCD and Monochrome Plasma Displays

To create a more readable display image on your laptop or notebook, you can make changes through the Scheme Palette.

If it is possible, use your Setup to designate your display as VGA color. Then open the System folder, click on **System Setup**, and click on the Scheme Palette icon. Choose the monochrome scheme (listed on the right side of the window).

This accomplishes two things. It optimizes the palette for grayscale and it gives you satisfactory output if you attach a VGA monitor to your laptop.

Fixes Due from IBM

A number of reported problems with the operating system, hardware and software incompatibility, and other annoyances have been reported to IBM, and fixes are in the works. Some may have been released by the time you read this.

Vertical scrolling in the OS/2 clipboard does not work. Use PGDN and PGUP until a fix is released.

If an application sends several sets of data to a public clipboard and if one of the sources generates a rendering problem, no data at all is sent to other WIN-OS/2 sessions. With the fix that is being created, only the problem data will not be sent.

When a metafile is sent to the OS/2 clipboard, it is converted to a bitmap and the image is enlarged. This means that only the middle of the image is in the clipboard window. A fix is in the works.

In DOS sessions, IRQ7 is not recognized, causing any device other than a printer that is attached to a parallel port (for example, tablets and network adapters) to be ignored. A solution is being worked on.

The virtual DOS machine under OS/2 only renders 1000 VDM interrupts per second, which is too slow for 9600 baud transmissions. Until the fix is released, you have to reduce your modem speed to 4800 baud or lower.

Miscellaneous Odds and Ends

To have the DIR command display directories in alphabetical order with the subdirectories listed first, edit CONFIG.SYS so that the SET DIRCMD= statement is followed by the parameter /O:GN. To do the same thing in DOS sessions, put DOSKEY in AUTOEXEC.BAT.

If you hold down the SHIFT key while you are resizing text windows, the size changes will be permanent.

If you are a true WordPerfect fan, it has been reported that if you run WordPerfect's File Manager in an OS/2-WIN full-screen window, you can use it as a replacement for running WIN and WIN's own program manager. You can launch applications with the RUN command or add applications to the Applications box in WPFM.

Judging by the questions and complaints received by OS/2 support personnel, it seems important to remind you that Windows programs cannot start DOS sessions or DOS applications.

CHAPTER

REXX

*T*he purpose of REXX is to provide a scheme for programming that is easy to use. Powerful program routines can be written using plain English words with an intuitive syntax. This makes it easy to automate tasks you perform repeatedly. Rather than reproduce the same set of keystrokes every time a specific task must be executed, it is much more productive to record them once and let the computer do the work.

As discussed in Chapter 8, OS/2 provides a batch language for just this type of repetitive work. However, in many cases REXX is a better solution for automating tedious tasks. REXX is a great deal more powerful than the native batch language, and its flexibility will allow you to do a lot more with less effort. Further, the REXX file extension of .CMD will permit you to separate OS/2-specific batch files from DOS batch files on the same drive.

Command Files

REXX files run only in OS/2 sessions (although REXX interpreters exist for DOS also), and they must have a filename extension of .CMD. When you type the name of a file with the .CMD extension at the OS/2 prompt, the operating system looks at the file for the "/*" in the first line, determines that it is a REXX batch program, and then executes the instructions using the REXX interpreter. Every REXX file may contain one or more of the following elements:

- Comments
- Strings
- Instructions
- Commands
- Assignments
- Labels
- Internal functions

Each element within a REXX program allows you to perform a specific task.

Comments

Comments provide a way to document your file, to explain what you want to do and what each step does and, if you wish, to indicate your name and the date you created the file. Some people add notes to indicate the dates and reasons for all the changes made as they improve and extend the power of the file. Commenting out any program, whether it is a simple batch file, a REXX file, or a complicated program, is an important element. It not only provides a clear sense of direction to anyone who has to change or use the files you create, but it also frequently helps when you look at the file yourself. Many people have found that when they look at their file months later, they can't remember why they wrote it the way they did.

All REXX procedures must begin with a comment that starts in the first column of the first line. This comment tells the operating system that the file it is going to read is a REXX procedure.

Comments are indicated via the use of special symbols:

/* is the indication of the beginning of a comment.

*/ is the indication of the end of a comment.

When the interpreter detects a /*, it knows to stop interpreting since there are no programming instructions to be read after that symbol. When it sees */, it begins interpreting instructions again.

Strings

A *string* is any assortment of characters that is placed inside a set of quotation marks, either double or single (an apostrophe). When the REXX interpreter sees the opening quotation mark, it stops interpreting the program and uses the text it sees until it comes across the closing quotation mark. The opening and closing quotation marks have to be of the same type—that is, either single or double. How the REXX interpreter uses the text depends upon what your instructions are regarding the text. You can use the text to tell the person using your batch file something, or you can use it to ask for information.

If you need to display a single quote, the easiest way to accomplish that is to enclose the string with double quotes. For example, you could use "Jack liked Mary's new car." Sometimes you'll need to display double quotes in a string. In that case, use two double quotes together. For example, "Mary said ""Boy, do you have a nice car."" displays as

Mary said "Boy, do you have a nice car."

Instructions

An instruction tells the system to do something. An instruction can be a simple one-word phrase or a more complicated set of directions involving assignments or labels (covered in the following paragraphs). Each instruction should begin on a new line in your file.

Commands

The ability to execute OS/2 commands is one of the main reasons to use REXX. As with batch files, OS/2 commands can be programmed ad infinitum, but unlike batch files, using REXX means a great deal more power can be attached to the instructions for executing OS/2 commands.

Assignments

Sometimes you need to keep track of a specific piece of information during the execution of a file. REXX allows you to do this by assigning the piece of information to a special place in memory. For example, you can write Customer = "Smith". The string "Smith" is stored as the value Customer in memory.

Variables

The value called Customer can be changed to "Jones" by assigning a new string. The variable acts like a box that you store the piece of information in until you need it again. Just like any other box, you can take the old piece of information out and put a new piece of information in. Because the string can be changed and therefore Customer can change its value, Customer is known as a variable. Every variable has a unique name, and every time you assign information to it, you assign it by referring to that name.

When you name a variable, the first character must be a letter of the alphabet or one of the characters !, ?, or _. After the first letter, you can also use the numbers 0 through 9.

In addition to a text string, you can store the value of an arithmetic expression in a variable, for instance, Sum = 1 + 2. The variable named Sum now contains a value of 3. If you make another assignment later, REXX will replace the value of 3 with a new value.

Labels

A *label* is a word that marks a statement to which you would like to directly move. The word must be followed by a colon to announce it is a label instead of a command. You can think of a label as a street sign in your file. If you want REXX to stop performing a specific task, you can tell it to go to another part of the file by announcing a label. REXX then looks for the right street sign.

Internal Functions

A *function* is a way to ask for a computation or information and have REXX bring back the result. You can take one or more pieces of information and use them to find out something else. This gives REXX a way to provide some shortcuts when certain tasks are necessary. For example, if you want REXX to figure out the maximum of three numbers, you would use the MAX function as follows: MAX(Number 1, Number 2, Number 3). When the REXX interpreter sees a word followed by a left parenthesis (with no space between), an expression of some kind, and then a final right parenthesis, it assumes that you are calling a function. REXX provides you with more than 50 built-in functions, some of which will be discussed in detail later in this chapter.

Language Components

There are three essential parts to any REXX program: control structures, commands, and functions. A *control structure* tells REXX how to execute your program. It allows you to create more sophisticated logic than simply one statement followed by another. A *command* is an instruction that you want REXX to perform. A *function* allows you to take a shortcut to get specific pieces of information.

These three parts of REXX combine to form a language. In many ways this language is similar to the macros you create for your word processor or spreadsheet. The big difference is that REXX works with the operating system, not with a specific software package.

Boolean Operators

Boolean operators are elements of the language that are used in almost every area of REXX programming. Boolean operators help REXX evaluate a given set of conditions and perform a specific task based on what it finds. There are only two values returned by Boolean operators, 1 for true and 0 for false.

Comparisons: >, <, =

REXX allows you to compare values. For example, if you wanted to see if it were true that one value is greater than another, you would type **Var1 > Var2**. Likewise, if you wanted to see if one value is less than another, you would type **Var1 < Var2**. The output of these comparisons is 1 for true or 0 for false.

NOT Operator (\)

You use the NOT operator to reverse the condition of an evaluation. For example, if you typed **\(1 = 1)**, REXX would evaluate the expression as false.

AND Operator (&)

The AND operator allows you to perform a logical union of two expressions. In effect you are saying, If expression 1 is true & (and) expression 2 is true, then return a value of true. If either expression is false, then the entire expression is false.

OR Operator (|)

The OR operator allows you to perform a logical intersection of two expressions. You are saying, If expression 1 is true | (or) expression 2 is true, then return a value of true. The only time you receive an output of false is when both expressions are false.

Control Structures

There are three basic forms of control structure supported by REXX. You can "nest" these control structures to perform more elaborate sequences of instructions. *Nesting* is the process of placing one control structure within another. Each structure is still its own unique element, but the structures work together to produce a specific result.

Conditional Statement

The *conditional statement* allows you to perform an action based on whether or not an expression is true or false. Think of a conditional statement as a light switch. You can turn the light either on or off depending on the position of the switch. The IF..THEN..ELSE control structure is the conditional statement for REXX.

```
IF <expression>
    THEN <statement>
    [ELSE <statement>]
```

The IF..THEN..ELSE control structure is one of the most common structures you'll need when creating a REXX program. Essentially, this control structure says that if the expression is true, then REXX will perform the statement appearing after the THEN clause. The ELSE clause is optional. REXX automatically performs the statement appearing after this clause if the expression is false. The following example shows how you would use the IF..THEN..ELSE control structure:

```
IF Var1 > 5
   THEN SAY "Input was greater than 5"
   ELSE SAY "Input was less than or equal to 5"
```

You can use a DO..END control structure if you need to perform more than one statement after the THEN or ELSE clause. The following example shows how you would use these two structures together:

```
SAY "Type your age and press Enter."
PULL Age
IF Age > 18
   THEN
      DO
      SAY "You are over 18."
      SAY "What would you like to drink?"
      PARSE PULL DrinkName
      SAY "Fixing you a " DrinkName
      END
   ELSE
      DO
      SAY "You are not over 18."
      SAY "I can't fix you a drink."
      END
```

Switch Statement

With a switch statement, you select from a group of actions based on a specific condition. Think of a switch statement as a soda machine. You insert a coin, press one out of a group of switches, and receive a specific kind of soda in return. The switch statement in REXX is the SELECT..WHEN..OTHERWISE control structure.

This is the best control structure to use when there is more than one possible choice that the user could make.

```
SELECT
   WHEN <expression 1>
      THEN <statement 1>
   [WHEN <expression 2>
      THEN <statement 2>...]
   [OTHERWISE
      <statement n>]
END
```

REXX looks at expression 1 first. If this expression is true, then it executes the statement following the first THEN clause. If the expression isn't true, REXX evaluates the second and following expressions. If REXX can't find any true expressions, then it looks for the OTHERWISE clause and executes any statements appearing after it. Once it executes one of the THEN clause statements, REXX exits the control structure. You only need to supply one WHEN clause with this control structure. Additional WHEN clauses are optional. The OTHERWISE clause is optional as well. However, if you don't provide an OTHERWISE clause, REXX will exit the control structure without doing anything if it doesn't find a true expression. The following example shows how you could use the SELECT..WHEN..OTHERWISE switch:

```
SAY "Type your age and press Enter."
PULL Age
SELECT
   WHEN Age < 13
      THEN SAY "You are a child."
   WHEN (Age > 12) & (Age < 20)
      THEN SAY "You are a teenager."
   OTHERWISE
      SAY "You are an adult."
END
```

Notice that you must always end a SELECT..WHEN..OTHERWISE control structure with an END clause. This is the only way that REXX knows that you finished the switch. Also notice that the OTHERWISE clause does not require a THEN clause. If you add a THEN clause, REXX will exit your program with an error.

Like the IF..THEN..ELSE control structure, REXX allows you to combine the SELECT..WHEN..OTHERWISE switch with the DO..END control structure. This allows you to follow a THEN clause with more than one statement.

Loop Statement

The final control structure is the loop statement. A *loop statement* allows you to perform one section of code one or more times based on a counter variable. For example, say you wanted to get three candy bars from a machine. First you'd place some money in the slot and then you'd pull the appropriate switch and retrieve your candy bar. To get three candy bars, you'd perform this sequence of steps three times. There are several loop statements for REXX, including the DO..LOOP, DO UNTIL.., DO WHILE.., and DO FOREVER control structures.

DO..LOOP This form of the DO..END loop is the most basic form of the control structure that you can use.

```
DO <number>
     <statements>
     [LEAVE]
  END
```

REXX executes the instructions within the control structure the number of times specified by number. The only way to exit the structure prematurely is to add a LEAVE clause. The LEAVE clause is an optional part of this control structure. The following example shows how to use the DO..END loop:

```
SAY "Enter a number."
PULL Counter
LastCount = 1
DO Counter
   SAY LastCount
   LastCount = LastCount + 1
   SAY "Do you want to count some more?"
   PULL Answer
   IF Answer = "NO"
      THEN LEAVE
END
```

You must add an END clause to the bottom of this control structure. Otherwise, REXX will not know when the control structure ends. This example also shows one way to use the LEAVE clause. Unless the user enters **NO** when asked if they want to count some more, REXX continues to process the loop. A variation of the DO statement allows you to automatically iterate a variable from one value to another. The following example shows you how to use this form of the DO..END loop:

```
DO Counter = 1 TO 10
   SAY Counter
END
```

DO WHILE   You won't always know how many times to execute a loop. Sometimes the number of executions depends on conditions that you can't control when you write the program. The DO WHILE..END loop checks an expression before it executes the statements within the control structure.

```
DO WHILE <expression>
      <statements>
      [LEAVE]
END
```

It continues to execute the instructions while the expression is true looping from END to WHILE. If the expression is false when the WHILE statement is reached, the control structure exits and REXX continues execution at the statement following the END clause. The following example shows how to use the DO WHILE..END loop:

```
SAY "Enter a filename you want to display."
PULL ListFile
DO WHILE \(ListFile = "")
   type ListFile
   SAY "Enter a filename you want to display."
   PULL ListFile
END
```

DO UNTIL   The DO UNTIL..END loop evaluates an expression after it executes a set of statements.

```
DO UNTIL <expression>
      <statements>
      [LEAVE]
   END
```

This assures that a loop will always execute at least once, no matter what happens. The DO UNTIL..END loop continues to execute a set of instructions until the expression you specify is true when the END statement is reached. The following example shows how to use the DO UNTIL..END loop:

```
Counter = 1
DO UNTIL Counter = 1 /* Prints 1. */
   SAY Counter
END
DO UNTIL Counter = 10
   SAY Counter
   Counter = Counter + 1
END
```

DO FOREVER   This loop continues to execute until the user manages to break out of it. As a result, you should always include a LEAVE clause as part of the code for this control structure.

```
DO FOREVER
     <statements>
     LEAVE
  END
```

You will not find many reasons to use the DO FOREVER..END loop.

Commands

Many people have trouble keeping commands and functions separate when creating a program. The thing to remember is that a function always returns a value, but it may not do any other work. A command always performs some type of work but never returns a value. REXX offers a wide assortment of commands that help you control the batch file environment.

CALL <Name>

One of the simplest forms of this command is to call a subfunction from within a main procedure or function. In many cases it is more convenient to break your program into small pieces. Each piece performs a specific part of a more complex task. For example, you could create a single routine for error trapping or displaying information onscreen. The following example shows a simple method of using the CALL command:

```
/* This is the main procedure. It displays a message to the
viewer, then requests some information. If the user doesn't sup-
ply the information, the main procedure calls an error handling
function to request it again. */
Who=""                      /* Initialize the variable. */
DO WHILE Who = ""           /* Do this until the user responds. */
   SAY "Hello! I am REXX"
   SAY "What is your name?"
   PARSE PULL Who
   IF Who = ""              /* Did the user provide a response? */
      THEN CALL Error       /* If not, call the error handling
                                                   function. */
      ELSE SAY "Hello" Who
END
EXIT
/* This is the error handling function. It displays an error
message, then returns so the main procedure can ask the user
for the requested information. */
Error:
SAY "Please type your name!"
RETURN
```

There are a few interesting points about this program. First, the error routine uses a label for identification. Notice that the function name is followed by a colon. Second, the function ends with a RETURN command, not the EXIT command. You want to return to the main procedure once the user presses the ENTER key. Using EXIT would simply return you to the OS/2 prompt.

EXIT

This call permits you to exit from the current program back to the calling program. In most cases, the calling program is the OS/2 command processor.

NOP

The NOP command stands for "no operation." Use this command when you don't want to do anything at all. For example, if you use a SWITCH control structure to select from a set of conditions, one condition could be to do nothing.

PARSE PULL Variable [, Variable2, ...]

The PARSE PULL command accepts input from the keyboard until the user presses ENTER. It places the input into the specified variables. PARSE PULL allows you to enter characters in either upper- or lowercase with no loss of formatting.

PULL Variable [, Variable2, ...]

The PULL command acts much like the PARSE PULL command. It places a value typed at the keyboard into variable. Unlike the PARSE PULL command, PULL converts all characters to uppercase. This is a good feature to use when you want to use the keyboard input as part of an expression for a control structure.

RETURN

Allows you to return from the current procedure to the calling procedure. This is the command you use to return from a subfunction to the function which called it. You could also use this command at the end of the program, but the EXIT command allows you to recognize the program ending point at a glance.

SAY <Expression>

The SAY command allows you to output the contents of an expression to the display. The expression can contain variables, expressions, or strings.

Functions

Functions always return a value. As a result, you normally set a variable equal to the value of the function. For example, if you wanted to find out the absolute value of a number, you could use the ABS function as follows:

AbsVal = ABS(SomeNumber)

Notice that there is no space between the left parenthesis and the function name. As an alternative to sending the output of a function to a variable, you can send it directly to the display using the SAY command.

ABS(Number)

Returns the absolute value of a number. Essentially, this makes negative numbers positive. Positive numbers remain unchanged.

BEEP(Frequency, Duration)

This function allows you to send a specific frequency to the speaker for a specified time. The first parameter is the frequency in Hertz. The duration entry determines how long you will hear the tone in milliseconds. For example, BEEP(1000, 250) sends a 1000 Hz signal to the speaker for a quarter of a second. The following example shows how you can enhance the error trapping routine of a previous example using the BEEP function:

```
/* This is the error handling function. It displays an error
message, then returns so the main procedure can ask the user
for the requested information. */
Error:
BEEP(1000,250)
SAY "Please type your name!"
RETURN
```

CENTER(String, Length, [Pad])

This function returns a string of Length with String centered within it. You can use the CENTER function to dress up your displays. The standard padding character (the character used to center the string) is a blank. However, you can specify any ASCII character using the optional Pad entry. The following example shows how you would use the CENTER function:

```
SAY CENTER("This is my menu", 80)    /* Center the heading on
                                        the screen */
```

DATE([Option])

This function returns the current date. It normally displays the date in a DD MMM YYYY format, as in 30 Sep 1992. However, you can specify an option to change the format. The following table shows the formats available:

B	Base Date	Returns the number of days since 01/01/0001
D	Days	Returns the number of days, including the current day, since the beginning of the year
E	European Formatted Date	Returns the short form of the European formatted date
L	Long Date	Returns the date in long format. This includes the full month name and a four-digit year
M	Month	Returns the current month in long form
N	Normal	Returns the date in normal format. You can accomplish the same thing by leaving the option blank
O	Ordered Form	Returns the date in a format suitable for sorting. It uses the YY/MM/DD format
S	Sorted Form	Returns the date in a format suitable for sorting. It uses the YYYYMMDD format
U	USA Format	Returns the date in the format used by the United States, MM/DD/YY
W	Weekday	Returns the day of the week in long form

TIME([Option])

Use this function to display the current time. The TIME function normally displays the time in military format, HH:MM:SS. Like the DATE function, you can add an option to change the form of the TIME function output. The following table shows the available formats:

L	Long Format	Shows the complete time in military format (24-hour clock), including hundredths of a second
H	Hours	Shows the number of hours since midnight

M	Minutes	Shows the number of minutes since midnight.
S	Seconds	Shows the number of seconds since midnight.
N	Normal Time	Use this option to display the time in normal format. You can obtain the same results by not using any option at all
C	Civilian Format	Shows the time in am/pm format (12-hour clock) instead of military format

Programming

Every REXX program starts the same way, with a comment field. Some people simply place a blank comment at the top of their REXX file, but you can use it for a lot more. If you create more than a few batch files to automate your everyday work, it becomes necessary to document them in some way. Using this initial comment to leave yourself a note about some of the details of this particular file can reduce confusion later and make your program easier for someone else who uses it. The more information you put here, the less frustration you'll have later when it's time to modify your program.

Expressions

One of the more powerful features of REXX is its ability to interpret expressions. There are two forms of expression that you will use quite often in your REXX programs. The first form is string concatenation. For example, if you use the following statements,

```
Var1 = "Hello"
Var2 = "World"
Var3 = Var1 + Var2
SAY Var3
```

you will see "Hello World" displayed on your screen. Concatenation is useful when you want to combine program text with user input. Often you'll use it as part of information or result screens.

The other form of expression is the result of an equation. REXX provides quite a few math operators, as shown in the following:

- ☐ **+** Addition

- ☐ **–** Subtraction

- ☐ ***** Multiplication

- ☐ **/** Division

- ☐ **%** Integer division. For example, 5 % 2 results in an output of 2. REXX truncates the decimal portion of the answer.

- ☐ **//** A double slash is the module operator. It returns the remainder of an integer division. For example, 5 // 2 returns an output of 1.

- ☐ **()** Parentheses change the normal order of precedence. REXX normally evaluates the multiplication and division portions of an expression first, then the addition and subtraction. It also evaluates an expression from left to right, just like you would normally read it. For example, 2 + 3 / 2 results in an output of 3.5. Using parentheses will force REXX to evaluate the part of the expression you want evaluated first. For example, (2 + 3) / 2 results in an output of 2.5 instead of 3.5.

  Of course, you can nest the parentheses as needed to achieve the desired result. For example, 2 + (3 + 4) / 2 results in an answer of 5.5, while (2 + (3 + 4)) / 2 results in 4.5.

Formatting

There are a variety of formatting techniques people use to increase the readability of their batch files. One system is not necessarily better than another. However, you should use a system of some sort to help you read your batch files.

Indentation is one technique people use to format their programs. For example, if you want to make a control structure obvious, you can format it as follows:

```
IF SomeExp
     THEN
```

```
    Do Something
ELSE
    Do Something Else
```

As you can see, this is a lot more readable than placing all the statements in a straight line. There is no doubt that this is a control structure, nor is there any doubt about where each element ends.

Another form of formatting is capitalization. For example, you could type all REXX commands in all uppercase, variables with initial capital letters only, and OS/2 commands in all lowercase. Using this formatting scheme reduces confusion when you edit your batch file. There is no doubt which words are variables, which are REXX commands, and which are OS/2 commands.

These are just a few ways that you can make your batch files easier to read and modify. As you become more proficient at creating REXX programs, you'll probably find other ways to improve the appearance and readability of your code.

Getting Down to Business

Now that you know what elements make a REXX program, it's time to start putting them together. Menuing systems are one of the projects that many people tackle using a batch programming language. While OS/2 reduces the need for using such a menuing system, you can still use one for commands that you must execute from the OS/2 prompt. The following program shows one simple way of using REXX to automate a process using a menuing system:

```
/* PURPOSE: This program shows you how to create a menuing sys-
tem using REXX. */

Answer = 0               /* Initialize our answer variable. */
DO WHILE \(Answer=3)     /* Do this procedure until the user
                                            enters Quit. */
    cls                  /* Clear the display */
    SAY DATE()
    SAY TIME()
    SAY CENTER("This is my menu", 80)   /* Center the heading. */
    SAY
```

```
      SAY "1. Display the current directory"
      SAY "2. Change drive and/or directory"
      SAY "3. Quit"
      SAY "Enter your selection"
      PULL Answer
      SELECT
         WHEN Answer = 1
            THEN CALL DispDir
         WHEN Answer = 2
            THEN CALL ChngIt
         OTHERWISE
            SAY "Goodbye"
      END
END
EXIT
/* This function displays the directory on screen, then returns
the user to the original menu. Some OS/2 commands require that
you enclose them in quotes. Otherwise, REXX assumes that they
are internal commands and processes them.*/
DispDir:
cls
dir "|more"     /* Surround MORE with quotes so it will execute
                                                     properly. */
SAY "Press any key when ready..."
PULL
RETURN
/* This function allows the user to change the current drive
and directory. */
ChngIt:
cls
/* Get the new drive from the user, then change it. */
SAY "Enter a new drive or press Enter to retain the current
drive."
PULL Drive
IF \(Drive = "")        /* If the user pressed Enter, ignore
                                              the change. */
   THEN Drive":"
/* Get the new directory from the user, then change it. */
SAY "Enter a new directory or press Enter to retain the current
one."
PULL Directory
IF \(Directory = "")    /* If the user pressed Enter, ignore
                                              the change. */
   THEN CD Directory
RETURN
```

As you can see, this menuing system is quite simple to create and it does automate the process of performing a task under OS/2. In many cases, a menuing system can do more than just help you when you don't remember a specific command. It can prompt you for the correct information. For example, in our example program, the menuing system prompts you for the information needed to change drive and directory. You don't have to remember the command itself, simply what you wanted to do with it.

Advanced REXX Functions

While it is beyond the scope of this book to provide detailed explanations and examples of some of the advanced REXX utility functions, you should examine them if you are comfortable with the process of programming.

For example, RexxUtil is a Dynamic Link Library that will provide you with many powerful functions. You can create message boxes; determine specific cursor positions for anything you display; get information about the state of the system; modify, add, or delete files and directories; create temporary files to hold information your program needs; and do a host of other tasks.

Learning REXX will also help you use many popular OS/2 programs. Applications from companies such as Lotus and Borland use REXX as their application extension language, letting you customize their programs via REXX.

The complete reference guide to REXX is found in the Information folder on the Desktop.

CHAPTER

Error Messages

*E*rror messages are, of course, an inescapable part of computing. Most of the time, the error messages are presented to you as a result of some action at the command line: you type a command and, instead of the expected result, the operating system sends you an error message. The nice thing about receiving an error message from OS/2, however, is that it is generally clear and concise.

Error messages can be classified in a number of ways: Those most frequently encountered are the result of simple errors at the command line. A little less frequent are error messages that occur during program loading or execution. The last category are those messages that, under most conditions, are seen by programmers. These classifications are subjective, not "official," and different people might put specific error messages into different categories.

It is beyond the scope of this book to present the full spectrum of error messages included in OS/2. This chapter covers all of the messages in the first category mentioned and some of the more frequent messages in the second category. If you want a full listing, especially of the messages that are more difficult to comprehend, you can get the OS/2 Toolkit, an invaluable resource for programmers and advanced users. OS/2 Toolkit is available from IBM.

Common Error Messages

The origin of most of the common error messages range from simple typing errors to missing or misplaced files. The messages presented here include the typical cause and some suggested solutions.

There are many error messages in which the text is similar or identical, although the message numbers are different. This is because many of the error messages are specifically responding to the individual command used at the command line. There is a number assigned to each error message in the form SYS*NNNN*, where *NNNN* is a number unique to that error message. You can get more information to help you solve the problem by asking for help and referencing the number, using the syntax **HELP *NNNN***. A DOS command session under OS/2 also offers this form of error message and the attendant help.

SYS0002: The system cannot find the file specified   This is the same as the familiar DOS message "File Not Found". Check for a typing error or spelling error, and make sure the file you are looking for is indeed in the current directory.

SYS0003: The system cannot find the path specified   You entered a path and there is no such subdirectory. Make sure you are entering a valid path for the current drive.

SYS0004: The system cannot open the file   The number of open files has reached maximum. Close another program and try again.

SYS0005: Access is denied   There are a number of causes for denying access to a file:

☐   The file may have a read-only attribute and you attempted to write to it or delete it. Use ATTRIB to change the read-only flag.

☐   The resource, for example a file or subdirectory, that you tried to access is being used by another process. Another possibility is that you (or the application) are attempting to access a named pipe, queue, or semaphore that is a shared resource being used. Waiting until the resource is released will usually work.

☐   You tried to access a resource or to effect an action, but you do not have the rights to do it. Perhaps you are using LAN Server Version 2.0 and you tried to accomplish something for which you do not have rights. Increase your user privileges to complete the task.

☐   The filename is incorrect. Retype the filename.

SYS0008: There is not enough storage available to process this command. All available storage is in use   Either the swap file is full or there has been a hardware error on the disk that contains the swap file. Close one or more programs and then retry the command. If you get this message frequently, make changes to the CONFIG.SYS file and reboot. The changes should be a reduction in the value of one or more of the following items:

BUFFERS=, TRACEBUF=, DISKCACHE=, THREADS=, RMSIZE=, DEVICE=VDISK.SYS

It might also be advisable to do some housecleaning and remove any expendable files from the hard disk that holds the swap file. Finally, you may need to add additional memory to your system.

SYS0015: The system cannot find the drive specified   Usually this means you have entered a drive letter as part of a path statement and that drive does not exist. If you get this error message during a RESTORE, you may be trying to restore to a read-only drive or to a redirected drive.

SYS0016: The directory cannot be removed   You are using the RD command on a directory that cannot be removed. Check your typing and make sure you entered the directory name correctly. If you did, remember that you cannot remove the current directory. Also check the attributes— the directory may be marked read-only. Perhaps there are files or subdirectories contained in the directory you are trying to remove. Delete those files and remove those subdirectories, and then try again.

Note   Also check to see if the directory has the same name as an OS/2 reserved device name. You can remove the device in order to remove the directory.

SYS0017: The system cannot move the file to a different disk drive The MOVE command only works within the same disk drive. Copy the file to the other drive and then delete it from the original drive.

SYS0019: The drive is currently write-protected   You cannot change or add anything to a write-protected drive. If this is a removable media drive (a floppy drive), remove the write-protection from the floppy disk.

SYS0020: The system cannot find the device specified   You used an incorrect device name in a command.

SYS0021: The drive is not ready   Either there is no diskette in the drive, the drive door is open, or another process is using the drive.

SYS0023: Data error (cyclic redundancy check)   This means that OS/2 cannot read or write the data correctly. If you are reading from or writing to a hard disk, try again; if the error occurs again, you probably have a hardware problem with that disk and you may need to reformat it. If you are trying to read or write with a diskette, make sure it is formatted. If it is, it may be bad; you should insert a new diskette and try again. There also may be a memory problem, so try a shutdown and reboot.

SYS0025: The drive cannot locate a specific area or track on the disk The diskette may be faulty, unformatted, or formatted with an incompatible operating system. Sometimes reinserting the diskette helps if you are sure it is not damaged and has been correctly formatted.

SYS0026: The specified disk or diskette cannot be accessed
The disk or diskette is not properly formatted.

SYS0027: The drive cannot find the sector (area) requested
The disk or diskette is either damaged, unformatted, or formatted for an incompatible operating system. This error will also occur if you put a high-density diskette into a double-density drive.

SYS0028: The printer is out of paper, or there is not enough space to create a spool file An "out of paper" message has been received from the printer or there is not enough room on the disk to create the spool file. The former message is sometimes a spurious message and could mean that the printer is turned off or the online button is not lit, or it can even occur in the event of a bad or loose cable connection. Check all of these possibilities and try again. If the problem is disk space, you will have to delete some files from the disk that has the spool directory.

 Note If you are printing through a network, there may be a disk space problem with the file server rather than with your local disk

SYS0029: The system cannot write to the specified device
The system encountered a problem trying to write to a device. Make sure the device is connected and turned on. If the device is a disk, be sure it is formatted. If all seems well, the device is probably in use by another process, so you should wait a little while and try again. This error could also be caused by a problem with the device driver, and you may have to contact the manufacturer for an update.

SYS0030: The system cannot read from the specified device   The system received an error when it tried to read from a device. See the solutions in the previous error SYS0029.

SYS0031: A device attached to the system is not functioning
A device is not working and the system cannot communicate with it. Make sure the device is turned on and connected properly. If the device is a diskette drive, be sure the door is closed, the diskette is inserted properly, and the diskette is formatted.

SYS0032: The process cannot access the file because it is being used by another process   The only solution to this self-explanatory error message is to wait and try again.

SYS0033: The process cannot access the file because another process has locked a portion of the file   This is almost the same as the previous error, except that you are trying to access a portion of a file that is already in use. Again, wait a few seconds and retry.

SYS0035: The program could not open the requested file
This error occurs when a program tries to open a file using File Control Blocks (FCBs) and the FCB limit is exceeded. Edit your CONFIG.SYS file to make the value of FCBS= larger. Shut down and reboot, then try the program again.

SYS0036: The system has detected an overflow in the sharing buffer   The sharing buffer maximum number of files has been exceeded. This is almost always a temporary condition, and when fewer programs are active the command will work again.

SYS0037: The system cannot write to the * write-protected drive**
The diskette is write-protected; remove the tape or move the button (depending on the diskette type) and try again.

SYS0038: The system cannot find the * device**   The system could not find the device you specified. Retype the correct device name.

SYS0039: The * device is not ready**   One cause of this error message is that the device you specified is not ready or is empty. Another cause is that a device driver for a COM port was specified but is not installed or has been disabled. If you have the former problem, insert a diskette in the drive, close the drive door, or wait until another process is finished with the drive. If it is the latter problem, check CONFIG.SYS for the COMx DEVICE statement. If there is one, shut down and reboot, watching for any error messages during bootup regarding COMx. Make sure there really is hardware for COMx. Try issuing a MODE COMx command to see if the system thinks COMx exists.

SYS0041: Data error (cyclic redundancy check) on *** The system cannot read or write the data. If you are reading from or writing to a hard disk, try again and if the error occurs again, you probably have a hardware problem with that disk and you may need to reformat it. If you are trying to read or write with a diskette, make sure it is formatted. If it is, it may be bad and you should insert a new diskette and try again. If the error occurred on a hard disk, retry the command. If the error occurs again, the hard disk may have to be reformatted.

SYS0043: Drive *** *cannot locate a specific area or track on the disk* The disk or diskette is either damaged, unformatted, or formatted with an incompatible operating system. Make sure the diskette is properly inserted, or format the diskette.

SYS0045: Drive *** *cannot find the sector requested* This error is caused by the same conditions explained in the previous error.

SYS0046: The *** *printer is out of paper* The printer has given the system an "out of paper" signal. This could also be a spurious message when the real culprit is a printer that is not turned on or not properly connected.

SYS0047: The system cannot write to the *** *device* The system received an error while writing to this device. Be sure the device is actually installed, is connected properly, and is turned on. It may be that the device is in use by another process, so wait a few seconds and try again. If the device is a diskette, make sure it is inserted properly and is formatted.

SYS0048: The system cannot read from the *** *device* The system received an error while reading from this device. See the previous error message for corrective actions.

SYS0049: The * device is not functioning**   This is a more general error message, but the corrective actions are the same as those in the two previous error messages.

SYS0050: The network request is not supported   You are trying to do something that cannot be done from your workstation or something that cannot be supported on the file server you specified. Be sure you are accessing the correct server for the task you need to perform. If you believe you are, contact the network administrator to make sure that the server and your workstation are both correctly configured for the task or application.

SYS0051: The remote computer is not available   You either specified the wrong computer name, or the remote computer is busy or turned off. Also check to make sure there are no problems with your cable.

SYS0054: The network is busy, or is out of resources   Either the network is busy processing other requests that interfere with your task, or the network has run out of resources. Wait and retry. If that doesn't work, have the network administrator check the network configuration to make sure enough network resources are available.

SYS0055: The specified network resource is no longer available
You either do not have access to the resource or the computer that has the resource is not turned on. Also, you may not have the correct rights for that network resource.

SYS0056: The network BIOS command limit has been reached
The network currently has too many NETBIOS requests waiting to be processed. Wait and try again.

SYS0057: A network adapter hardware error occurred   The network interface card in your computer is having a problem. It could also be a problem with the cable connecting the card to the network.

SYS0059: An unexpected network error occurred   Your workstation received an error message from the network that was not expected in this situation. There are numerous causes for this, depending upon the task, the software being used, and the network type. Contact your network administrator to investigate the problem further.

SYS0060: *The remote adapter is not compatible* Your computer cannot communicate with the specified remote computer because the hardware adapters are not compatible.

SYS0061: *The printer queue is full* When the queue file is full, the printer cannot accept any additional print requests. Wait a few seconds and try again.

SYS0062: *Space to store the file waiting to be printed is not available on the server* The server that is connected to the printer does not have enough space available to store the file waiting to be printed. Wait a few seconds for the space to become available and try again.

SYS0063: *Your file waiting to be printed was deleted* The file you sent for printing was deleted by another user on the server. Find out who did it and demand to know why. If the explanation isn't acceptable, avenge the action by tattling to the network administrator.

SYS0064: *The specified network name is no longer available* The network resource you specified was either taken off-line or is no longer available. Make sure that the server that shared the resource is turned on. Also check your rights on the server.

SYS0065: *Network access is denied* You attempted to access a resource that is not available to you. Make sure you have an account on the server or that your account has the necessary rights and privileges.

SYS0070: *The remote server has been paused or is in the process of being started* The server you are attempting to access is either in a paused state or is still in the process of being started. Wait and try again.

SYS0073: *The diskette is write protected* Remove the write-protection and retry the command.

SYS0074: *A device attached to the system is not functioning* A device is turned off or improperly connected. If the device being accessed is a diskette, the diskette may not be inserted properly or may not be formatted.

SYS0075: *There is not enough memory to run this XGA application*
The reason for this error is that the XGA Virtual Device Driver requires locked memory to guarantee successful I/O (input/output) transfer by the XGA coprocessor. The easiest and fastest way to correct this error is to select End program/command/operation.

Then press CTRL+ESC or ALT+ESC to switch the XGA application to the background. Close down one or more active programs. Return the XGA application to the foreground by selecting it from the Window List.

SYS0082: *The directory or file cannot be created*   You used the MD command to make a directory that already exists or you tried to create a file that already exists. This error will also occur if the root directory is full and the file you are trying to create is to be put on the root directory, if there is not enough room on the disk to create a file or directory, or if the filename or directory name is a reserved name.

SYS0084: *Storage to process this request is not available*
The system has more requests to process than it can handle at the moment. Wait and retry.

SYS0086: *The specified network password is not correct*
The password you entered is not correct for the account or application resource you named. Retype your password. If that does not work, contact your network administrator.

SYS0088: *A write fault occurred on the network*   An error occurred while data was being written to the disk. Make sure there is enough free disk space available and that you have the necessary rights.

SYS0089: *The system cannot start another process at this time*
The system has reached the maximum number of running processes. End another process or wait until it is finished, and then retry.

SYS0108: *The disk is in use or locked by another process*   A process has gained exclusive use of this disk or diskette, so you will have to wait and retry.

SYS0111: *The file name is too long*   A filename cannot exceed 255 characters.

SYS0112: There is not enough space on the disk The disk or disk-ette is full. Delete some files and retry.

SYS0123: A file name or volume label contains an incorrect character The system does not accept the following characters:

\ / [ ] : | < > + ; = . ? * "

Retype the filename or volume label.

SYS0142: The system cannot perform a JOIN or SUBST at this time
You are trying to JOIN or SUBST a drive that is in use. Wait and retry.

SYS0144: The directory is not a subdirectory of the root directory
A directory specified in the JOIN command must be a subdirectory of the root directory. Specify a different directory if you must.

SYS0146: The path specified is being used in a substitute
You are trying to join to a path that is being used in a substitute. Change the path.

SYS0150: System trace information was not specified in your CONFIG.SYS file, or tracing is disallowed Your CONFIG.SYS file does not contain a TRACE= or TRACEBUF= statement, or tracing is disallowed by the trace utility. If you need the function, add the appropriate statements to CONFIG.SYS.

SYS0171: A program in this session encountered a problem and cannot continue An application has disabled the interrupts and did not reset them in a reasonable period of time. This is a programming problem, and you must contact the software company or the programmer.

SYS0182: The operating system cannot run *** There are numerous messages with this text. In almost every case it is a problem with the programming code, and you must contact the software company or programmer. Each specific cause for this message has a different message number. Enter **HELP *NNNN*** to get more information.

SYS0191: *** cannot be run in an OS/2 session   The specified file or program is either a DOS application program or not compatible with OS/2. If the former, switch to a DOS session and try again. If the latter, contact the software company or the programmer.

SYS0206: The file name or extension is too long   The filename or the extension is longer than permitted.

SYS0240: The network connection is disconnected   Some form of transmission error has caused the connection to the remote machine to be disconnected. Running the application again will usually reestablish the connection.

SYS0250: The move or rename operation is not allowed   You cannot move or rename a parent directory to one of its subdirectories.

SYS0251: The move or rename operation is not allowed   The move or rename operation is not allowed because COMMAND.COM or CMD.EXE is in the source directory, the source directory is in use, or the directory is part of a SUBST or JOIN macro. Correct whichever one of these conditions applies.

SYS0252: The specified file system name is not correct   The file system name you specified could not be found. Check your typing. You may have to add an IFS= statement containing the correct file system name to CONFIG.SYS. If so, remember to shut down and reboot.

SYS0253: The specified device name is not correct   Device name could not be found in the path you gave.

SYS0254: An incorrect extended attribute name was used
The extended attribute name contains a character that is not permitted.

SYS0255: The extended attribute list size is not correct   The extended attribute list size does not match the size that was specified.

SYS0256: The extended attribute list is too long   The extended attribute list is too long; you must use a shorter extended attribute list.

SYS0258: *A timeout occurred before the requested changes could be completed* The application program timeout did not allow the requested number of changes to occur. If this is not user-configurable, contact the software company or the programmer.

SYS0266: *The specified file was not copied* For some reason, a file was not copied. Possibly the source and target files are not in the same file system.

SYS0276: *The extended attributes are corrupted* The extended attributes for the specified disk or diskette are not usable. You should run CHKDSK /F on the disk or diskette.

SYS0277: *No more space is available for extended attributes* The number of files containing extended attributes has reached the system limit. Delete any unneeded files containing extended attributes.

SYS0278: *The system cannot find the extended attribute* A file contains a reference to an extended attribute that does not exist. It may be that the disk partition is damaged or the extended attribute system file has been modified improperly. Run CHKDSK /F on the disk or diskette.

SYS0279: *The system detected an extended attribute read error* The system cannot find a cluster in the extended attribute system file. Either there is a problem with the disk or there is damage to the extended attribute system file. Run CHKDSK /F on the disk or diskette.

SYS0280: *Extended attributes cannot be created on this disk or diskette* Extended attributes could not be put on the disk or diskette because no free directory entry exists in the root directory, or not enough space is available. Remove unneeded files from the root directory and retry.

SYS0281: *The extended attribute system file cannot be opened* The system could not open the extended attribute system file. The file could be missing, and if it is, it may be unrecoverable. Try running CHKDSK /F on the disk or diskette.

SYS0282: *The target file system cannot save extended attributes*
You tried to save extended attributes using a file system that does not have the ability to save them. Use a file system that can save them or use the EAUTIL /S command to save the file without saving the extended attributes.

SYS0283: *The target file system cannot save extended attributes*
This error message is similar to the previous one except that there is no option to save the file or directory without the extended attributes via the EAUTIL /S command. You must use a file system that will save extended attributes.

SYS0332: *The specified queue name is already in use* A process tried to create a queue using the same name as that of an existing queue. Contact the software company or the programmer.

SYS0333: *The specified queue element does not exist* A process attempted to read or peek at an item that is not in the queue. Contact the software company or programmer.

SYS0334: *Not enough memory is available to process a queue request* The total amount of memory for queues in the system has been exceeded. Cancel one or more of the applications that use queues. If there is only one application running, contact the software company or programmer.

SYS0515: *Too many device drivers are registered with the Session Manager* The Session Manager function has too many device drivers registered; you must remove one or more device driver statements from CONFIG.SYS. Then restart your system and retry the command.

SYS0525: *The specified disk cannot be formatted* Either another process is accessing the disk you specified or you have not logged on with sufficient privileges to format the disk. End the process that is accessing the disk or log on with an ID that gives you the privileges you need.

SYS0526: *The system detected an error and cannot format the specified disk for HPFS (High Performance File System)* This error is sometimes caused by a bad disk, a bad disk device driver, or an incompatible disk, disk drive controller, or device driver. Restart your computer and try running FORMAT again. If the computer will not start from the hard disk, use OS/2 or DOS from a diskette. Then format the disk for the FAT (File Allocation Table) file system.

If the hard disk will take the FAT format, the problem is with the disk device driver that you are using with HPFS. If the format does not work, the disk is probably unusable.

SYS0527: HPFS (High Performance File System) data cannot be copied to the specified disk   The disk you want to format is either corrupt or not large enough for the HPFS files. Run FORMAT again and if it fails, use FDISK to increase the size of the partition, or format the partition for the FAT file system.

SYS0528: The specified disk did not finish formatting   An operating system error occurred while the disk was being formatted, and the format is not complete. The best solution is to restart the computer and retry.

SYS0529: Not enough memory is available to run FORMAT
The memory needed to run FORMAT is currently not available. Close any programs that you no longer need and retry.

SYS0530: You must specify a hard disk with the FORMAT command
This error message occurs when you have specified HPFS with the FORMAT command. HPFS partitions can be created only on hard disks and you must indicate a hard disk letter. If you are trying to format a diskette, you must format for a FAT file system.

SYS0531: You can specify only one drive letter with FORMAT
HPFS formats are only to be used for one hard disk partition at a time.

SYS0540: The disk did not format for HPFS   The disk cannot be formatted for HPFS because the HPFS File System Driver is not loaded. Load the File System Driver and retry.

SYS0543: *** is not a valid parameter with the CHKDSK command when checking a hard disk   You entered the command CHKDSK with a parameter that is incorrect. Enter **HELP CHKDSK** for the valid parameters.

SYS0544: CHKDSK cannot access drive *** CHKDSK cannot read data from the drive you specified. Either the drive does not exist or another process is using it. If you used the /F parameter, make sure no other process is using the drive.

SYS0546: Not enough memory is available to run CHKDSK
CHKDSK requires more memory than is available. Close some processes and retry.

SYS0547: CHKDSK cannot write recovered data to the disk
CHKDSK located lost files but did not write the recovered information to the disk yet. Make sure there is room on the disk by deleting any files you don't need.

SYS0548: Warning! Not enough memory is available for CHKDSK to recover all lost data CHKDSK is trying to recover lost data but not enough memory is available to recover all of the data. End one or more programs that are running in other sessions or as background processes, and then retry.

SYS0549: Not enough disk space is available to run CHKDSK using the /F parameter CHKDSK is fixing errors as it finds them, but there is not enough disk space to write the recovered data to the disk. Make room on the drive by deleting unneeded files, and then retry.

SYS0550: CHKDSK did not recover any data CHKDSK did not recover any data on the disk because it could not identify any of the directories or files. First, restart the system and try CHKDSK again. If that does not solve it, try restoring files from a backup. If that fails too, you may have to format the disk.

SYS0551: Warning! CHKDSK cannot find the root directory of the specified disk but will still attempt to reconstruct the file system
CHKDSK is trying to recover lost data even though it is unable to find the root directory of the disk. Probably, some of the data will not be recovered. After the CHKDSK process is completed, examine the disk to see if all of the files were recovered. If not, try running CHKDSK /F:3 to recover them.

SYS0552: *The system found file system errors on the disk specified*
CHKDSK detected file system errors on the disk and those errors were not corrected. Use the CHKDSK command with the /F parameter.

SYS0562: *The system detected lost data on disk* *** Lost data was detected on the disk. Use the /F parameter to recover the data.

SYS0565: *Warning! CHKDSK cannot read critical HPFS data on the specified disk. Do not turn your computer off before you back up files. Back up all files on this disk immediately!* It is important to pay attention to this message. Do not turn your computer off until you create a backup copy of all files on the disk. It might be that the disk is unusable and the file system files unreadable, and once you turn off your computer, you probably will not be able to access this partition. If this is your primary partition, that means you will be unable to restart your system. Use the OS/2 BACKUP command or a backup program to back up all files and directories on the disk. Then, FORMAT with the /FS:HPFS parameter to reformat the drive. Finally, restore your data from the backup copy.

SYS0566: *The specified disk is being used by another process*
CHKDSK cannot run on a partition while another process is accessing the partition. End all programs and retry.

SYS0576: *CHKDSK found extended attributes in a temporary replacement sector but could not relocate the data* When HPFS cannot write data to the proper place on the disk, it writes the data to a temporary replacement sector. Not enough disk space is available to move the data to the correct location. Delete unneeded files to make room and then retry.

SYS0579: *CHKDSK found an access control list in a temporary replacement sector but could not relocate it to its correct place*
This message, like the one above, is caused by insufficient disk space, and the remedy is the same—make room on the disk and retry.

SYS0588: *CHKDSK found data in a temporary replacement sector but could not relocate it to its correct place* Again, insufficient disk space is the problem. Use the remedy noted above.

SYS0590: CHKDSK found data in a temporary relocation sector
Data was found in a temporary relocation sector during a CHKDSK process. Use the /F parameter to recover the data.

SYS0593: * is not a valid parameter with the RECOVER command**
The only valid parameter of the RECOVER command is the name of the file that you want to recover. Make sure you have used the correct path name.

SYS0594: RECOVER cannot find the specified file   RECOVER cannot find the file you specified on the disk. Make sure you typed the filename correctly.

SYS0596: Not enough memory is available to run RECOVER
RECOVER requires more memory than is currently available. Close one or more programs and retry.

SYS0597: RECOVER cannot write the recovered data to the specified disk   The disk is either full or bad. Delete unneeded files to make room and retry.

SYS0598: RECOVER cannot create a temporary file   RECOVER can create up to 10,000 files named FILEnnnn.REC (where "nnnn" is a number). You attempted to exceed that number. Delete or rename one or more existing FILEnnnn.REC files and retry.

SYS0599: Warning: RECOVER cannot read extended attributes
One or more attributes may have been deleted because RECOVER is unable to read a list of extended attributes. There is nothing you can do to solve this.

SYS0603: No information about bad blocks was written to the specified disk   RECOVER was unable to write information about bad blocks to the disk because another process was accessing the disk. No action is required.

SYS0604: RECOVER cannot delete the original file *. The contents of the original file were recovered in *****   Duplicate files now exist on your disk, so you must delete the original file and rename the recovered file.

SYS0605: RECOVER cannot create a new file named ***. The contents of the original file were recovered in *** Duplicate files now exist on your disk. This was probably caused because a read-only attribute of a file is set, or you have insufficient file access permission. Check the attributes on the original file and check your access rights. If you have the appropriate permission, delete the original file and rename the recovered file.

SYS0606: An unexpected operating system error occurred
RECOVER detected an operating system error. Restart your system and retry.

SYS0607: *** is not a valid parameter with the SYS command
You must specify the drive that you want the system data transferred to.

SYS0608: The HPFS (High Performance File System) cannot be installed on the current drive by the SYS command The command assumes that the current drive is the source drive. The source and target drives cannot be the same. Specify a different drive as the target drive.

SYS0609: Only drives formatted for HPFS (High Performance File System) can run HPFS SYS You tried to use SYS on a drive that is not formatted for HPFS. You can only use this version of SYS on HPFS formatted drives.

SYS0610: The file *** cannot be created by the SYS command
The system files cannot be written to the target disk. Check to see if the disk is full or write-protected, or if a file already exists with the read-only attribute set. Use the appropriate remedy, depending on the problem you find.

SYS0612: The system detected a syntax error in the IFS= statement of the CONFIG.SYS file The IFS= statement contains illegal characters. Edit CONFIG.SYS to correct the IFS= statement, and then restart the system.

SYS0613: Not enough memory is available for the cache to start
The cache requires a minimum of 64K to start. This minimum amount was not available. Reinstall a new version of HPFS.

SYS0626: The system detected a disk error on the HPFS (High Performance File System) volume in drive *** An error was found on the HPFS volume in the specified drive. This is usually caused by the disk not being formatted correctly. Reformat the HPFS volume.

SYS0627: Drive *** was improperly stopped. From the OS/2 command prompt, run CHKDSK with the /F parameter on the specified drive An HPFS drive gives this message if the system lost power or was turned off before the **Shutdown** choice in the Desktop was used. Run CHKDSK with the /F parameter on the specified drive using the following steps:

1. Insert the Installation diskette in drive A.

2. Press CTRL+ALT+DEL.

3. At the prompt, insert Diskette 1.

4. At the logo screen, press the ESC key to display the OS/2 command prompt.

5. Type **CHKDSK ***: /F** at the command prompt; then, press the ENTER key and follow the instructions on the screen.

6. When CHKDSK finishes, remove Diskette 1.

7. Press CTRL+ALT+DEL to restart the system.

 Note If you receive this message after your system is started, you need only use step 5.

SYS0629: *** is not a valid parameter to use with the FORMAT command when formatting a hard disk You entered an invalid parameter for FORMAT. Enter **HELP FORMAT** to see the valid parameters.

SYS0630: The High Performance File System (HPFS) format could not modify the CONFIG.SYS file When a volume is formatted for HPFS, the IFS= statement in CONFIG.SYS is modified. Your CONFIG.SYS file was not modified because the drive or drives formatted for HPFS were not included with the /AUTOCHECK: parameter in the IFS= statement.

You will have to edit CONFIG.SYS to make sure the letters of all drives that are formatted for HPFS are included with the /AUTOCHECK: parameter in the IFS= statement of the CONFIG.SYS file.

SYS0637: The FORMAT command cannot be executed at this time
Too many FORMAT commands are running concurrently. When one of the FORMAT processes is finished, retry.

SYS0638: The *** Virtual Device Driver does not support *** access
A DOS application is trying to access a function that is not supported by the Virtual Device Driver. Do the following:

1. Save data.

2. End the application.

3. At the DOS prompt, type **EXIT** to end the virtual DOS machine session.

SYS0639: The keyboard is not locked. If you want to lock your keyboard and mouse, display the Desktop pop-up menu; then, select Lockup now   KP.COM and other keyboard-lockup utility programs are not supported in DOS mode. To set the keyboard and mouse lockup password, display the Desktop pop-up menu; select **LOCKUP NOW** and enter a password.

SYS0651: DOS support is not active because the DEVICE statement for the Virtual *** device was not specified in the CONFIG.SYS file
DOS support was specified in CONFIG.SYS by setting the PROTECTONLY statement to NO, but the Virtual *** device driver was not specified. This device driver must be specified for DOS support. Take the following steps:

1. Continue with start-up.

2. Add the DEVICE statement for the Virtual *** device driver to CONFIG.SYS.

3. Restart the system.

SYS0652: *The specified drive letter is in use and cannot be re-mapped or deregistered*   The drive letter you want to access is currently in use and cannot be remapped or deregistered at this time.

SYS0653: *The syntax used for mapping drives is incorrect. You must specify two drive letters*   You used the mapping symbol (=) in the command, but did not specify the two drive letters to map.

SYS0654: *The syntax used for drive sequence is incorrect. You must specify two drive letters*   You used a sequence symbol (-) in the command, but did not specify the first and last letters of the sequence.

SYS0655: *The syntax for deregistration is incorrect. The deregistration symbol (!) must precede a drive letter*   You used a deregistration symbol (!) in the command, but did not specify the DOS drive letter to deregister.

SYS0656: *The FSFILTER.SYS device is not installed*   FSACCESS requires the installation of the FSFILTER.SYS device driver. Edit the Virtual Machine (VM) Boot CONFIG.SYS file and add DEVICE=FSFILTER.SYS as the first device driver statement. Close the VM Boot session and restart the session.

SYS0657: *The parameter specified is not a drive letter*   FSACCESS requires a drive letter as a parameter.

SYS0659: *There is not enough space on the target disk to complete this operation. Space available: ***KB Space needed: ***KB*   Additional disk space on the target disk is needed in order to complete this operation. Delete unneeded files to make space on the disk.

SYS0663: *VEMM.SYS is required for EMM386 on OS/2*   To load the EMM386 device driver in a DOS session, you must install the OS/2 VEMM.SYS device driver. Be sure there is a DEVICE= statement in the OS/2 CONFIG.SYS file that loads the VEMM.SYS device driver. If there isn't, you will have to reinstall OS/2 and select DOS Support as an installation option.

SYS0664: *VXMS.SYS is required for HIMEM on OS/2*   In order to load the HIMEM device driver in a DOS session, you must install the

OS/2 VXMS.SYS device driver. Check for a DEVICE= statement that loads the VXMS.SYS device driver in the OS/2 CONFIG.SYS file. If it is not there, reinstall OS/2 and select DOS Support as an installation option.

SYS0665: VMOUSE.SYS is required for MOUSE on OS/2 In order to load MOUSE.COM in a DOS session, the OS/2 VMOUSE.SYS device driver must be present. Check the OS/2 CONFIG.SYS file to be sure there is a DEVICE= statement that loads the VMOUSE.SYS device driver. If there isn't, reinstall OS/2 and select DOS Support as an installation option.

SYS0666: EMM386 requires OS/2 Version 2.0 or above The OS/2 EMM386.SYS device driver does not provide services for earlier versions of OS/2.

SYS0667: HIMEM requires OS/2 Version 2.0 or above. Use the DOS version of the driver The OS/2 HIMEM.SYS device driver does not provide XMS services for earlier versions of OS/2. Use the DOS version of the driver.

SYS0668: MOUSE requires OS/2 Version 2.0 or above OS/2's MOUSE.COM does not provide services for earlier versions of OS/2. Use the DOS version of the driver.

SYS0670: The specified disk or diskette cannot start The disk or diskette specified by the VM boot path DOS setting, is not able to start in a VM boot session. This could be because the disk or diskette has not been formatted for startup or the startup program is trying to use invalid instructions. Make sure the VM boot path setting is set to a disk or diskette that has a startable DOS system.

SYS0693: The system could not read an HPFS (High Performance File System) structure from drive ***. To prevent possible system instability or loss of data, backup critical files from the drive and run CHKDSK /F The HPFS had a disk error while updating the system's temporary and reserved allocation pool. This may have left the system in an inconsistent state. Backup critical files from the affected drive and run CHKDSK /F on the drive as soon as possible.

SYS0700: The baud rate *** is not supported by the serial port hardware The baud rate had the correct syntax, but the serial port hardware does not support the baud rate you specified. Check the specifications for the hardware and specify a different baud rate.

SYS0722: No baud rate has been specified The baud rate is a required parameter.

SYS1003: The syntax of the command is incorrect There are several syntax mistakes that could produce this error message:

☐ An incorrect parameter was specified.

☐ An incorrect separator was specified.

☐ A required parameter is missing.

☐ Too many parameters were entered.

☐ The parameters were entered in the wrong order.

Type **HELP** followed by the command name to see syntax information.

SYS1006: The file is too big to be sorted A file larger than 63KB cannot be sorted. There is no remedy.

SYS1010: The number of lines (records) in the file has exceeded the limit of the SORT command The number of lines in a file has a maximum determined by the formula (file size + 768)/4. Either reduce the number of lines in the file or split the file into smaller files.

SYS1019: The system cannot find the drive specified An incorrect disk drive letter was used.

SYS1024: Warning! The directory is full The root directory is full and cannot store the files requested. Delete unneeded files from the root directory of the disk.

SYS1034: The system cannot find the command processor in the path specified The system cannot find CMD.EXE in the specified path. Make sure that CMD.EXE is in the path specified. You may need to change the PROTSHELL= parameter in CONFIG.SYS and restart the system.

SYS1035: The system cannot accept the path or file name requested An incorrect path or filename was entered with the RENAME, TYPE, MKDIR, MOVE, or RMDIR command.

SYS1036: The system cannot accept the date entered An incorrect date format was entered. Use the format MM/DD/YY, MM-DD-YY, or MM.DD.YY.

SYS1039: The system cannot find the batch label specified The label specified in the GOTO command could not be found in the batch file. Remove the GOTO command or edit the batch file to put the desired label in the correct location.

SYS1041: The name specified is not recognized as an internal or external command, operable program, or batch file This is the OS/2 version of "Bad command or file name". Any command entered at the command line must be an OS/2 internal or external command, a batch file, or the filename of an executable file that launches software. Check your spelling first, and if that is correct, make sure the command or file that you are trying to initiate is in the current path.

SYS1044: The system cannot accept the time entered An incorrect time format was entered. Reenter the time using 00:00:00 as the format.

SYS1045: The application program is not compatible with the version of the operating system being used Usually incurred on systems that have older versions of OS/2 in addition to version 2.0, this error message indicates that the program requires a different version of the operating system. Use Operating System/2 Version 2.0 and restart the system, or install the proper version of the application program on the system.

SYS1057: The file or path name entered is not valid in a DOS session The DOS application could not be launched because the filename or the path is not valid in a DOS session. The filename and all the path names must be limited to the DOS 8.3 filename format (FAT). Either rename the file or path using DOS file naming conventions (FAT), or move the file to a path that is valid in a DOS session.

SYS1058: The FAT (File Allocation Table) file system cannot replace a cluster that failed on a write operation. Your data was saved, and is in the root directory of drive *** in the HOTFIX.DAT file
An area of your hard disk is defective. Retrieve the data in the HOTFIX.DAT file, do a backup, and then reformat the drive.

SYS1059: The system cannot execute the specified program   The operating system encountered an unknown error while attempting to start up the program. Call the software company or programmer.

SYS1061: The system detected a file error   The file you tried to write to is read-only or the directory is full. If the former, use the ATTRIB command to change the read-only attribute; if the latter, delete unneeded files to make room.

SYS1066: The contents of the target file were lost   When the destination file and one of the source files share the same name, the shared name must be the same as the first source file listed for the COPY command. There is no remedy.

SYS1069: UNC path names are not supported by this command
A uniform naming convention network path name does not work with this command. Use a command that supports UNC, or correct the path name.

SYS1078: The file cannot be copied onto itself   You named the target file the same as the source file. Most of the time, this happens because you neglect to name the target file and the source file becomes the default target. If you type **COPY FILENAME** without a target, you will receive this error message.

SYS1081: CMD.EXE has halted   A permanent copy of CMD.EXE was running, and either a program tried to cancel it or CMD.EXE was started using a redirected input file and the end of that file was reached. There is no remedy; you will have to restart the system.

SYS1083: A duplicate file name exists, the file cannot be found, or the file is being used   The target filename specified with the RENAME or MOVE command already exists or is in use by a process, or the source file cannot be found. Check the target filename or wait until a process has finished using the file.

SYS1102: The system cannot create the directory   The JOIN command was unable to create the directory you specified. Retry the command, making sure the directory name is correct.

SYS1103: The system cannot find the directory specified   The directory you specified does not exist on your system. Create it and retry.

SYS1107: The system cannot complete the process   The command is either a file that can be run only in a DOS session or is an invalid executable file. If the file is a DOS file, switch to a DOS session and then retry the command. If the file is an invalid executable file, check your spelling.

SYS1141: The system cannot find the files specified: ***   The source path specified does not contain the files requested. Check the path statement.

SYS1184: The system cannot copy the file   The source and target files cannot have the same name.

SYS1185: Internal error *** occurred during XCOPY   An unexpected error occurred during XCOPY processing. Restart the system before trying again.

SYS1186: XCOPY cannot access the source file   You have one of the following problems:

- [ ] There is a Cyclic Redundancy Check error.

- [ ] The file is in use by another process.

- [ ] Too many files are open.

- [ ] The diskette is not a DOS diskette.

You will have to ascertain which problem exists and then retry.

SYS1187: XCOPY cannot access the target file   You have one of the following problems:

☐   The disk is full.

☐   The file or drive is in use or locked by another process.

☐   Too many files are open.

☐   The target file is a read-only file.

☐   A disk error occurred.

Determine which problem you have, fix it, and try again.

SYS1192: XCOPY cannot access the source or target drive   E i t h e r the disk is in use by another process or there has been a disk error. If the former, wait and retry. In the latter case, if the problem involves a diskette, make sure it is inserted properly or format it.

SYS1193: The processor is disabled because OS/2 does not support the 80287 math coprocessor   OS/2 does not support the 80386 processor with the 80287 math coprocessor. Upgrade to an 80387 math coprocessor.

SYS1195: The command "***" on line *** of the CONFIG.SYS file is not recognized. Line *** is ignored   The command specified is not a recognized configuration command. Edit CONFIG.SYS to change or remove the incorrect command and restart the system.

SYS1196: The parameter "***" on line *** of the CONFIG.SYS file is not acceptable for the *** command. Line *** is ignored   The parameter is not a correct keyword or numeric value for the configuration command. Edit CONFIG.SYS to correct or remove the parameter and restart the system.

SYS1197: The *** command requires a parameter that is not specified on line *** of the CONFIG.SYS file. Line *** is ignored
The specified command requires a parameter. Edit CONFIG.SYS to correct or remove the incorrect command and restart the system.

SYS1204: An Input/Output privilege level is required for the program or device driver *** Input/Output privilege level 2 is required by an application or device. To permit this, add the statement IOPL=YES to CONFIG.SYS and restart the system.

SYS1210: The process cannot be completed. You are using an incorrect version of the operating system The version of the operating system in your system is not the expected level. Use the VER command to determine the level of Operating System/2 you are using. You should be using Operating System/2 Version 2.0.

SYS1217: The file cannot be decompressed with this version of the OS/2 UNPACK command A file must be decompressed with the same version of OS/2 that was used to compress it.

SYS1231: The system cannot accept the drive specified or a hard disk An incorrect drive was specified, or a hard disk was specified and this program cannot accept a hard drive.

SYS1234: The source diskette is bad or incompatible with the drive type The diskette and drive type are incompatible with each other, or the diskette is unusable.

SYS1235: Target diskette is bad or incompatible with the drive type The diskette and drive type are incompatible with each other, or the diskette is unusable.

SYS1248: A subdirectory or file *** ***already exists*** A subdirectory or file with the same name already exists in the target directory.

SYS1261: An error occurred while reading from the source diskette During a DISKCOPY, the system detected an error while reading from the source diskette. The function will attempt to proceed normally. There is no action required.

SYS1262: An error occurred while writing to the target diskette. Information on the target diskette might be distorted During a DISKCOPY, the system detected an error while writing to the target diskette. The function will attempt to proceed normally. Reformat or change the diskette and retry.

SYS1274: The size of the requested partition exceeds 2,048 MB or is beyond cylinder 1023 of your disk The OS/2 FAT file system can only support partitions up to 2,048 MB and/or before cylinder 1023. If the drive does not provide a translation feature that permits you to get around this problem, you will have to repartition the hard disk.

SYS1275: The /S parameter is not supported in this release of OS/2 The /S parameter has been removed from the FORMAT command in version 2.0.

SYS1276: The FORMAT command has detected an incorrect parameter You have entered an incorrect parameter. Type HELP FORMAT for the information you need.

SYS1279: The format was unsuccessful A disk error occurred while the disk was being formatted. Review the error messages displayed, and take the corrective action.

SYS1280: The disk is unsuitable for a system disk The area on the disk that holds system information is not usable. Either retry the FORMAT command using another diskette or repartition the hard disk.

SYS1281: Track 0 cannot be formatted Either track 0 is defective or the diskette and drive type are incompatible. If the former, throw away the disk; if the latter, put the correct size diskette into the drive or repartition the hard disk.

SYS1291: An error has occurred while reading the system file *** FORMAT could not read the files that are required for a system transfer. Retry from another OS/2 diskette or recopy the system files to your default disk and retry.

SYS1296: FORMAT cannot write the file system to the target disk The area on the disk where the system information is stored is not usable. Retry the FORMAT command with a different diskette or repartition the hard disk.

SYS1297: An incorrect parameter was specified for formatting the hard disk A parameter was used that is only valid for formatting diskettes and cannot be used for formatting a hard disk.

SYS1298: An incorrect combination of parameters was specified
FORMAT parameters were entered that cannot be used together.

SYS1303: The system is currently unable to format drive *** The system cannot support the device as configured. A Virtual Disk (VDISK.SYS) is already formatted. Check the DEVICE= command in CONFIG.SYS.

SYS1310: A drive letter must be specified The FORMAT command was entered without a drive letter.

SYS1311: The system files are missing The system files cannot be found on the default drive.

SYS1313: An error has occurred while reading or writing to the hard disk partition Either the partition table of the hard disk does not contain an OS/2 partition, or the partition is unusable. You will have to repartition the hard disk.

SYS1316: The version of extended attributes is not correct
The format of the extended attributes on this disk or diskette is not correct for this version of OS/2.

SYS1319: Incorrect volume label entered for drive *** An incorrect volume label for the hard disk to be formatted was used. Type **VOL** to determine the current volume label and then use that label when the FORMAT command prompts for the label.

SYS1330: The system cannot accept the ****** parameter One or more of the parameters entered for the CHKDSK command is not correct. Type **HELP CHKDSK** for the correct CHKDSK parameters.

SYS1333: CHKDSK cannot access the specified drive The drive specified is not correct, the diskette is not in the OS/2 format, or the diskette is unusable.

SYS1335: *** allocation error, size adjusted The file had a different size than the number of clusters associated with the file and the file size was adjusted automatically. Be aware that this error may be an indication of hard disk problems.

SYS1337: *Disk error writing the File Allocation Table* *** There was a disk error during an attempt to update the File Allocation Table on the specified drive. The table number will be 1 or 2, depending on which of the two copies of the File Allocation Table could not be written. If the message appears for both copies, format the disk. The disk is unusable if the formatting fails.

SYS1340: *** *has an incorrect cluster* During a CHKDSK, it was found that the file *** contains an incorrect pointer to a data block. Use the /F option to truncate the file at the last valid data block. No corrective action can occur if CHKDSK is used without the /F option.

SYS1341: *The system cannot read the current directory*
CHKDSK attempted to read the current directory. It found an unrecoverable error on the disk. The disk is unusable.

SYS1342: *** *allocation size error* During a CHKDSK, it was found that a file has a different size than the number of clusters associated with the file. To correct the file size, type **CHKDSK /F**.

SYS1343: *** *is cross-linked on cluster* *** During a CHKDSK, it was found that the File Allocation Table points to the same data block for these files. The files are assigned to the same space on the disk or diskette. Make copies of the specified files and delete the original files. You should look at the files because they may need editing (if they are data files).

SYS1347: *** *directory is totally empty. Tree past this point is not processed* During CHKDSK, a subdirectory was found that does not contain a . or .. entry. The usual cause is that the operating system was not able to update the disk properly because the system was shut down prematurely. Try the RECOVER command to recover files on the damaged disk.

SYS1349: *** *is an incorrect subdirectory* Incorrect information was found in subdirectory ***. CHKDSK will attempt to correct the error if you used the /F option.

SYS1350: The system cannot recover . entry, processing continued
A subdirectory did not properly contain a . entry. This usually occurs when the operating system is not given a chance to update the disk properly. Try the RECOVER command to recover the files on the damaged disk.

SYS1351: The system cannot recover the .. entry. Tree past this point not processed A subdirectory did not properly contain a .. entry. This usually occurs when the operating system is not given a chance to update the disk properly. Try the RECOVER command.

SYS1352: *** has a bad link, attribute, or size
end with one or two dots. One dot indicates that the current directory is in error. Two dots indicate that the parent directory is in error. If you did not enter the /F option with CHKDSK, no corrective action will be taken. Enter **CHKDSK /F** and CHKDSK will try to correct the error.

SYS1359: *** bytes disk space would be freed
was noted that some disk space is marked as allocated and is not associated with any file. Using CHKDSK without the /F option does not free up any space, so enter **CHKDSK /F**.

SYS1360: No recovered files can be added to the root directory
CHKDSK was trying to create files from the lost data blocks it found, but the root directory is full and the lost chains could not be recovered into files. Copy some of the files that were recovered to another disk and delete them from the disk you are checking. Run CHKDSK again to recover the remainder of the lost data.

SYS1374: File Allocation Table is bad on drive *** Multiple errors occurred while writing to a disk drive. The disk may be unusable. You will have to format the disk.

SYS1376: A disk error occurred while writing to directory entry ***
A disk error was found while CHKDSK /F was trying to update the directory entry. The directory entry ******* may not be usable. There is nothing you can do.

SYS1377: *The system is unable to write to the root directory on drive* ***   A diskette error was found while CHKDSK /F was trying to update the root directory. Check to see that the diskette was inserted properly. If so, the diskette may have been write-protected or unformatted.

SYS1397: *System trace information was not specified in your CONFIG.SYS file*   The CONFIG.SYS file does not contain a TRACE= or TRACEBUF= statement. Enter the appropriate system trace statements into CONFIG.SYS and restart the system before trying the command again.

SYS1433: *The system cannot find the input device specified*   An incorrect input device name was entered.

SYS1434: *The system cannot find the output device specified*
An incorrect device name was entered.

SYS1457: *The system is unable to transfer system files at this time*
Wait for another process to end and then retry.

SYS1458: *The system cannot find the operating system files*
The operating system files do not exist on the default drive. Reenter the command using the correct default drive for the operating system files.

SYS1461: *The system cannot accept the target drive*   An incorrect target drive was entered, or no drive specification was given at all, or the disk is not formatted.

SYS1465: *The VDISK specified in the CONFIG.SYS file cannot be installed*   The DEVICE=VDISK statement in CONFIG.SYS contains incorrect parameters. Correct the DEVICE=VDISK statement and restart the system.

SYS1466: *The system does not have enough storage to initialize a virtual disk*   VDISK requires more storage than is currently available. You can change the amount of space requested in the DEVICE=VDISK statements in CONFIG.SYS or edit CONFIG.SYS to reduce the values given for the BUFFERS=, TRACEBUF=, DISKCACHE=, or THREADS=

statements. Another option is to add memory to your system. (Remember, you have to restart the system if you change CONFIG.SYS.)

SYS1470: The system cannot accept the drive *** specified for the SWAPPATH= statement in the CONFIG.SYS file. The default drive *** will be used   The drive you specify for the SWAPPATH= statement must be a single letter followed by a colon (and optionally, a path), and the drive must exist on your system. Correct CONFIG.SYS and restart your system.

SYS1471: The system cannot accept the path *** specified for the SWAPPATH= statement in the CONFIG.SYS file. The system will attempt to use the subdirectory \OS2\SYSTEM of the startup drive   The path you specified is incorrect. The path must be the name of a subdirectory that exists on the specified disk. Correct CONFIG.SYS and restart your system.

SYS1472: The system cannot create file ***   The hard disk or diskette may be full. Swapping requires a minimum of 512KB free space, and you may have to delete unneeded files to make room. The error will also occur if the diskette is write-protected. You can also change the SWAPPATH= statement in CONFIG.SYS to specify a different drive. Remember to restart your system after changing CONFIG.SYS.

SYS1474: The system does not have enough storage to activate swapping   There is not enough system memory or disk storage available. You can edit CONFIG.SYS to reduce the value specified in the BUFFERS=, TRACEBUF=, DISKCACHE=, THREADS=, or RMSIZE= statements. You can also reduce the size allocated for a virtual disk in a DEVICE=VDISK.SYS statement, install more memory, or delete unneeded files from the swap disk. Remember to restart your system if you change CONFIG.SYS.

SYS1476: The system cannot accept the path *** specified for the SWAPPATH= statement in the CONFIG.SYS file. The system will attempt to use the root directory of the startup drive   The   path specified is incorrect; it must be the name of a subdirectory that exists on the disk.

If you want to use a specific path for the swap file, change the SWAPPATH= statement in CONFIG.SYS and restart your system.

SYS1477: Warning! The partition containing the SWAPPER.DAT file is full. You may lose data   This is a serious error message and you must act on it immediately. It means that your system needs additional virtual memory for an application, but cannot expand the size of the swap file to meet the request. You must reduce the virtual memory requirement by closing applications or increase the amount of available space on the partition by deleting unneeded files.

SYS1502: An unrecoverable I/O error occurred when the system attempted to read the swap file and reload a segment. The system is shut down. To get help for this message go to any machine with OS/2 1.31 or OS/2 2.0 installed and type: help 1502 | more
A portion of the swap file is mapped to a bad sector on the hard disk. The system cannot read the specific segment in this area of the swap file. The solution depends on the location of your swap file, named SWAP-PER.DAT.

If the swap file is located on the C: partition (the default location), do the following:

1. Restart the system using an OS/2 or DOS startup diskette.

2. Backup to diskette any non-OS/2 system files located on the C: partition.

3. Reinstall OS/2 and select the option to format the C: partition. (Do not do this if you want to use the Dual Boot Option.)

4. Restore any files you backed up in Step 2.

If the swap file is located on a partition other than C, follow these steps:

1. Restart the system using an OS/2 or DOS startup diskette.

2. Edit the CONFIG.SYS file and change the SWAPPATH statement so that the swap file is located on the C: partition.

3. Restart OS/2 from the hard disk as usual.

4. If requested, perform an error recovery. You may have to reformat the partition that contained the bad sector.

SYS1505: A virtual disk could not be installed There are not enough drive letters available to install a virtual disk. You can try to make drive letters available by modifying the disk partitions. Use FDISK or delete DEVICE=VDISK statements in the CONFIG.SYS file.

SYS1509: The system cannot run the specified program The operating system detected an error when starting the program. Make sure the program exists and can be found (check the path or make sure you are in the right directory). Another option is to close an application and try again, in case there was a memory problem.

SYS1511: The program cannot continue processing A function needed by a program is not available or is in use. Wait and retry.

SYS1520: * additional diskette drive(s) did not install** All drive letters are being used by the hard disks. Delete any unneeded logical partitions.

SYS1521: There are too many parameters specified in the * command on line *** of the CONFIG.SYS file. Line *** is ignored** The specified command in the CONFIG.SYS file has more parameters than are permitted. Edit CONFIG.SYS to correct or remove the incorrect command and restart the system.

SYS1523: "*" was found where "***" was expected in the *** command on line *** of the CONFIG.SYS file. Line *** is ignored** A required symbol has been left out or is misplaced. Edit CONFIG.SYS to correct or remove the incorrect command, and then restart the system.

SYS1525: The system cannot accept the option selected An option for PRINT was selected that does not exist. Options /B, /C, /T, and /D: are the only ones the system accepts.

SYS1526: The system cannot accept the combination of parameters entered Multiple parameters entered with PRINT cannot be used together, or no parameter was specified.

SYS1529: The system cannot print the file to the device specified
Correct printer device names are PRN, LPT1, LPT2, and LPT3.

SYS1531: The spooler is not running   A /C or /T option was requested with PRINT, but the spooler is not running. Retry without those options.

SYS1532: DOS sessions cannot accept the /C or /T parameter
The /C or /T parameter can only be used in an OS/2 session.

SYS1572: You used an invalid FDISK parameter   The parameter you used is not valid for the FDISK command. /D is the only parameter you can use.

SYS1601: The MODE parameters are incorrect   The MODE command accepts only the following parameters:

☐   For parallel printer modes:

    MODE LPT# chars,lines,P

    MODE PRN chars,lines,P

☐   For video modes:

    MODE display,rows

☐   For asynchronous modes for DOS sessions:

    MODE COM#:baud,parity,databits,stopbits

☐   For asynchronous modes for OS/2 sessions:

    MODE COM#:baud,parity,databits,stopbits,

    TO=ON I OFF,XON=ON I OFF,IDSR=ON I OFF,ODSR=ON I OFF,

    OCTS=ON I OFF,DTR=ON I OFF I HS,RTS=ON I OFF I HS I TOG

☐ For diskette verification:

MODE DSKT VER=ON I OFF

SYS1613: The MODE parameter *** is not correct   The value for the printer parameter is incorrect. The only acceptable values are LPT# (where # is 1, 2, or 3) or PRN.

SYS1614: The MODE parameter CHARS *** is not correct   The value for the printer characters parameter is incorrect. Only 80 and 132 are valid.

SYS1615: The MODE parameter LINES *** is not correct   The value for the printer lines/inch parameter is incorrect. Only 6 or 8 may be used.

SYS1616: The MODE parameter *** is not correct   The value for the COM# parameter is incorrect. Only COM# 1 to 8 are valid.

SYS1617: The MODE parameter BAUD *** is not correct   The value for the BAUD parameter is incorrect. Only the following values can be entered as parameters:

110, 150, 300, 600, 1200, 1800, 2400, 3600, 4800, 7200, 9600, 19200, 38400, 57600, 76800, 115200, 138240, 172800, 230400, 345600.

Note   BAUD rates higher than 19200 are only valid on certain systems.

SYS1619: The MODE parameter *** is not supported for DOS sessions   You are operating in the DOS environment, but the parameter specified is for an OS/2 session. The following MODE parameters can be used in OS/2 sessions only:

TO=, XON=, IDSR=, ODSR=, OCTS=, DTR=, RTS=

SYS1620: The COM port specified is not installed   MODE detected a COM port that is not installed. Enter a correct port number.

SYS1622: The MODE parameter ROWS * is not correct** The value for the video mode rows parameter is incorrect. Only 25, 43, and 50 are valid.

SYS1624: The MODE parameter DISPLAY is missing When you enter a ROWS parameter for the MODE command, you must also enter a DISPLAY parameter. These are the valid display parameters:

40, 80, BW40, BW80, CO40, CO80, MONO

SYS1625: The MODE COM "*" parameter is not correct** The values for the asynchronous communications MODE parameters are incorrect. Here are the valid parameters:

COM#	1-8
BAUD	110, 150, 300, 600, 1200, 1800, 2400, 3600, 4800, 7200, 9600, 19200, 38400, 57600, 76800, 115200, 138240, 172800, 230400, 345600
PARITY	N(one), O(dd), E(ven), M(ark), S(pace)
DATABITS	5, 6, 7, 8
STOPBITS	1, 1.5, 2 (1.5 STOPBITS is correct only if DATABITS is set to 5)
P	
TO	ON, OFF
XON	ON, OFF
IDSR	ON, OFF
ODSR	ON, OFF
OCTS	ON, OFF
DTR	ON, OFF, HS
RTS	ON, OFF, HS, TOG

SYS1627: The MODE parameter * is not correct** The value for the diskette verification parameter is incorrect. Only DSKT VER=ON, OFF are valid.

SYS1642: The source and target drives entered are the same
This error occurs during RESTORE and reminds you that a disk cannot be restored onto itself.

SYS1643: The number of parameters entered is incorrect Using RESTORE, more than 11 parameters or less than 2 parameters were entered.

SYS1645: No files were found to restore All of the backup diskettes were searched, and there were no files matching the path and file(s) you specified. You probably inserted the wrong diskette.

SYS1651: The system cannot restore a file in an incorrect order
The diskettes you use during RESTORE must be inserted in the same order in which they were backed up.

SYS1664: The system cannot write to the BACKUP log file. Press ENTER *to continue, or press* CTRL+BREAK *to cancel* The /l parameter was specified but there is not enough room on the disk to create the log file. Press CTRL+BREAK to end the BACKUP log file procedure or press ENTER to continue without adding more entries to the log file. If you used CTRL+BREAK, you can delete unneeded files and retry.

SYS1667: No source drive was specified A source drive must be entered with the BACKUP command.

SYS1668: No target drive was specified A target drive must be entered for the BACKUP command.

SYS1671: The source and target drives entered are the same A disk cannot be backed up onto itself.

SYS1672: The system cannot run the FORMAT command Either the system could not find FORMAT.COM during BACKUP or there is not enough storage in the system. Use a formatted diskette.

SYS1676: The system cannot find the FORMAT utility During BACKUP, it was discovered that the FORMAT utility is not in the current directory or cannot be found in the path. Copy FORMAT to a location that can be found.

SYS1688: The file cannot be backed up at this time The file is being used by another process. Wait and retry.

SYS1690: The target disk cannot be used to back up files The system cannot create files on the target disk. Try a different diskette.

SYS1693: The system cannot create the directory You have one of the following problems:

☐   The directory cannot be created because it already exists.

☐   The directory path cannot be found.

☐   The root directory is full.

☐   A file already exists with the name you are trying to use.

☐   The directory name contains unacceptable characters or is an OS/2 reserved filename.

SYS1694: The path name is too long During XCOPY, the path specified was greater than 63 characters.

SYS1703: The system encountered an error while accessing file *** During XCOPY, a file was found to contain errors or was in use by another process.

SYS1704: XCOPY cannot be performed because the number of parameters entered is incorrect The source directory was not specified, or a parameter was entered more than once.

SYS1707: A version of DOS earlier than DOS 3.20 was detected This utility requires DOS version 3.20 or higher.

SYS1711: The Dual Boot feature file *** cannot be found Either the file is missing or the Dual Boot feature is not installed. Make sure that the file is present at the location specified in the error message. If the file is in the correct location, reinstall the Dual Boot feature.

SYS1712: The specified operating system is already on the current drive   The requested operating system is the same as the current operating system. The BOOT command is only used when you want to switch from the startup operating system to the other operating system.

SYS1713: The operating system did not start *** as requested
An error occurred during the attempt to change the startup operating system. Reinstall both operating systems.

SYS1714: Warning! Make sure all your programs have completed or data will be lost when the system is restarted   The BOOT utility made changes to your hard disk and replaced the C:\CONFIG.SYS and C:\AUTOEXEC.BAT files in preparation for the next reset. This means that if you restart the system while programs are running, those programs will automatically be ended and no changes will be saved. Be sure to end all programs properly and restart your system.

SYS1716: Warning! You should now restart your system by pressing CTRL+ALT+DEL   The program made changes to your hard disk and replaced files C:\CONFIG.SYS and C:\AUTOEXEC.BAT in preparation for the next reset.

SYS1718: The system cannot find the file "***" specified in the *** command on line *** of the CONFIG.SYS file. Line *** is ignored
The file containing the specified device driver, program, or data file cannot be found. Install the appropriate file and restart your system.

SYS1719: The file "***" specified in the *** command on line *** of the CONFIG.SYS file does not contain a valid device driver or file system driver. Line *** is ignored   The file specified does not contain a valid device driver or file system driver, or it has a DOS device driver and a DOS session was not started. Try one of these solutions and then restart your system:

☐   Edit the CONFIG.SYS file to correct or delete the incorrect command.

☐   Edit the CONFIG.SYS file and remove the PROTECTONLY=YES command.

☐   Install the correct device driver or file system driver.

☐   Install all the dynamic link libraries required by the device driver.

SYS1727: The system does not have enough storage for the DISKCACHE buffers   There is not enough storage available for the storage specified by the DISKCACHE statement. You can add more memory or reduce the values in CONFIG.SYS of the following statements:

DISKCACHE=, BUFFERS=, TRACEBUF=, THREADS=, RMSIZE=

You might also want to try to reduce the size allocated for a virtual disk in the DEVICE=VDISK.SYS statement. Remember to restart your system after changing CONFIG.SYS.

SYS1728: The value specified in the DISKCACHE statement in your CONFIG.SYS file is too small   The value entered in the DISKCACHE statement in CONFIG.SYS is too small for the amount of total DASD (hard disk size) in your system.

SYS1731: The BOOT command was not able to restart the system   An error prevented the BOOT command from automatically restarting the system. If you are running OS/2, the C:\OS2 directory probably does not contain the DOS.SYS file. If you have just run BOOT /DOS, the OS/2 CONFIG.SYS file might have an incorrect DEVICE= statement. Make the necessary changes and restart your system.

SYS1736: The DOS.SYS device driver cannot be found   The BOOT command cannot access a function of the DOS.SYS device driver. The device driver may be missing or not in the proper directory. If the DOS.SYS device driver is not in the C:\OS2 directory, use the UNPACK command to copy it from the OS/2 Installation Diskette to the C:\OS2 directory. Make sure the OS/2 CONFIG.SYS file contains a DEVICE=C:\OS2\DOS.SYS statement.

SYS1738: The system has detected an error when starting   The storage in the system cannot be allocated, or else a hardware error occurred. Run the diagnostics diskette to determine the cause of the problem.

SYS1748: The system cannot open the keyboard   The operating system had an error opening the keyboard. There are probably too many files or programs open.

SYS1750: The system cannot accept the keyboard type specified
The keyboard installed for the system is not compatible. Compatible types of keyboards are Personal Computer AT and Personal Computer Enhanced keyboards.

SYS1773: The system cannot accept the START command parameter *** You entered an incorrect parameter or a bad combination of parameters with the START command.

SYS1779: The Presentation Manager print device specified is not installed or is not ready The Presentation Manager detected an error while trying to write to this device. Make sure the device is installed, connected, and turned on. Check to see that the device is in the proper receive mode.

SYS1798: Your application tried to access a communications port, ***, which is in use by another application. Press Retry the operation if you would like to switch to the application which currently controls the communications port and end it. The OS/2 operating system will pause to give you time to end this application before reassigning the port to the waiting program. Press the Ignore choice if you would like the application to continue without access to ***. Press the End the program choice if you would like to end the application that is waiting to access ***. Warning! If you select this choice, both your application and its DOS command prompt session will end. You may lose data A communications port can be used by only one application at a time. End a program by selecting it from the Window List and then closing it.

SYS1799: Your application tried to access a parallel port, ***, which is in use by another application. Press Retry the operation if you would like to switch to the application which currently controls the parallel port and end it. The OS/2 operating system will pause to give you time to end this application before reassigning the port to the waiting program. Press the End the program choice if you would like to end the application that is waiting to access ***. Warning! If you select this choice, both your application and its DOS command prompt session will end. You may lose data A parallel port can be used by only one application at a time. End a program by selecting it from the Window List and then closing it.

SYS1801: OS/2 Procedures Language 2/REXX is not installed A REXX command file was not processed because OS/2 Procedures Language 2/REXX is not installed.

SYS1802: *** cannot be executed as a detached process A Presentation Manager program cannot be executed using the DETACH command. Use the START command.

SYS1803: Chaining was attempted from a REXX batch file CMD.EXE does not support chaining in REXX batch files. Check the REXX batch file for other batch filenames and precede them with the keyword CALL.

SYS1806: The system cannot start the session in the foreground The START command used the /F parameter, but CMD.EXE was not able to start the program in the foreground. The session did start, but it is not the foreground session. Switch to the session created by the command in order to make it the foreground session.

SYS1812: The process ended when it tried to use a non-existent math processor A math coprocessor is not present in your system. Either install one or use a version of the software that does not require one.

SYS1816: The batch file cannot be found The batch file that was running cannot be found, or it has been deleted. Replace or rebuild the batch file and retry.

SYS1818: Insufficient memory is available to examine extended attribute chains. Processing continues CHKDSK requires more memory to examine the extended attribute chains for the file or directory. All the extended attribute chains on this disk will be ignored. You can install more memory to prevent this in the future. Meanwhile, close an application or reduce the values of the following statements in CONFIG.SYS:

BUFFERS=, TRACEBUF=, DISKCACHE=, THREADS=, RMSIZE=, DEVICE=VDISK.SYS

SYS1827: The system cannot process this request.   A nonrecoverable error has occurred. Try to save all your programs and data and then restart your system.

SYS1828: The system cannot start the selected program   The maximum number of programs is currently running so you must close an application before starting a new one.

SYS1830: The system cannot set the mouse button assignments The mouse may not be installed properly. Check the mouse software configuration. If you make corrections, be sure to restart your system.

SYS1901: The query status function for COM port is not available for DOS sessions   The system can only establish the status of the COM port from an OS/2 session. Switch to an OS/2 session and retry.

SYS1902: The infinite retry option, P, is not valid in the OS/2 session. It has been ignored   The ASYNC parameter, P, has been specified in the OS/2 session but is only valid in DOS sessions. Either switch to a DOS session or set the infinite timeout setting to TO=ON in the OS/2 session.

SYS1924: A program in this session encountered a problem and cannot continue   The software disabled interrupts and did not reset them. An error in a ring 2 subroutine is causing it to return to ring 3 without resetting the interrupts. Contact the software company or the programmer.

SYS1996: EDLIN cannot open the specified file   The system has too many open files. Either wait for a program to end or increase the value of the FILES= statement in CONFIG.SYS and restart the system.

SYS1998: EDLIN will not edit a file with a .BAK extension   Files with the extension .BAK are backup files, and the replacement file is assumed to exist. If a replacement file doesn't exist, rename or copy the .BAK file and give it a different extension.

SYS1999: The disk is full and all the edits were lost   During EDLIN, The E (End Edit) command ended because the disk does not contain enough free space to save the entire file. Any editing of the file has been lost. Remove unneeded files to make room, and begin the edit again.

SYS2001: EDLIN cannot continue because of a syntax error
Except for the Edit Line command, all EDLIN commands are a single letter, usually preceded and/or followed by parameters.

SYS2005: EDLIN cannot continue because the line is longer than 253 characters   The replacement of a string with the R (Replace Text) command caused the line to expand beyond the 253-character limit. Split the line up.

SYS2008: EDLIN cannot continue unless a destination line number is specified   A destination line number is missing from an M (Move Lines) or C (Copy Lines) command.

SYS2009: EDLIN does not have enough room to merge the specified file
The T (Transfer Lines) command could not merge the entire contents of the file because of insufficient storage.

SYS2063: Not enough storage is available to create the DOS environment   Not enough space is available to create the DOS environment, or the specified DOS environment size is too large. Edit CONFIG.SYS to decrease the value of the RMSIZE command or add PROTECTONLY=YES. Then restart your system.

SYS2064: There is not enough storage to create the DOS environment
There is not enough storage available to create the DOS environment, or the specified DOS environment size is too small. Edit CONFIG.SYS and remove any unnecessary DEVICE commands, increase the value of the RMSIZE command, or add PROTECTONLY=NO.

SYS2068: *** messages were lost   The system had so many error messages to display during system initialization that it ran out of room to display them. If you correct the errors for the messages that were displayed and restart the system, any additional error messages will be displayed.

SYS2085: *** is no longer required. This command is not necessary
This command performs no required function in this version of OS/2. It is not necessary to execute this command and it can be removed from your batch file.

SYS2102: The network is not started   Either the network is not mounted or your CONFIG.SYS file is not correct.

SYS2150: The print queue does not exist   The queue that you specified is not valid. Check your spelling.

SYS2151: The print job does not exist   There is no print job matching the print job identification number you entered. Either the job has finished printing or it has been deleted from the print queue.

SYS2154: The print queue already exists   You attempted to create a print queue with a name that is already in use. Use a different name.

SYS2155: No more print queues can be added   The system does not have enough memory to add another print queue. Delete an existing queue and then add the new one.

SYS2156: No more print jobs can be added   The system does not have enough memory to add another print job. Wait and retry.

SYS2157: No more print devices can be added   The system does not have enough memory to add another printer. Delete an unneeded printer and then create the new one.

SYS2158: The print device has no active jobs and cannot accept control operations   The specified printer is not in use.

SYS2159: The print device request contains a control function that is not valid   The control function sent is invalid. Contact the software company or programmer.

SYS2161: The spooler is not running   The spooler has not been started.

SYS2162: The operation cannot be performed while the print device is in its current state The change you requested cannot be made because the port is already assigned to a printer, or a job is active on the printer. Wait until all jobs have finished printing.

SYS2164: The operation cannot be performed while the print job is in its current state The change you requested cannot be made because of the status of the job, which may either be printing or paused. Wait until the job status changes and then retry.

SYS2165: A spooler memory allocation failure occurred The spooler is out of memory. Delete a print queue or a print job.

SYS2166: The printer driver does not exist The printer driver you specified has not been installed for the print queue.

SYS2167: The data type is not supported by the queue driver
The data type for this print job is not supported by the queue driver of the queue. Use a different queue driver for jobs that have this data type.

SYS2242: The password given has expired The password you entered is no longer valid. Contact the system administrator to get a new password.

SYS2250: The connection cannot be found This network connection does not exist.

SYS2401: There are open files on the connection You tried to delete an active network connection which has open files or requests pending. Close all files and end all programs before deleting the connection.

SYS3003: The specified environment size is not valid In COMMAND.COM, the correct syntax for establishing the environment size in bytes is /E:*nnn*, where *nnn* is from 160 to 32768. Either you specified a number that is too small or too large or there is a character other than a number in your specification. COMMAND.COM has started, so there is no need for immediate action, but you should correct your environment statement before shutting down.

SYS3004: The CTTY command is not supported in OS/2   OS/2 does not support redirecting of standard input, standard output, and standard error to any device other than the console (default). If you used CTTY to start a new copy of COMMAND.COM, your call to COMMAND.COM must be changed.

SYS3007: The PATH= statement contains an invalid drive or path Your PATH= statement contains a reference to an invalid drive or path. If you type **PATH** at the command line, the current path is displayed. Correct it from the command line for now and change the startup files to the correct path for the future.

SYS3010: A memory allocation error has occurred   Either there is not enough memory to load COMMAND.COM or the memory control blocks have been corrupted. Enter **EXIT** to end the current copy of COMMAND.COM and retry.

SYS3011: The .EXE file that starts the program you specified contains an error   There is an internal error in an .EXE file. The program cannot be run as it now exists. Contact the software company or the programmer.

SYS3012: The program cannot fit in memory   Not enough memory is available to process this command. Type **EXIT** to end the current copy of COMMAND.COM and retry.

SYS3013: A load module error has occurred   An attempt to start an .EXE or .COM file failed. The following error conditions have already been checked and eliminated:

❑   File not found

❑   Access denied

❑   Insufficient memory

❑   Bad load module format

The program cannot be run. Contact the software company or the programmer.

SYS3014: The name specified is not recognized as an internal or external command, an operable program, or a batch file   You typed a command and it does not match any DOS command, executable command (an .EXE or .COM file), or batch file. Check your spelling.

SYS3016: This session was halted because COMMAND.COM cannot be loaded   The session was halted because there is no permanent copy of COMMAND.COM to return to. Close the DOS session; no other activity can be accomplished. You should correct the COMSPEC variable to prevent this from occurring again.

Note   You cannot change copies of COMMAND.COM by changing COMSPEC. You must load a secondary copy into memory.

SYS3019: ON or OFF must be specified   The BREAK, ECHO, or VER command tried to use a parameter other than ON or OFF.

SYS3022: An error occurred when writing to a device   An input/output error occurred while trying to write to a device. The device cannot handle the number of bytes requested. You need to reduce the amount of data you are sending to the device.

SYS3030: The second drive letter is missing   The ASSIGN command requires two drive letters.

SYS3031: The invalid character, ***, was used to specify a drive
The character you entered for an ASSIGN is not valid as a drive specification either because it is not a letter or because a drive with that letter is not on the system.

SYS3032: The invalid character, ***, was used as a separator
The character you entered with ASSIGN is not a valid separator. These are the only separators permitted:

space, tab, comma, semicolon, plus sign, equal sign, line feed

SYS3038: You cannot use the LABEL command at this time because you previously used a JOIN, SUBST, or ASSIGN command   A drive cannot have its label altered if any of the real-mode drive redirection commands (JOIN, SUBST, or ASSIGN) are active. If you want to change the label, change the drive back to its default setting.

SYS3074: The file, ***, is a read-only file and cannot be deleted
Read-only files cannot be deleted or altered unless the read-only attribute is removed.

SYS3076: The file cannot be renamed because you specified a drive
The RENAME (REN) command cannot change the drive of a file, so the second parameter cannot contain a drive letter.

SYS3078: A file name must be specified   You must specify a filename when using the following commands: RENAME, ERASE, VDISK.

SYS3083: There is not enough memory available to store the DOSKEY macro. The request was ignored   Your request to add or modify a macro exceeds the buffer space that is available. If you want to increase the buffer space, use the /BUFSIZE option when starting a copy of DOSKEY. The default buffer size is 512 bytes. To start a new buffer, type **DOSKEY /REINSTALL /BUFSIZE=size**

Note   This will discard all of the current command history and macro definitions.

SYS3084: An incompatible DOSKEY is installed. Your request was ended   A copy of DOSKEY is already installed in this DOS session but it does not match the version of DOSKEY previously installed. If you want to use the new version of DOSKEY, use the DOSKEY /REINSTALL command. Otherwise, you must use the version of DOSKEY that was already installed.

SYS3140: The system detected a Software generated error   The system stopped. Run the diagnostics supplied with your system to learn the cause of the problem.

SYS3141: The system detected a bus timeout error   The system stopped. Run the diagnostics supplied with your system to learn the cause of the problem.

SYS3142: The system detected a fail-safe timer error The system stopped. Run the diagnostics supplied with your system to learn the cause of the problem.

SYS3143: The system detected an I/O check error The system stopped. Run the diagnostics supplied with your system to learn the cause of the problem.

SYS3144: The system detected a hardware memory error on the system board The system stopped. Run the diagnostics supplied with your system to learn the cause of the problem.

SYS3145: Bad or missing command interpreter Press ENTER to close the DOS session.

SYS3192: The path or parameter is incorrect An invalid path or an unrecognized parameter was entered with the UNDELETE command.

SYS3200: The file, ***, cannot be undeleted There was an error while trying to restore a deleted file to its original path. Be sure the disk or diskette is not damaged and then retry.

SYS3201: The file, ***, cannot be discarded There was an error while trying to discard a file in the temporary storage directory. Be sure the disk or diskette is not damaged and then retry.

SYS3203: No matching files were found During UNDELETE, no files matching the specified path were found. Enter **UNDELETE [drive:]*** **/LIST /S** for a list of all the recoverable files on the disk.

SYS3206: An error occurred while creating directory *** There was an error while trying to restore the path of a previously deleted file. The file cannot be processed. Make sure the disk or diskette is not damaged, the disk has room, and you have not reached the maximum number of directories.

SYS3322: A hardware configuration error has been found The system found that configuration memory does not contain the correct information for your hardware configuration (setup). Use the appropriate setup program to correct the information.

APPENDIX

Command Reference

*T*his summary of the commands available for use at the command line is intended as a quick reference. To access more detailed instructions along with lists of available parameters and options and examples of use, at the command line type **HELP** followed by the command in question.

This appendix lists the commands alphabetically.

ANSI Permits or prevents extended display and keyboard support in the DOS environment of OS/2. If you type **ANSI** at the command line, it displays its current status. Use ANSI control sequences to redefine keys, change the cursor, and alter display color attributes.

APPEND Sets a search path for data files that are not in the current directory.

You will see APPEND used frequently in the AUTOEXEC.BAT file. Enter **APPEND** at the command line to display the APPEND statement in your AUTOEXEC.BAT file. Enter **APPEND ;** to cancel the APPEND command.

The first time you use APPEND it is an external command, and you might have to give the entire drive and path for it. Once loaded, it remains in memory and the path is no longer needed.

The search sequence for a specified file is as follows:

1. Search the specified directory, or the current directory if not specifying a directory.

2. Search the directories indicated by the current APPEND command.

ASSIGN Assigns a drive letter to a different drive. Enter **ASSIGN** at the command line with no parameters to reset all drives to their original letters.

The following commands do not work in a DOS session on drives that have ASSIGN in effect:

CHKDSK
DISKCOMP
DISKCOPY

FORMAT
JOIN
LABEL
PRINT
RECOVER
RESTORE
SUBST

ATTRIB   Displays the attributes of the filename that follows the command. It is also used to turn on or off the read-only attribute, the archive bit, the system flag, and the hidden attribute of a file, for a group of files, or for all files in a directory. These are its parameters:

+R, –R, +A, –A, +S, –S, +H, –H

BACKUP   Backs up one or more files to diskette. After BACKUP fills a diskette, it prompts you to insert a new one. BACKUP works only within the current directory unless you use the /S parameter, which copies files in all directories beneath the current one.

BACKUP can back up files on disks of different types. If the source is a diskette, make sure it is not write-protected because BACKUP resets the archive bit on the backed-up files.

BACKUP does not back up system files (COMMAND.COM and CMD.EXE), hidden system files, or any open dynamic link library files (.DLL).

BACKUP creates two files, called BACKUP.XXX and CONTROL.XXX, in the root directory of the diskette. The BACKUP.XXX file contains the files and the CONTROL.XXX file saves paths, filenames, and other information.

BACKUP saves any extended attributes associated with a file or directory as long as you are using OS/2.

BOOT   Switches between the DOS and OS/2 operating systems that have been installed on the same hard drive (C).

The BOOT command can be run from an OS/2 command prompt or a DOS command prompt as well as from native DOS. It is accessible under these conditions:

☐ DOS Version 3.2 (or a later version) is installed and operating on drive C before OS/2 is installed.

☐ Drive C is not formatted during OS/2 installation.

☐ The High Performance File System is not installed on drive C.

The BOOT command takes effect when you reboot the system.

BREAK   Tells DOS to check whether or not the CTRL+BREAK keys have been pressed before carrying out a program request. Enter **BREAK** at the DOS command prompt to display the current status. If BREAK is ON, processing is slower, but CTRL+BREAK is responded to more quickly. If you think you need the ability to break out of programs frequently, the tradeoff is worthwhile. In OS/2 sessions, BREAK is always ON and cannot be changed.

CACHE   Defines the parameters that the HPFS uses when writing information to a disk. This command is specified as part of a RUN statement in the CONFIG.SYS file or it can be entered at a command prompt.

If you type **CACHE** at the command line without a parameter, the current values for CACHE will be displayed.

CD or CHDIR   Changes the current directory or displays its name. Enter **CD** to move to the root. Use two dots (..) to move up one directory.

CHKDSK   Analyzes directories and files, displays the file system type, and creates a disk status report. It also displays the volume label and the volume serial number of the disk.

CHKDSK also gives a memory storage report. It does not work in DOS sessions on drives that have an ASSIGN, JOIN, or SUBST command in effect, nor does it work on network drives.

CHKDSK can detect *lost clusters* on your disk; these are parts of files that the operating system did not save completely. If lost clusters are found you are asked if you want to convert them to files. If you type **Y** (Yes), CHKDSK converts them into files that you can examine. If you type **N** (No), CHKDSK deletes these parts of files from your disk without warning. The files created from lost chains follow this naming convention: FILE*nnnn*.CHK (where *nnnn* is a sequential number starting with 0000).

CLS Clears the window or entire screen of any information and puts the system prompt into the upper-left portion of the window or screen.

CMD Starts the OS/2 command processor, CMD.EXE, found in the C:\OS2 subdirectory. To return to the previous command processor use the EXIT command.

COMMAND Starts the DOS command processor, COMMAND.COM, which is located in the C:\OS2\MDOS subdirectory. To return to the previous command processor, use the EXIT command. If COMMAND.COM is not found in the current directory, OS/2 searches the environment for the value of COMSPEC. This system variable, in the environment when a DOS session is started, describes the path the system uses to load the command processor.

You can change the value for COMSPEC with the SET command. However, if you make any changes to the environment with the SET command, the change is known only to the current command processor. Returning to the primary DOS command processor with the EXIT command causes a resumption of the environment that was in existence with the original command processor.

COMP Compares the contents of two files. Entering this command begins a step-by-step menu that enables you to compare files. The files can be on the same directory or drive or on different directories and drives. If you give only a drive letter for the second file, without a filename, COMP assumes that the second filename is the same as the first.

After comparing the files, COMP moves to the next pair of files that match the two filenames. When no more files that match the first parameter are found, you are asked if you want to compare more files. Type **Y** (Yes) to compare two more files, or end COMP by typing **N** (No).

If the file sizes are different, COMP informs you and asks if you want to continue. If you continue, COMP processes both files based on the length of the smaller of the two files.

During a comparison, an error message appears for any location that contains mismatching information in the two files. If there are more than ten mismatches, processing ends.

If the file to be compared is on a diskette, enter **COMP** without any parameters. You are asked for the filename, at which point you insert the diskette and enter the name of the file to be compared.

COPY   Copies one or more files. These parameters and options are used most often:

☐   *Append (+) files* Use this option to merge multiple files into one file, or to add one file to the end of another.

☐   *Change the date and time (+ ,,)* Use this to change the date and time of a file, or to update the date and time of a file after it is copied.

☐   *A device name* Use this to specify a device (for example, printer) as the target of the copy process.

You can copy files from one diskette or hard disk to another or copy files within directories. If you copy one or more files to a subdirectory, the subdirectory must already exist. You cannot copy a file to itself.

COPY preserves extended attributes when the file is copied with the /F parameter, as long as you use OS/2 2.0.

CREATEDD   Creates a dump diskette for use with the Stand-Alone Dump procedure.

Caution   Only users with advanced technical knowledge should attempt to use CREATEDD.

The CREATEDD utility program prepares a diskette for an OS/2 memory dump. If a dump requires more than one diskette, the first diskette must be prepared with CREATEDD but remaining disks need only be formatted.

DATE   Displays the date in the system and gives the opportunity to change it. When you create or change a file, the current system date is attached to that file.

OS/2 lets you choose between using a slash (/), a period (.), and a dash (-), as the valid date separator.

DDINSTAL   Provides a way to install new device drivers after the operating system has been installed.

Enter the command to start a step-by-step procedure to install device-driver files. These files are provided on a separate diskette, called a Device Support diskette, that contains a file with the extension .DDP (device-driver profile), which controls the installation process. The DDINSTAL program uses the information from the device-driver profile to add any necessary statements to CONFIG.SYS and to copy the driver files to the hard disk.

Remember   Anything added to CONFIG.SYS does not take effect until you reboot the system.

DEBUG   Use this command to access the DOS DEBUG environment. You can then enter all DEBUG commands in response to the DEBUG prompt, which is a hyphen (-). Refer to your DOS manual for more information about the DEBUG command.

DEL   *See* ERASE.

DETACH   Starts and simultaneously detaches an OS/2 program from its command processor.

Any program started with DETACH must be able to process outside the control of the command processor. The program should not issue any input or output calls to the keyboard, the mouse, or the display.

You can detach any program that does not require the screen—for example, internal commands and batch (.CMD) files. OS/2 detaches CMD.EXE when it runs internal commands or batch files.

Use DETACH with redirection instructions to redirect a program's standard input and output to devices other than the keyboard and the display. This permits the program to run without any interactive processes.

DIR Displays the files and subdirectories in a directory. Options include the following:

DIR.. lists the files in the parent directory of the current directory.

DIR>PRN sends the directory listing to the printer.

The DIR command produces a display that gives the name, size (in bytes), and the date and time the file was last written to the disk. It also shows the disk volume label and volume serial number, as well as the total number of files, the number of bytes used in the files displayed, and the amount of free space (in bytes) remaining on the disk. Hidden files are not displayed.

DISKCOMP Compares the contents of two diskettes. Entering this command begins a step-by-step procedure to compare the contents of diskettes in different diskette drives. DISKCOMP will not work in DOS sessions if drives have an ASSIGN, JOIN, or SUBST command in effect.

Use DISKCOMP only between diskettes of the same size and storage capacity.

DISKCOPY Copies the contents of the diskette in the source drive to the diskette in the target drive. If the target diskette is not formatted, the format will be done during the copy. Neither the source nor the target drive can be a hard disk or a virtual drive.

DISKCOPY does not work in DOS sessions on drives that have an ASSIGN, JOIN, or SUBST command in effect. The media type and size of both diskettes must be the same.

Because of the OS/2 multitasking operating environment, DISKCOPY locks the diskettes to prevent any other program from accessing them while copying is being performed.

DPATH Gives programs the search path to data files that are outside the current directory. The DPATH environment variable can only be set using the SET command in OS/2 sessions.

Type **DPATH** at the command line to display the current value of DPATH.

Type **DPATH ;** to clear the DPATH environment variable.

Note: Not all programs are written so that they will search the DPATH directory list.

DPATH differs from the APPEND command in how it operates. DPATH tells applications which directories to search in order to find data files; it is up to the applications to recognize DPATH. With APPEND, programs are able to find files without recognizing that the APPEND command is in effect.

EAUTIL Allows you to remove extended attributes from a file and later put them back. With this facility, you can use the file with applications or file systems that do not recognize or cannot process extended attributes. By saving extended attributes to a hold file, you can retain them until the file they were in originally is returned to a file system that can use extended attributes.

ERASE or DEL These interchangeable commands delete one or more files. Read-only and hidden files, such as operating system files, cannot be deleted.

If you try to delete all the files in a directory, the system displays the name of the directory, along with this message:

```
Are you sure (Y/N)?
```

EXIT Closes the current command processor (CMD.EXE or COMMAND.COM) and returns to the previous one, or to the desktop if no previous session existed.

FDISK Enables you to create or delete a primary partition or a logical drive in an extended partition.

Use the FDISK command to establish or change partitions.

FDISKPM Presents the same functions as FDISK, except FDISKPM is a Presentation Manager program with menus and graphic displays to guide you through the tasks.

FIND Searches for a specific string of text in a file or files and sends the string to your output device.

You must type the string in quotation marks in the exact format (uppercase or lowercase) in which it is written in the text. When searching for strings that contain quotation marks, an extra set of quotation marks must be entered both before and after the string.

You must specify the specific filename you want the FIND command to search. Global characters such as the asterisk (*) or question mark (?) do not work.

FORMAT   Formats a disk in the specified drive so that it accepts OS/2 files by marking the directory and file allocation tables on the disk. It also checks the disk for defects.

If you format a drive for the HPFS, FORMAT checks the IFS statement in the CONFIG.SYS file to determine if the drive is listed with the /AUTOCHECK parameter. If the drive is listed, FORMAT does not update the IFS statement. If the drive is not listed, FORMAT adds the drive letter.

If you format a diskette or hard disk that already contains information, all the information is erased.

You must set up an OS/2 partition on hard disks before formatting them. FORMAT does not recognize a hard disk as being an OS/2 disk if an OS/2 or a DOS partition does not exist.

Do not attempt to format a diskette to an incorrect capacity. Any data stored on a diskette formatted in such a way will not be reliable.

FORMAT does not work on drives that have an ASSIGN, JOIN, or SUBST command in effect, nor on network drives.

FSACCESS   Used to reassign drive letters and to make drives accessible or inaccessible. The current drive cannot be remapped.

When a specific version of DOS is started from an image file on the hard drive instead of from a DOS boot diskette, the physical diskette drive A is not available. Typing **FSACCESS A:** maps drive letter A to the physical drive A.

GRAFTABL   Provides additional characters for graphics mode in a DOS session; the GRAFTABL command has no effect on OS/2 sessions. GRAFTABL allows the ASCII extended character set to be displayed when using graphics.

HELP Provides help at the command line. Entering **HELP** at the command line shows the HELP options available for the current mode of operation.

Entering **HELP** followed by a command filename will bring help about that command.

If you encounter a system error message after attempting a command, enter **HELP** followed by the error message number for an explanation of the error.

JOIN Logically connects a drive to a directory on another drive. This makes it possible to access a drive by a directory name instead of a drive letter. You can join a drive only at the root directory.

If the directory name does not exist, OS/2 creates a directory on the drive you specify. A directory that already exists must be empty for the JOIN to work. Once you issue the JOIN command, the first drive name is no longer valid; if you attempt to access it, the operating system gives an error message.

KEYB When followed by a keyboard layout name, this command selects a keyboard layout to replace the current keyboard layout for all OS/2 and DOS sessions.

If your CONFIG.SYS file contains a keyboard DEVINFO statement, you can switch keyboard layouts using KEYB. If there is no keyboard DEVINFO statement in CONFIG.SYS you will see an error message.

Typing **KEYB** without a layout parameter displays the current keyboard code-page information, whether there is a DEVINFO statement in your CONFIG.SYS file or not.

KEYB is useful to access the characters of another keyboard layout. KEYB can be run only from an OS/2 full-screen command prompt; entering the command from an OS/2 Window may bring unexpected results.

KEYS Allows previously issued commands to be retrieved and edited via the cursor keys. The maximum amount of memory for the command queue is 64KB. When the queue is full, the oldest command is discarded when a new command is entered from the keyboard.

Entering **KEYS ON** or **KEYS OFF** at the command line sets an environment variable named KEYS with a value of ON or OFF. CMD.EXE checks the KEYS environment variable when it starts, and determines if KEYS is set to ON.

Note   Typing **KEYS ON** disables ANSI extended keyboard support in OS/2 sessions.

LABEL   Puts a volume identification label on a disk. You type the label following the command (for example, **LABEL A:MYDISK**). If you enter the command without a parameter, the current label is displayed and LABEL asks if you want to change it. Type a volume label up to 11 characters long and press ENTER. If you press ENTER without entering a label, the volume label remains unchanged.

LOADHIGH or LH   Loads Terminate and Stay Resident (TSR) DOS programs into an available upper memory block (UMB) for a DOS session.

You can load a DOS TSR program into an upper memory block (UMB) by typing **LH** or **LOADHIGH** at the DOS command line. If no UMB is available, the TSR program will be loaded into low memory (below 640KB). To enable UMBs, a DOS=UMB statement in the CONFIG.SYS file is necessary.

MAKEINI   If you receive an error message stating that the OS2.INI file has been corrupted, use this command to replace it.

MD or MKDIR   Creates subdirectories. Enter the command followed by the name of the directory you are creating. Do not use the backslash (\) symbol if you are in a subdirectory and want to create another subdirectory below the current one. Use a space between the command and the new directory name.

MEM   Shows the amount of used and free memory in the DOS environment.

MODE   Sets operation modes for devices. There are four different MODE commands:

COM#   Sets asynchronous communications modes

DISPLAY   Sets the display modes for video adapters

LPT#   Sets parallel printer modes

DSKT   Sets diskette input/output write verification

MORE   Sends data to the standard output device (usually the display) one full screen at a time. After each screen, OS/2 pauses with the message —More— until you press any key to continue with the next screen of data.

MOVE   Moves one or more files from one directory to another directory on the same drive. You can use wildcards for both source and target files. If you do, the names of the files will be displayed as the files are being moved.

PATCH   Permits you to apply IBM-supplied patches in order to repair software.

Caution   PATCH should be used only by those who can determine the need for a patch, know how to make a patch, and understand the effect the patch has on operations.

If you select the /A option (to apply patches shipped by IBM automatically) to make fixes to IBM-supplied code, verification is performed before the patch is applied. This may not occur on non-IBM-supplied patches.

If you apply a patch manually by typing **PATCH** without any options, you are asked to supply an offset to indicate where the patch is to be made. PATCH shows the contents of the location specified and allows you to enter the patch. Both the offset and the patch contents must be entered in hexadecimal notation. The operating system displays the 16 bytes at that offset and you can change any or all of them or quit without making any changes. If you specify automatic mode (/A), PATCH gets the information needed from a patch information file received from IBM.

PATH   Sets the search path for commands and programs. Type **PATH** at the command line to see the path currently in effect. Enter **PATH ;** to delete the path.

Setting PATH in the CONFIG.SYS and AUTOEXEC.BAT files means you do not have to set it from the command line each time you turn on your system.

OS/2 searches directories in the PATH for commands or batch files that were not found in the current directory. PATH only applies to files that can be run, such as files with the following extensions: .COM, .EXE, and .BAT (for DOS sessions), or .CMD (for OS/2 sessions).

When you install OS/2 the installation program places the following PATH statement in your CONFIG.SYS file:

SET
PATH=C:\OS2;C:\OS2\SYSTEM;C:\OS2\MDOS;C:\OS2\INSTALL;C:\;

The installation program also creates the following PATH statement in your AUTOEXEC.BAT file for use with DOS sessions:

PATH C:\OS2;C:\OS2\MDOS;C:\;

PICVIEW   Launches the OS/2 Picture Viewer program in order to display a picture file. You can either open Picture Viewer from the Productivity folder or type the command at an OS/2 command prompt. If you enter **PICVIEW** without a filename at the OS/2 command prompt, the Picture Viewer window appears and you can select the file you wish to see. If you type **PICVIEW** with a filename, PICVIEW displays that file immediately. Exit from the Picture View menu to return to the OS/2 command line.

PMREXX   Shows the output from REXX procedures and also provides an input field for them. This is a Presentation Manager window application that permits you to browse through the output of any of your REXX procedures. Start the PMREXX program by typing **PMREXX** followed by a target procedure name that generates an output or input function.

Using PMREXX adds the following features to REXX:

☐   A window to display the output of a REXX procedure. It would, for example, display the SAY instruction output, the STDOUT and STDERR outputs from secondary processes that are started from a REXX procedures file, and the REXX TRACE output (not to be confused with OS/2 tracing).

❏ An input window for the PULL instruction (in all of its forms) and the STDIN data for secondary processes that are started from a REXX procedures file.

❏ Browsing, scrolling, and clipboard capability for REXX output.

❏ A selection of fonts for the window.

PRINT Prints or cancels printing of one or more files. You can enter more than one filename at the command line. Wildcards are permitted. The files are queued for printing in the order in which you enter them.

PROMPT Changes the system command prompt. Typing **PROMPT** alone at the command line resets the system prompt to the system default. You can also set the PROMPT command in the CONFIG.SYS file.

The default OS/2 system prompt is the current directory of the default drive enclosed within bracket symbols. In DOS sessions, the default system prompt is the default drive letter followed by the > symbol.

PSTAT Shows process, thread, system-semaphore, shared-memory, and dynamic-link library information. Entering **PSTAT** at the command line displays:

❏ Current processes and threads

❏ System semaphores

❏ Shared memory for each process

❏ Dynamic-link libraries

PSTAT helps determine which threads are running in the system, their current status, and current priorities. It can also help determine why a particular thread is blocked (waiting for a system event), or why the thread's performance is slow (low priority compared to other threads). It gives the process ID that has been assigned from each process, which can be used with the TRACE utility.

RECOVER   Recovers files from a disk that has defective sectors. Entering **RECOVER** tells OS/2 to read every sector of the specified disk. Bad sectors are marked and data will no longer be put on those sectors.

You cannot use RECOVER on a disk that has either the RECOVER.EXE file or the OS/2 message file OSO001.MSG (which is found in the \OS2\SYSTEM subdirectory). Copy those files to diskette and delete them from the disk you are going to recover.

RECOVER cannot be used on the disk used to boot OS/2, so you will have to boot from the OS/2 Install diskette. For step-by-step instructions, enter **HELP RECOVER** at the command line.

Caution   RECOVER can be a complicated, dangerous procedure.

REN or RENAME   Changes a filename without changing the contents of the file. In OS/2 sessions, you also can change the name of a directory.

You cannot specify a path in the second filename, so the file stays in the same directory after you rename it. Wildcards are permitted.

REPLACE   Replaces files on the target drive with files of the same name from the source drive. The replacement may be selective. In addition, it adds files selectively from the source drive to the target drive. Hidden and system files cannot be replaced.

REPLACE will copy the source file's extended attributes to the target file.

RESTORE   Restores files that were backed up using the BACKUP command. RESTORE works only within the source directory unless you specify the /S parameter, which copies files in the source directory and in any directories below the starting one. It can restore files from disks of different types.

The RESTORE command does not restore COMMAND.COM, CMD.EXE, or the hidden system files.

You must restore files to the same directory they were in when BACKUP was used. You cannot restore to a different directory.

If you use wildcards, RESTORE will ask you to insert the next diskette after it has restored any files that match the specifications on the current diskette.

RESTORE will copy the extended attributes of a backed-up source file or directory.

RD or RMDIR Removes empty subdirectories. You cannot remove the root directory or the current directory.

The directory you want to remove must be completely empty; it cannot contain any subdirectories or hidden files.

SET Used in the CONFIG.SYS file in addition to being available to you at the command line. Type **SET** at the command line to see the current environment variables. Use SET followed by a string to set a new environment variable. If the variable in the SET command already exists in the environment, the command processor will replace its value with the new value that is in the second string. If you enter **SET** with only the variable and the equal sign (=), the command processor will remove that environment variable or parameter name and any associated value from the environment.

SETBOOT Gives you the ability to set up the Boot Manager for a hard disk. SETBOOT allows you to enter parameters at the command line so you can take advantage of the Boot Manager.

SORT Reads data from standard input, sorts it, and then writes it to standard output. When you are sorting large files, it might take a bit of time for processing to be completed.

The standard input and output devices cannot be redirected to the same filename.

Characters are sorted according to their ASCII values, except that lowercase letters are handled as if they were uppercase.

SPOOL Redirects printer output from one device to another. This could be redirection from a parallel printer to a serial printer, or even from one parallel printer to another.

In order to spool to a serial printer, the COM.SYS device driver must be added as a device in CONFIG.SYS.

START   Begins an OS/2 program in another session. The primary use for START is to start programs automatically at system startup via instructions in STARTUP.CMD, but it is also available to you at the command line.

Type **START** at the command line without any parameters to start an OS/2 command processor. If you use the /WIN, /FS, or /PM parameter, your program will run in the foreground. If you do not use one of these parameters, use the /F parameter to make the program run in the foreground session.

START will run full-screen applications or applications running in a window. START determines the type of application and runs it in the appropriate session. You have the option to override that determination with the /FS, /WIN, /PM, or /I parameters. However, you cannot start a batch file (.CMD) with the /PM parameter.

SUBST   Substitutes a drive letter for a drive and path so you can access that drive and path by using only a drive letter.

SWAPPATH   Specifies the size and location of the swap file. You use the swap file (SWAPPER.DAT) to store data segments that the system has removed from physical memory to satisfy another request for memory. With SWAPPATH you specify the location and size of the swap file.

A swap file can be placed in either a subdirectory or a separate partition. A separate partition is recommended, because it is possible for the swap file to become quite large. The default location is SWAPPATH=C:\OS2\SYSTEM.

SYSLEVEL   Shows you the operating-system service level. A "Please wait..." message appears while SYSLEVEL checks the current corrective service level of your system.

Once the corrective service level has been determined the results will be displayed on your monitor.

SYSLOG Permits you to view or print the contents of the system error-log file. SYSLOG is a Presentation Manager application that runs in a window. You can use SYSLOG to stop or start error logging, format the contents of the error-log files, print the log files, or redirect error logging to a different filename.

TIME Shows the time in the system and offers an opportunity to change it.

Enter **TIME** at the command line to display the system time and be prompted to change it.

Time is specified in hours and minutes, using a 24-hour clock separated by a colon or period.

TRACE Selects and sets the tracing of system events.

Caution TRACE should be used only by people technically proficient in OS/2.

OS/2 processes TRACE statements in the order in which they appear in the CONFIG.SYS file; the outcome of the statements is cumulative. If any part of a statement is incorrect, it is ignored.

If you do not specify TRACE in the CONFIG.SYS file, events are not traced. However, you can allocate a trace buffer by putting a TRACEBUF statement in CONFIG.SYS. This is what permits you to trace events by entering **TRACE** at the OS/2 command line.

You use the Trace facility to record a sequence of system events, usually for debugging reasons. After the trace data is recorded, the System Trace Formatter retrieves it from the system trace buffer and sends the data to your display, printer, or to a file.

An OS/2 enhancement to the Trace utility permits you to trace a given process or set of processes so you can focus on their events. Analyzing the trace data is easier because only events of the specified process are reported.

TRACEFMT Shows formatted trace records in reverse time-stamp order.

Caution The TRACEFMT command is to be used only by those technically proficient with OS/2.

TREE Displays all the directory paths found on the specified drive. You also have the option of asking for a list of the files in the root directory as well as the files in each subdirectory by entering **TREE C: /F** (substitute a different drive for drive C if appropriate).

TYPE Sends the contents of one or more files to the screen. In a DOS session, only one file can be displayed.

You use TYPE to display ASCII or text files. Other files, such as program files, may appear unreadable because of the presence of nonalphabetic or nonnumeric characters.

In an OS/2 session, TYPE displays files consecutively on the screen if you specify multiple filenames. TYPE will display the filename before displaying the contents of the file.

UNDELETE Recovers files that have been deleted. When files are deleted they are placed in a directory, the location of which is set by the DELDIR statement in CONFIG.SYS, as is a maximum size for the directory. If the number of deleted files exceeds the maximum size of that directory, files are automatically removed in first-in-first-out order.

If the file being undeleted is still recoverable, it is restored to its original path. If a duplicate filename exists, you are prompted to rename it.

UNDELETE can be used in both DOS and OS/2. Files that are available for recovery are reported as used bytes on the disk.

UNPACK Unpacks compressed files and copies any files that are not compressed but that are located on an OS/2 installation diskette. Compressed files have "@" as the last character in their filenames.

Because UNPACK uses the filename from the original uncompressed file, do not specify a destination filename. UNPACK also preserves the date, time, and file attributes of the original uncompressed file.

UNPACK also copies files that are not compressed and handles file attributes the same way the COPY command does. You can unpack a diskette that contains a combination of compressed and uncompressed files.

VER Displays the operating system version number. It can be entered at either the OS/2 or DOS command line.

VERIFY Confirms that any data written to a disk has been written correctly. Type **VERIFY** at the command line to display the current status of VERIFY (On or Off).

When you have VERIFY On, verification is done for file system I/O write actions for both hard disks and diskettes.

This command has the same purpose as the /V parameter in the COPY and XCOPY commands.

VIEW Displays online documents created with the Information Presentation Facility (IPF) compiler. VIEW displays IPF files that have an .INF extension. It can display the entire file or individual topics located in the file.

VMDISK Creates a file that contains the image of a DOS startup diskette. After creating an image, you can create a DOS session by starting from this image file.

VOL Displays the disk volume label and serial number if they exist. From a DOS command session, VOL displays the label for one disk. From an OS/2 command session, if you specify more than one drive, VOL displays the information consecutively.

XCOPY Selectively copies groups of files, which can include lower-level subdirectories. Specify the drive, path, and filename for the source and target drives. If you do not give a path, XCOPY starts from the current directory. If you do not name a file or group of files, *.* is assumed.

XCOPY works only within the source directory unless you specify the /S parameter, which also copies files in all directories below the starting directory.

XCOPY will not replace a read-only file with another file, nor will it copy hidden or system files.

The /M parameter copies files whose archive bit is set, and then turns off the archive bit of the source file. This makes XCOPY useful for backing up recent work.

If the specified target path does not exist, XCOPY creates the directories before copying. You can specify a different filename for the target.

XCOPY will copy the extended attributes of a source file to the target file.

Configuration File Reference

Many of the characteristics of OS/2 can be tailored through commands in the CONFIG.SYS file. This is the first file OS/2 reads as it is booted, and it determines which functions you will have as you work. If you make any changes to CONFIG.SYS, they will not take effect until you have shut down OS/2 and rebooted.

Note   Statements in CONFIG.SYS are not restricted to the number of characters you can see in the typical screen window. You can have up to 255 characters in a line.

AUTOFAIL=[YES | NO] (default NO)

Inserting AUTOFAIL=YES into the CONFIG.SYS file instructs OS/2 that when a "hard error" occurs (that is, an error that requires changes to the system before it can continue reliably), OS/2 should display error codes rather than the default information window. This is most meaningful for system administrators and technical support people.

BASEDEV=path \ filename arguments

Base device drivers are programs that control the low-level interface to key hardware pieces, which OS/2 requires to begin the boot process. These include the fixed disk, the diskette, and the printer. OS/2 inserts BASEDEV statements into your CONFIG.SYS automatically during initial installation and adds or changes those statements when you make changes using Selective Install. Consequently, it is unusual for the user to modify these statements.

BREAK=[ON | OFF] (default OFF)

This setting tells OS/2 whether to monitor DOS sessions continuously to see if CTRL+C or CTRL+BREAK was pressed. Keeping the default of OFF means improved operating system performance because checking for these keystrokes takes place only when I/O is taking place.

BUFFERS=number

Disk buffers are a temporary storage area between the fixed disk and main memory. Similar to a mini-cache, buffers can be especially useful in constrained memory situations where little space can be assigned to a cache. On the other hand, each buffer uses 512 bytes of storage, so assigning 64 buffers, for example, uses 32K of memory.

CACHE

This appears as: RUN=C:\OS2\CACHE.EXE /LAZY:[ON | OFF] /MAX-AGE:time /DISKIDLE:time /BUFFERIDLE:time. See Chapter 13 for details on this statement.

CODEPAGE=codepages (default varies based on OS/2 version)

Being an international product, OS/2 supports several different languages. Languages are implemented in computers via *code pages*, which are grids that lay out the set of characters supported. These have been largely standardized to make it easier for people to develop software for international applications.

The U.S. English code page is 437. The International code page, which contains a set of the most common characters across all languages, is number 850. Versions of OS/2 2.0 shipped in the U.S. will by default load those two code pages in the CONFIG.SYS. The user can then change between those two at any time using the CHCP command from an OS/2 command prompt. Versions of OS/2 shipped in other countries will have code page 850 as well as others specific to the national language.

COUNTRY=number,drive:path\filename

This is another part of the country-specific configuration. The COUNTRY command determines how OS/2 displays such information as date and time, numeric information, and the sequence by which information is sorted.

For example, many countries use the 24-hour format for displaying time. Many countries write the date with the day of the month preceding the name of the month, as in 20 August, 1992. And, OS/2 needs to know where in the sort sequence to put the special characters required for non-English languages. It enables your system to handle the large number of characters required for some Asian languages.

Each national language version of OS/2 inserts a different version of the COUNTRY statement as the default in your CONFIG.SYS. For U.S. English, you should have COUNTRY=001,C:\OS2\SYSTEM\COUN-TRY.SYS.

DEVICE=drive:path\filename

This statement instructs OS/2 to load a device driver. There are several key device drivers included with OS/2. In addition to those listed in this book, there are a number of device drivers listed in the \OS2\MDOS directory that are OS/2 emulations of common DOS device drivers.

DEVICE=C:\OS2\COM.SYS

This statement allows OS/2 to communicate with devices attached to the serial ports, such as modems, mice, or printers. If you have a specialized driver for a device attached to a serial port, make sure that driver is loaded before COM.SYS is loaded.

DEVICE=C:\OS2\EXTDSKDD.SYS /D:drive /T:tracks /S:sectors /H:heads /F:format

This statement allows you to access external disk drives, those not physically inside your computer. It allows you to establish a drive letter for the external drive as well as specify the physical characteristics of the diskette, such as number of tracks, number of sectors per track, number of heads, and format. Get the details on the physical capabilities of your drive from the documentation that came with it.

DEVICE=C:\OS2\MOUSE.SYS

This statement is used in conjunction with the POINTDD.SYS driver to establish mouse support for OS/2. If you are not using an IBM PS/2 mouse or a compatible product, you must add the parameter /TYPE=mousetype to this statement to specify the type for your mouse. An additional DEVICE= statement is required to load the device specific software for your mouse. These statements are all maintained automatically by OS/2 when you use the installation and Selective Install functions.

DEVICE=C:\OS2\PMDD.SYS

This statement is required in your CONFIG.SYS file. It is the support needed for putting the pointer on the desktop.

DEVICE=C:\OS2\POINTDD.SYS

This statement is required to allow pointer functions in OS/2 text mode sessions.

DEVICE=C:\OS2\VDISK.SYS

It is sometimes valuable to simulate a physical disk drive in memory. This allows much quicker response time when accessing the files on the virtual drive, due to the speed of RAM versus disk. On the other hand, use of a virtual disk could increase swapping, which may remove all of the performance gains. Virtual disks lose their contents when the system is rebooted.

DEVICE=FSFILTER.SYS

This statement is used in the CONFIG.SYS of DOS boot diskettes or images that you wish to boot within OS/2. The file system filter device driver allows the DOS version to access OS/2 files.

DEVICEHIGH=drive:path\filename

This statement loads DOS device drivers, and specifies that they should be loaded into high memory. This leaves conventional memory free for your applications.

DEVINFO=SCR,type,codepage file

This required entry identifies the types of adapter/displays you are using and gives the name of a file containing codepage information related to that device. If you have more than one display, there may be more than one type of parameter specified. OS/2 inserts this statement into CONFIG.SYS automatically. It is unusual for the user to modify this statement manually.

DEVINFO=KBD,country,codepage file

Another required entry, this statement identifies the country for which the user's keyboard is configured, and gives the name of a file containing codepage information related to that keyboard. OS/2 inserts this statement into the CONFIG.SYS automatically. It is unusual for the user to modify this statement manually.

DEVINFO=[PRN | LPT #],device,codepage file

As with the other DEVINFO statements, this identifies the file containing codepage information specific to your printer.

DISKCACHE=size,lazywrite,drives

This statement activates and defines the size of the disk cache for drives formatted as FAT. OS/2 determines a default based on your hardware and inserts it into your CONFIG.SYS. If you have no FAT drives, you can remove this statement. For details on tuning this command, see Chapter 13.

DOS=[HIGH | LOW],[UMB | NOUMB] (default=LOW,NOUMB)

This statement allows you to configure the DOS support provided with OS/2. The default setting matches the configuration found as the default with many versions of DOS. It doesn't, however, provide the greatest amount of memory to DOS sessions. The HIGH | LOW parameter determines whether or not some portions of DOS are loaded into high memory, memory above the 640K boundary. Some older applications might have compatibility problems with the HIGH setting, but in general it provides more conventional memory to the program without causing problems. The UMB setting refers to Upper Memory Blocks. Upper memory blocks are extended memory devices designed to allow DOS programs to address memory between 640K and 1MB.

If UMB is specified, OS/2 will control the upper memory blocks, and can load applications there. If NOUMB is specified, the program cannot be loaded into upper memory blocks, but can allocate storage there. If you have compatibility problems with a DOS program, this is an area to review.

FCBS=total,locked (default 16,8)

File control blocks (FCBs) are used by DOS programs to contain specific information about the files being used. The first parameter specifies the total number of files expected to be open at any one time. If more than that maximum is requested, the least-recently used block will be discarded, and the newest file will replace it. The second parameter allows you to specify the number of FCBs that will be locked into memory and not discarded as new files are opened.

FCBs were used by programs written for early versions of DOS and are not used by most recent programs. It is unusual for the user to modify this statement.

FILES=number

This statement specifies the number of files to be allocated for DOS sessions. Some applications require a large number, a fact that will be specified in the program's documentation. This statement is not necessary for nor applicable to OS/2 sessions.

IFS=filename,parameters

The IFS statement governs OS/2's use of an installable file system. Any file system other than FAT is considered an additional, installable file system and must be listed in an IFS statement.

The most common IFS is the High Performance File System (HPFS) included with OS/2 2.0. If you format a partition as HPFS, OS/2 will insert the required IFS statement into your CONFIG.SYS automatically. For HPFS, the additional parameters are related to disk caching, and are described in more detail in Chapter 13.

IOPL=[YES|NO|name] (default YES)

One of the benefits of OS/2 is its Crash Protection. This takes several forms, one of which is that programs are removed from the lowest layers of the system, and thus cannot access hardware or memory directly.

Some programs, however, cannot execute properly without more direct access to the system. By granting a program access to the I/O Privilege Layer, you may somewhat compromise your Crash Protection, but allow applications to execute as expected. Specifying YES means that any program that attempts to do so will be granted access to the I/O Privilege Layer. Specifying NO restricts everything other than OS/2 and device drivers from the IOPL. You can also list the names of specific executable modules to which you wish to grant access. This is a good compromise between allowing your application to run and maintaining system integrity.

LASTDRIVE=letter (default Z)

OS/2 applications can use any drive letter in the system. DOS programs, however, are governed by this statement. Earlier versions of DOS defaulted to a last drive letter of C or D, requiring a change when additional disks, tapes, CD-ROM, and so on were added to the system. Making this letter the highest you use will save a small amount of conventional memory for programs. The difference is slight, however, and can cause confusion if you later add additional hardware. It generally makes sense to leave this parameter at Z.

LIBPATH=path;path;path...

For software developers, one of the benefits of OS/2 is its support of Dynamic Link Libraries (DLLs). It provides developers with a simplified means of connecting pieces of their applications. When their application tries to access one of these DLLs, it looks in the LIBPATH for the list of directories through which to search.

OS/2 inserts a quite lengthy LIBPATH into CONFIG.SYS during installation, and you should not remove any of the subdirectories listed there. As you install OS/2 applications, they will often add their directory to your LIBPATH statement.

Tip If you have problems with a program generating an error message such as "File not found," chances are good that the directory containing the program's DLLs are not in the LIBPATH. Add the subdirectory, reboot OS/2, and try again.

MAXWAIT=seconds

As a multitasking operating system, OS/2 has a very intelligent scheduler that determines which program should run at any point in time. Some programs, however, may try to take all of the computer's power and deny time to other programs. OS/2 gives you the best throughput for all applications by preempting those programs, allowing others to get time as well. The MAXWAIT parameter specifies the maximum number of seconds a program can sit idle waiting for other programs before OS/2 changes its priority to a higher setting so it receives processor time as well.

MEMMAN [SWAP | NOSWAP,MOVE | NOMOVE,PRO-TECT] (default SWAP,PROTECT)

The MEMMAN statement allows you to configure some of the memory management features of OS/2. Specifying NOSWAP causes programs and data not to be swapped to disk in heavy memory usage situations. While this speeds up performance, it should only be used if you are certain you have enough memory to hold all the programs you want to run. OS/2 is quite large by itself, and may not start successfully if the NOSWAP parameter is used on systems with less than 12MB of physical memory.

The MOVE | NOMOVE parameters are provided simply for compatibility with 16-bit versions of OS/2. The 16-bit versions swap based on segments, which could be of differing sizes. Consequently, segments might need to be moved around to make space for another segment. OS/2 2.0 takes advantage of the paging mode of Intel processors number 386SX and higher. That means that it stores memory in 4K pages. Since each page is the same size, pieces don't need to be moved to make room for larger segments.

The PROTECT parameter gives programs the ability to get to protected memory. Many programs require this, so use caution when choosing to remove this parameter.

PATH=path;path;path...

When working in command line sessions, it can become annoying to have to remember the path to each program, and change the current directory each time you want to load a program. The path statement specifies the subdirectories that will be searched when you enter a program name. If the program is not found in the current directory, those specified in this command will be checked from left to right until a program or command file matching the command you entered is found.

PAUSEONERROR=[YES | NO] (default YES)

If you are modifying your CONFIG.SYS file, with this statement you can have OS/2 pause during the boot process if it encounters any error situation. Some power users may have statements in their CONFIG.SYS that they know will generate an error message (which the users choose to ignore). In that case, OS/2 allows you to specify that it not pause on those errors. However, most users find it's best to leave this in the default

YES position so they are informed of any unusual circumstances that may arise.

PRINTMONBUFSIZE=port_1_buffer_size,port_2_buffer_size... (default 134 bytes)

If you are not in a memory-constrained situation, you can improve the performance of print tasks by expanding the buffer for the parallel port to which the printer is attached. The maximum buffer is 2048.

PRIORITY=[DYNAMIC | ABSOLUTE] (default DYNAMIC)

OS/2 is constantly monitoring the programs you have running to try to give you the best overall performance for your system. If you have enabled dynamic priority (the default), OS/2 may adjust the priorities of programs frequently in order to help ensure that the keyboard and mouse are responsive while continuing the programs running in the background. Setting priority to absolute disables this valuable feature of OS/2, and should only be done by system administrators with a complete understanding of the jobs being performed at the workstations.

PRIORITY_DISK_IO=[YES | NO] (default YES)

OS/2 automatically gives a priority boost to programs that run in the foreground. This boost helps ensure that the keyboard and mouse are responsive to the user. You can choose whether to give operations involving reading or writing to the fixed disk the same priority boost using this statement in CONFIG.SYS. For most users, leaving this at the default YES setting will produce the best overall system performance.

PROTECTONLY=[YES | NO]

This command determines whether support for DOS applications will be enabled when OS/2 is booted. The default is set based upon whether you installed DOS/Windows support when you loaded OS/2 originally.

Setting this parameter to YES causes OS/2 to omit loading DOS support, saving a good deal of memory for OS/2 applications.

PROTSHELL=shell_file,arguments (default PMSHELL.EXE)

The PROTSHELL statement determines the user interface shell to be loaded to control the desktop of the OS/2 session. This parameter is provided to allow for future after-market interfaces that may be provided by other vendors. In the absence of such products, it's best to leave this command at its default setting.

REM text

REM stands for REMark, which allows you to put informational statements into CONFIG.SYS. If you add statements, it is often useful to add a remark as well to jog your memory as to the purpose of those statements the next time you look at CONFIG.SYS. To disable a command in CONFIG.SYS, enter **REM** at the front of the line rather than deleting the line. In the long run you'll save time with this method because if you need that function later, all the parameters are still there at your fingertips. All you have to do is remove the REM at the front of the line.

RMSIZE=number_of_K_bytes (default 640)

This statement determines the amount of conventional memory to be allocated to DOS sessions. There are some programs that need this value to be lowered, for reasons of compatibility. This is unusual, though, and for most people the default value is correct.

RUN=drive:path\filename

Some programs need to be run during the system startup process. This applies to special-purpose programs such as CACHE.EXE. You cannot load Presentation Manager programs from CONFIG.SYS. If there are other applications that you want started automatically, they should be copied into the System Startup folder on the desktop.

SET variable=value(s)

OS/2 keeps track of certain implementation-specific items for your system in an area called the *environment*. The environment is made up of a series of variables with key names and values appropriate for your specific needs. These environment variables are initialized through the use of the SET statement.

OS/2 puts a series of SET statements into CONFIG.SYS based on what it determines your hardware to be and choices you make during installation. Other applications may instruct you to add SET statements to your CONFIG.SYS, or may do so automatically. Make sure you study the documentation provided with the software before modifying the default SET statements.

SHELL=shell_file,arguments (default COMMAND.COM)

The SHELL statement determines the command processor that is loaded in DOS command sessions. The default is OS/2's COMMAND.COM emulator, but others can be specified such as the 4DOS shell from JP Software.

THREADS=number (default 64)

In a multitasking system, a program can spin off separate units of execution, each of which can be performed concurrently. These units of execution are called *threads*. Setting this parameter too low can force some activities to take place serially rather than concurrently, slowing performance. The maximum setting is 4095. There is some overhead required for thread management, so setting this value much higher than necessary is not wise. For most people, the default value is adequate.

TIMESLICE=minimum,maximum (default is dynamic)

This statement allows you to specify the minimum amount of time in milliseconds that can be given to a process before its time is yielded to another thread. The maximum specifies the greatest number of milliseconds a thread can have before being preempted by OS/2. The lowest allowable minimum is 32 milliseconds, and the greatest maximum value is 65536. Leaving this statement out of the CONFIG.SYS allows OS/2 to adjust these values dynamically to provide the best overall performance.

TRACE=[ON | OFF],events (default OFF)

Tracing allows your service representative or technical supervisor to track key events in the execution of your system. This can help in diagnosing problems. It adds a lot of overhead to your system, and should only be done at the direction of a trained service representative.

TRACEBUF=size (default 4K)

This statement allows you to specify the size of the buffer into which trace events are recorded. Like the TRACE statement, this should only be used at the direction of a trained service representative.

APPENDIX

OS/2 Files

*D*uring installation, OS/2 puts its files into several subdirectories so your disk will be logically organized.

The information in this appendix works on the assumption that OS/2 is installed on drive C. Substitute the correct drive letter if you have installed OS/2 on an extended drive. The directory names may differ slightly since the HPFS takes advantage of long names and FAT systems are limited to the 8.3 filename and directory name format. Some files discussed here are system files or hidden files, and will not show up in a directory listing.

C:\ (Root Directory)

The root directory is kept as clean as possible, containing only the configuration file (CONFIG.SYS) and the DOS session startup file (AUTOEXEC.BAT). If you set up an OS/2 startup file (STARTUP.CMD), it should go here as well.

C:\NOWHERE

This directory is used for OS/2 internal purposes, and you should not see any files listed here.

C:\OS!2 2.0 Desktop (HPFS) or C:\OS!2_2.0_D (FAT)

This directory is the top-level entry of the directories used by the Workplace Shell to keep track of information regarding the Desktop. There is an entry in this directory for each icon on the desktop, as well as subdirectories for some OS/2 folders. The entries in this area typically represent only the icon and physical location of the object, not the actual executable programs.

***C:\OS!2 2.0 Desktop\Information (HPFS) or C:\OS!2_2.0_D\INFOR-
MAT (FAT)*** This subdirectory contains the entries for all online documentation items you installed, as well as the system README file and
any other items you have moved into the Information folder.

***C:\OS!2 2.0 DESKTOP\MINIMIZED^WINDOW VIEWER (HPFS) or
C:\OS!2_2.0_D\MINIMIZE (FAT)*** This area is used to store representations of the icons of all applications that have been minimized.

***C:\OS!2 2.0 DESKTOP\NETWORK (HPFS) or C:\OS!2_2.0_D\NET-
WORK (FAT)*** This subdirectory is present only if you are running in a
connected environment, and contains the representation of icons for the
network attachments and devices you have installed.

***C:\OS!2 2.0 DESKTOP\OS!2 SYSTEM (HPFS) or C:\OS!2_2.0_D\SYS-
TEM (FAT)*** The subdirectories here are the objects in the OS/2 System
folder:

DRIVES
STARTUP
GAMES
COMMAND PROMPTS (HPFS) - COMMAND_ (FAT)
PRODUCTIVITY (HPFS) - PRODUCTI (FAT)
SYSTEM SETUP (HPFS) - SYSTEM_S (FAT)

***C:\OS!2 2.0 DESKTOP\TEMPLATES (HPFS) or C:\OS!2_2.0_D\TEM-
PLATE (FAT)*** The entries in this subdirectory represent the icons of the
objects present in the Templates folder. The Bitmap, Icon, and Pointer
templates are starter files for those objects, since their file extensions are
automatically associated with the Icon Editor. The Data File template is
an empty file associated with the System Editor. The Folder is an empty
subdirectory, representing an empty window into which the user can
move objects.

C:\OS2

This is the main area for all of the OS/2 executable programs.

C:\OS2\APPS   This subdirectory contains all of the productivity applications and games that you have installed.

The following are the game files:

NEKO.EXE (Cat and Mouse)
REVERSI.EXE (Reversi)
OS2CHESS.EXE (Chess)
JIGSAW.EXE (Jigsaw)
KLONDIKE.EXE (Klondike Solitaire)
SCRAMBLE.EXE (Scramble)

The following are the application files:

CLIPOS2.EXE (Clipboard Viewer)
EPM.EXE (Enhanced Editor)
ICONEDIT.EXE (Icon Editor)
PICVIEW.EXE (Picture Viewer)
PMDALARM.EXE (Alarms)
PMDCALC.EXE (Calculator
PMDCALEN.EXE (Calendar)
PMCHART.EXE (Chart)
PMDDARC.EXE (Planner Archive)
PMDDIARY.EXE (Daily Planner)
PMDLIST.EXE (Activities List)
PMDMONTH.EXE (Monthly Calendar)
PMDNOTE.EXE (Notepad)
PMDTARC.EXE (To-Do List Archive)
PMDTODO.EXE (To-Do List)
PMDTUNE.EXE (Tune Editor)
PMMBASE.EXE (Database)
PMSPREAD.EXE (Spreadsheet)
PMSEEK.EXE (Seek and Scan Files)
PMSTICKY.EXE (Sticky Pad)
PULSE.EXE (Pulse)
CTLSACDI.EXE (Terminal Emulation)
SOFTTERM.EXE (Terminal Emulation)

In addition to the programs, the data files created as you use these applications will also be kept in this subdirectory.

C:\OS2\APPS\DLL This subdirectory contains the Dynamic Link Libraries (DLLs) required to run the OS/2 productivity applications and games.

C:\OS2\BITMAP This subdirectory contains a bitmap of the OS/2 logo. If you selected additional bitmaps during installation, they will be here as well.

C:\OS2\BOOK This subdirectory is for the online documentation you have installed. The online command reference and the REXX documentation are stored here. Some applications will also copy their online help here during installation.

C:\OS2\DLL Dynamic Link Libraries (DLLs) are a key to OS/2 development. This subdirectory has been set aside to contain all of the DLLs OS/2 requires for its normal operations. There are also subdirectories within this directory for each of your printers. They contain the device drivers specific to your hardware. This directory also contains the screen display information for the fonts you installed.

 Caution Most files in this directory are critical to OS/2. Do not delete one of these files unless you are absolutely certain it is unnecessary.

C:\OS2\DRIVERS This is the area for any specialty device drivers needed for your hardware configuration.

C:\OS2\HELP This is the storage place for all the online help modules for OS/2 as well as the productivity applications and games you installed. There are subdirectories for the OS/2 Glossary (OS2\HELP\GLOSS) and the Tutorial (OS2\HELP\TUTORIAL).

C:\OS2\INSTALL The Selective Install program is located here (INSTALL.EXE) as well as information that allows OS/2 to keep track of the items installed, and their service levels (INSTALL.LOG, SYSLEVEL.*).

The device driver installation program (DDINSTAL.EXE) is also here as are backup versions of the original desktop configuration (CONFIG.SYS, OS2*.INI).

This subdirectory also contains the program to migrate DOS and Windows applications (MIGRATE.EXE) as well as a database of known

DOS and Windows programs to search your disk for when migrating (*.DAT), and information about the DOS settings for those applications (DATABASE.TXT). If you are an extremely knowledgeable user, you can even modify the database and prepare it for use with PARSEDB.EXE.

Finally, there are programs here that allow remote installation of OS/2 across a network (RSP*.*, *.RSP).

C:\OS2\MDOS   This subdirectory contains OS/2 DOS emulation software. There are versions here of all of the programs found in DOS 4, as well as many of the features found in DOS 5, such as Quick Basic. There are some additional programs here to patch DOS programs to enable them to run properly under OS/2. These fixes are documented in the README file.

Also in this subdirectory are virtual DOS device drivers. These are rewritten device drivers designed to provide the same function as their DOS counterparts, but do so within OS/2.

C:\OS2\MDOS\WINOS2   This subdirectory contains WIN-OS/2, the OS/2 version of Windows. It is a complete version of Windows itself, excluding some of the mini-applications included in Windows. As with Windows, there is a SYSTEM subdirectory with the low-level components. Documentation of these files and their purposes is included with Windows.

C:\OS2\SYSTEM   This subdirectory houses a collection of miscellaneous low-level OS/2 functions. This is also the default location of the swap file (SWAPPER.DAT). The location of the swap file can be changed by modifying the SWAPPATH statement in CONFIG.SYS and rebooting the system. You can then erase SWAPPER.DAT from this directory.

 Caution   If any other file is removed from this directory, OS/2 cannot continue to run properly.

C:\OS2\SYSTEM\TRACE   System error tracing files and programs are contained here. These are used by service personnel to help track down any problems that occur in your system.

C:\PSFONTS

This directory is for information related to proportionally spaced fonts. At installation this directory contains no files; it is set aside for any new ATM fonts you add to your system. There is also an empty subdirectory, \PSFONTS\PFM, to contain the printer font metrics (details about the actual width of each character) of your added fonts.

C:\SPOOL

This is the area used by the print spooler to hold jobs being sent to the printer. It contains a subdirectory for each printer queue you have installed. It is in those subdirectories that your printed output is spooled.

APPENDIX

Changing Your Hardware

*E*ven if you have the best hardware currently available, you will eventually want to upgrade, replace it, or add an additional hardware device. Once you do this, your old drivers may no longer work. OS/2 provides the means for changing the device drivers used to support your hardware without reinstalling the operating system. If OS/2 doesn't support a piece of hardware you need to use with its built-in drivers, contact the manufacturer for an OS/2 driver. OS/2 allows you to install these custom drivers with very little work.

Using Selective Install

Changing your mouse, keyboard, display, or country setup is easy with OS/2. Double-click on the Selective Install icon found in the System Setup folder. The application displays a dialog box containing check boxes for each device type. Simply check the ones you want. OS/2 asks which drivers you want to install. Answer the questions and OS/2 will make the appropriate changes for you.

Once you make these selections, turn off your computer, install the new hardware, and then reboot your machine. OS/2 uses the new hardware you installed.

Adding a New Printer

Adding a new printer to your system is fairly easy. Start by physically attaching the printer to your system. Then follow these steps to install the appropriate driver:

1. Place the first printer driver disk in a floppy drive (either drive A or drive B). Your OS/2 package includes five printer driver disks.

2. Open the disk to icon view. Check each of the driver icons (files with the .DRV extension) on the disk for the appropriate printer type. For example, Disk 1 contains drivers for the IBM null, LaserJet, and PostScript printers. (It also contains a blank folder for Toshiba

printers.) Continue this process with each floppy in the printer driver set until you find the driver you need for your printer.

3. Double-click on the Driver icon. OS/2 displays a list of specific printer names for that printer driver type.

4. Once you find the correct driver and verify that it supports your printer, drag the printer icon from within the driver list to the desktop. OS/2 automatically installs support for the printer on the drive. Once it installs OS/2 support, the installation routine asks if you want to install support for this printer in WIN-OS/2 as well. Select either Yes or No depending on your need to support the printer. In most cases the install routine will ask you for another disk.

Of course, this procedure assumes that IBM provides a printer driver for your printer. If you need to get a printer driver from the manufacturer, use the Device Driver Install program found in the System Setup folder to install the driver.

Installing Other Device Drivers

Sometimes you'll need to install a device driver other than those supplied with OS/2. The simplest way to do this is to insert the disk with the device driver into a floppy drive, then double-click on the Device Drive Install icon in the System Setup folder. OS/2 automatically scans your floppy drives for disks with the appropriate information. It then displays a list of device drivers it found. Double-click on the device you wish to install and follow any prompts that OS/2 displays.

Unfortunately, some device drivers do not install from within the Workplace Shell. If you get the message, "A profile control file could not be found in the source directory," then you can't use the Device Driver Installation utility provided in the System Setup folder. In most cases you need to go to the OS/2 command prompt and perform a special set of instructions. The documentation provided with the driver should give all the details for a command line installation. If it does not, contact the manufacturer.

Adding a Second Hard Drive

To install a second data drive, use the following procedure:

1. Turn your machine off and install the disk drive in your machine.

2. Turn the machine on and reconfigure your system's CMOS, and then boot OS/2. (You normally access the system CMOS setup by pressing a set of control keys during bootup—for example, CTRL+ALT+ESC for Award BIOS machines or DEL for AMI BIOS machines.)

3. Some drives require a low-level format. These drives include most MFM and RLL drives. IDE, ESDI, and SCSI drives do not require a low-level format. When using an MFM or RLL drive, use either DEBUG or a program such as SpeedStor to low-level format the drive if your CMOS setup menu does not have a low-level format option. (When using DEBUG, simply type **G=C800:0005** and press ENTER at the debug prompt; then follow the instructions provided by the BIOS formatter.)

4. Use FDISK to partition the drive. This tells the drive how you want it separated into logical drives. In most cases you will want to create one large partition.

5. The FORMAT command will format the hard drive for you. Simply type **FORMAT <*drive letter*> /FS: file system (default FAT)** to start the process.

Caution   Make absolutely certain you do not format the system drive.

Replacing Your Hard Drive

To install a new OS/2 system drive, make sure you back up your current hard disk, then follow the procedures found in the OS/2 documentation for installing OS/2 on the new drive. Once the installation is complete, restore your data and applications from the backup you made of the old drive.

Index